THE NEW DEAL

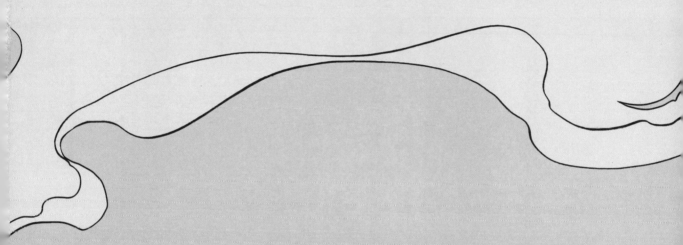

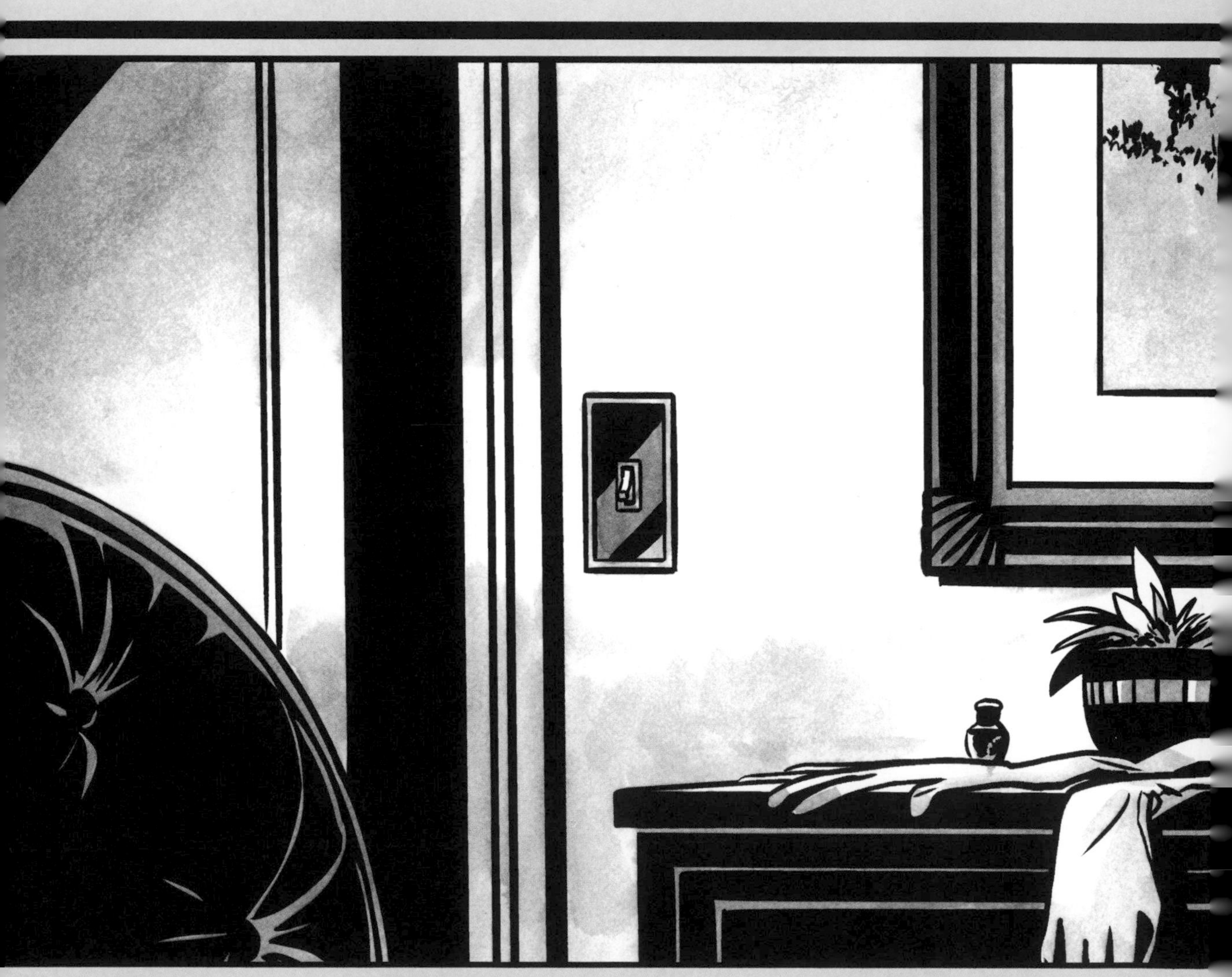

JONATHAN CASE

THE NEW DEAL

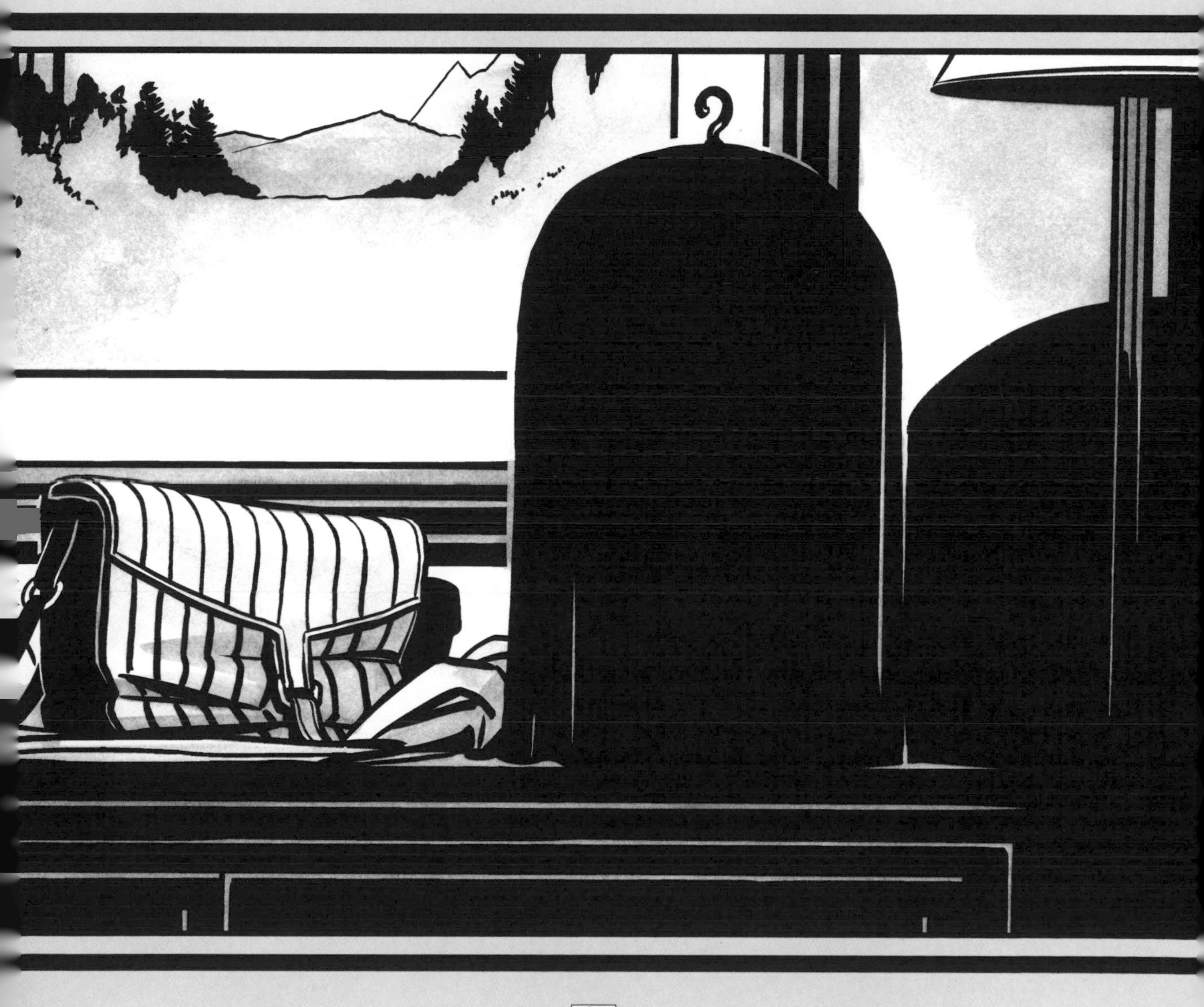

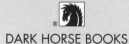

DARK HORSE BOOKS

PRESIDENT & PUBLISHER
MIKE RICHARDSON

EDITOR
SIERRA HAHN

ASSISTANT EDITOR
SPENCER CUSHING

COLLECTION DESIGNER
ETHAN KIMBERLING

DIGITAL ART TECHNICIAN
MATT DRYER

SPECIAL THANKS TO
Sierra, Spencer, Scott, Kari, and the rest of the Dark Horse crew, my family
and community, and especially Sarah: I couldn't do this without you.

Published by Dark Horse Books
A division of Dark Horse Comics, Inc.
10956 SE Main Street
Milwaukie, OR 97222

First edition: September 2015
ISBN 978-1-61655-731-7

10 9 8 7 6 5 4 3 2 1
Printed in China

International Licensing: (503) 905-2377
Comic Shop Locator Service: (888) 266-4226

Neil Hankerson, Executive Vice President | Tom Weddle, Chief Financial Officer | Randy Stradley, Vice
President of Publishing | Michael Martens, Vice President of Book Trade Sales | Scott Allie, Editor in
Chief | Matt Parkinson, Vice President of Marketing | David Scroggy, Vice President of Product Devel-
opment | Dale LaFountain, Vice President of Information Technology | Darlene Vogel, Senior Director
of Print, Design, and Production | Ken Lizzi, General Counsel | Davey Estrada, Editorial Director | Chris
Warner, Senior Books Editor | Cary Grazzini, Director of Print and Development | Lia Ribacchi, Art
Director | Cara Niece, Director of Scheduling | Mark Bernardi, Director of Digital Publishing

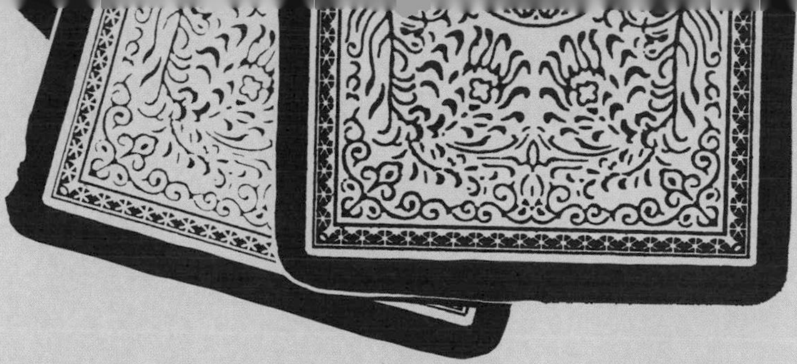

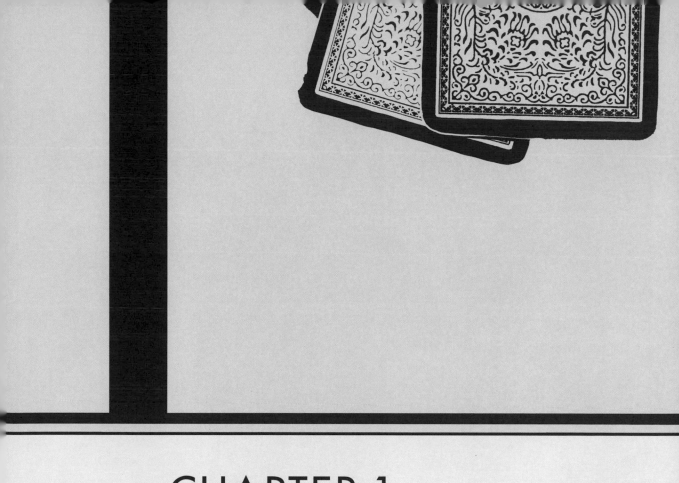

CHAPTER 1

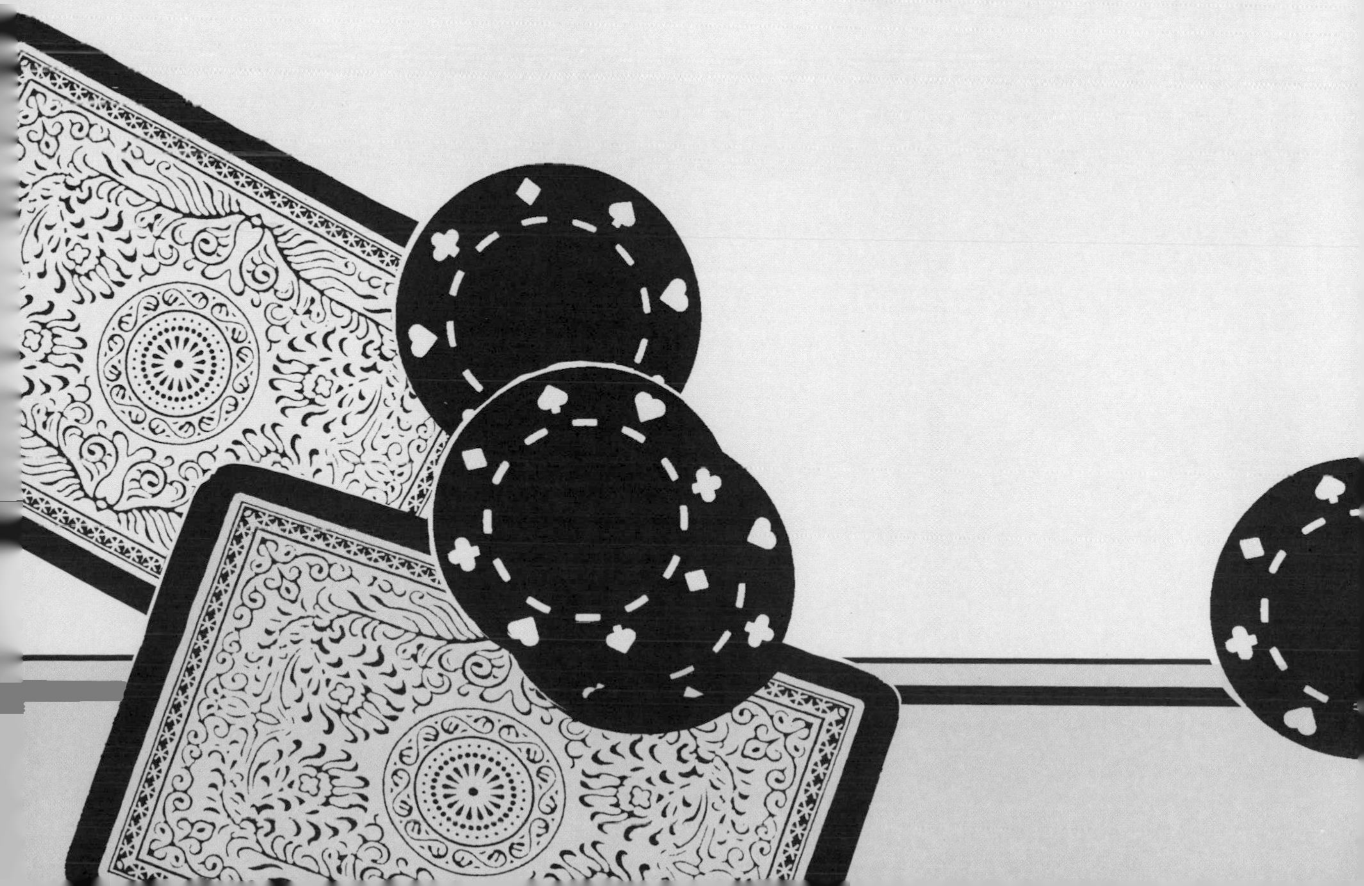

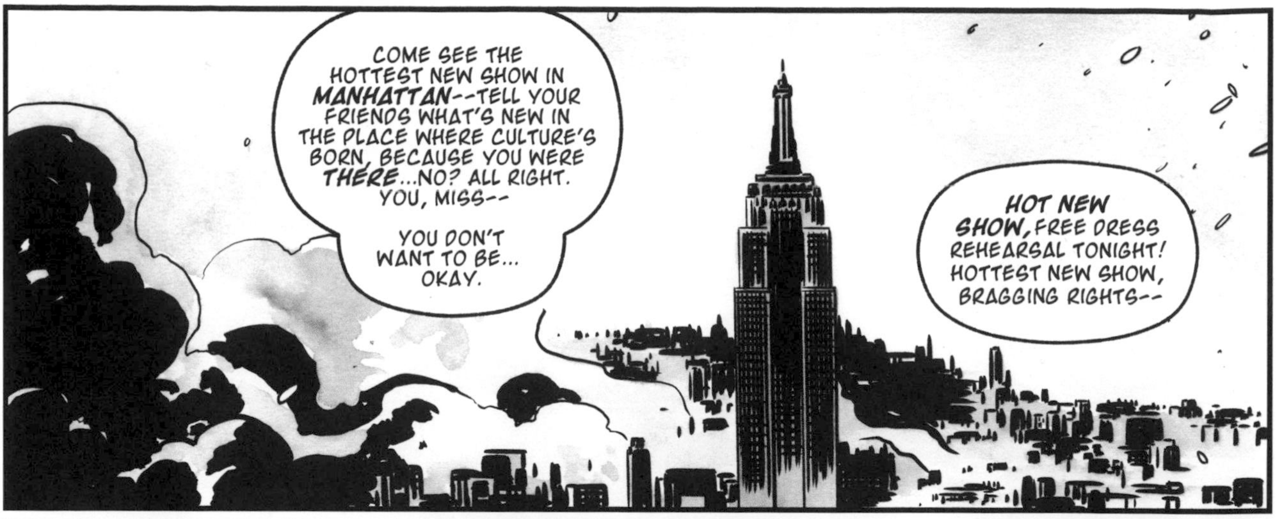
COME SEE THE HOTTEST NEW SHOW IN MANHATTAN--TELL YOUR FRIENDS WHAT'S NEW IN THE PLACE WHERE CULTURE'S BORN, BECAUSE YOU WERE THERE...NO? ALL RIGHT. YOU, MISS--
YOU DON'T WANT TO BE... OKAY.
HOT NEW SHOW, FREE DRESS REHEARSAL TONIGHT! HOTTEST NEW SHOW, BRAGGING RIGHTS--

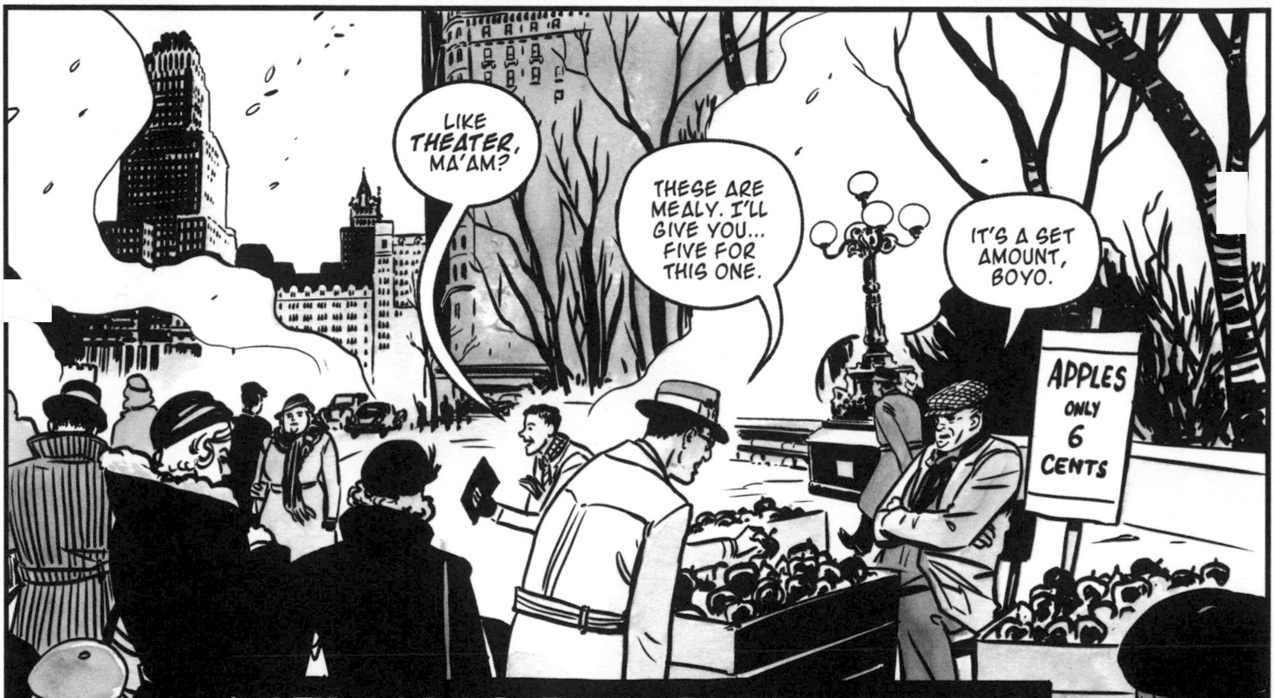
LIKE THEATER, MA'AM?
THESE ARE MEALY. I'LL GIVE YOU... FIVE FOR THIS ONE.
IT'S A SET AMOUNT, BOYO.
APPLES ONLY 6 CENTS
NEW YORK CITY, 1936

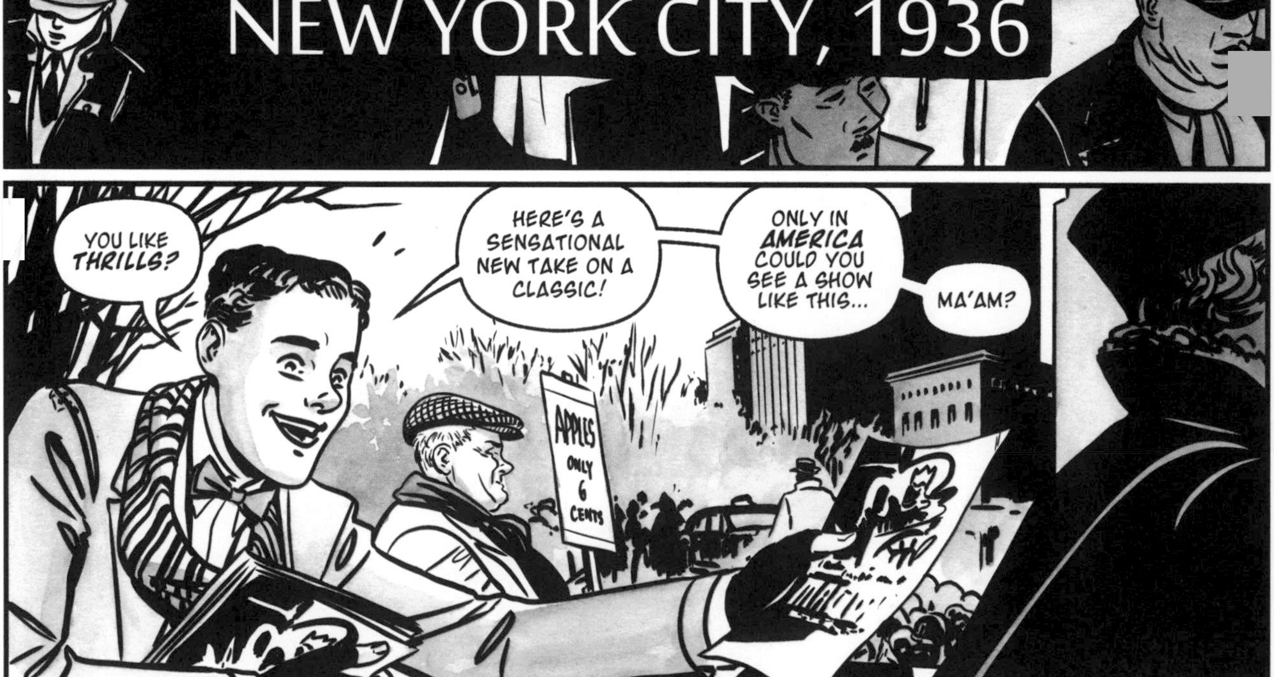
YOU LIKE THRILLS?
HERE'S A SENSATIONAL NEW TAKE ON A CLASSIC!
ONLY IN AMERICA COULD YOU SEE A SHOW LIKE THIS...
MA'AM?
APPLES ONLY 6 CENTS

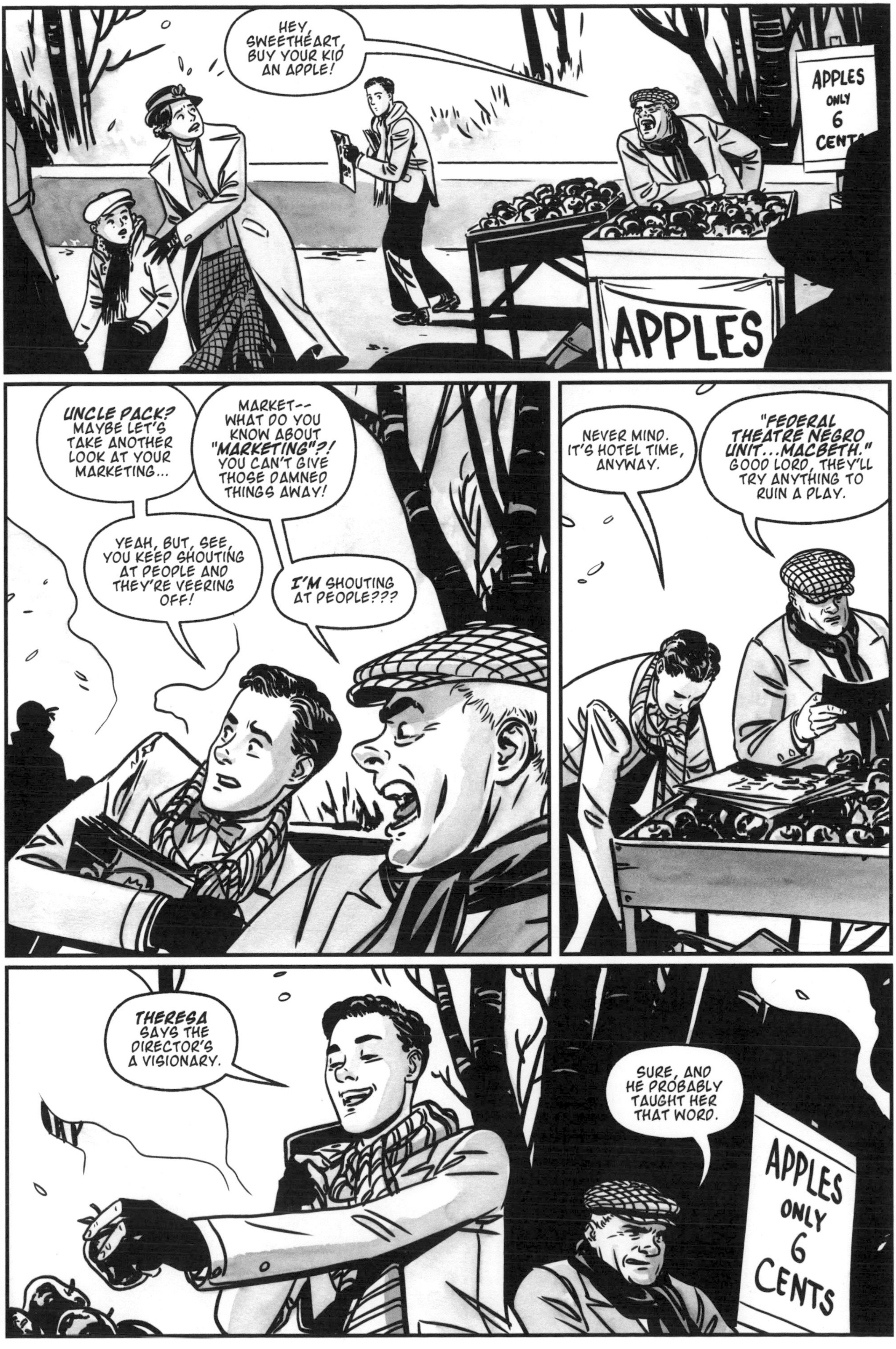

HEY, SWEETHEART, BUY YOUR KID AN APPLE!
APPLES ONLY 6 CENTS
APPLES
UNCLE PACK? MAYBE LET'S TAKE ANOTHER LOOK AT YOUR MARKETING...
MARKET-- WHAT DO YOU KNOW ABOUT "MARKETING"?! YOU CAN'T GIVE THOSE DAMNED THINGS AWAY!
YEAH, BUT, SEE, YOU KEEP SHOUTING AT PEOPLE AND THEY'RE VEERING OFF!
I'M SHOUTING AT PEOPLE???
NEVER MIND. IT'S HOTEL TIME, ANYWAY.
"FEDERAL THEATRE NEGRO UNIT...MACBETH." GOOD LORD, THEY'LL TRY ANYTHING TO RUIN A PLAY.
THERESA SAYS THE DIRECTOR'S A VISIONARY.
SURE, AND HE PROBABLY TAUGHT HER THAT WORD.
APPLES ONLY 6 CENTS

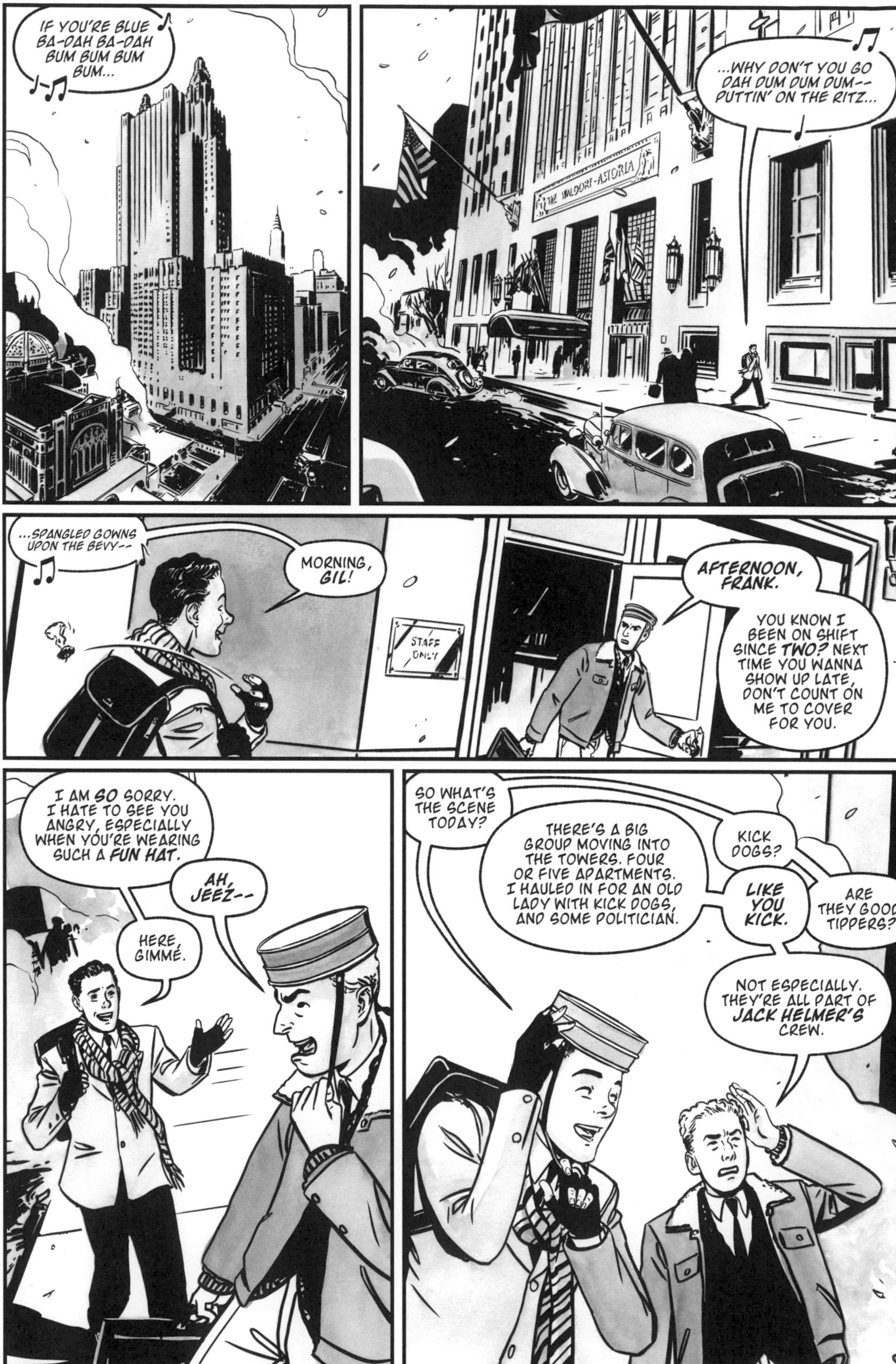
IF YOU'RE BLUE BA-DAH BA-DAH BUM BUM BUM BUM...
...WHY DON'T YOU GO DAH DUM DUM DUM-- PUTTIN' ON THE RITZ...
THE WALDORF-ASTORIA
...SPANGLED GOWNS UPON THE BEVY--
MORNING, GIL!
STAFF ONLY
AFTERNOON, FRANK.
YOU KNOW I BEEN ON SHIFT SINCE TWO? NEXT TIME YOU WANNA SHOW UP LATE, DON'T COUNT ON ME TO COVER FOR YOU.
I AM SO SORRY. I HATE TO SEE YOU ANGRY, ESPECIALLY WHEN YOU'RE WEARING SUCH A FUN HAT.
AH, JEEZ--
HERE, GIMME.
SO WHAT'S THE SCENE TODAY?
THERE'S A BIG GROUP MOVING INTO THE TOWERS. FOUR OR FIVE APARTMENTS. I HAULED IN FOR AN OLD LADY WITH KICK DOGS, AND SOME POLITICIAN.
KICK DOGS?
LIKE YOU KICK.
ARE THEY GOOD TIPPERS?
NOT ESPECIALLY. THEY'RE ALL PART OF JACK HELMER'S CREW.

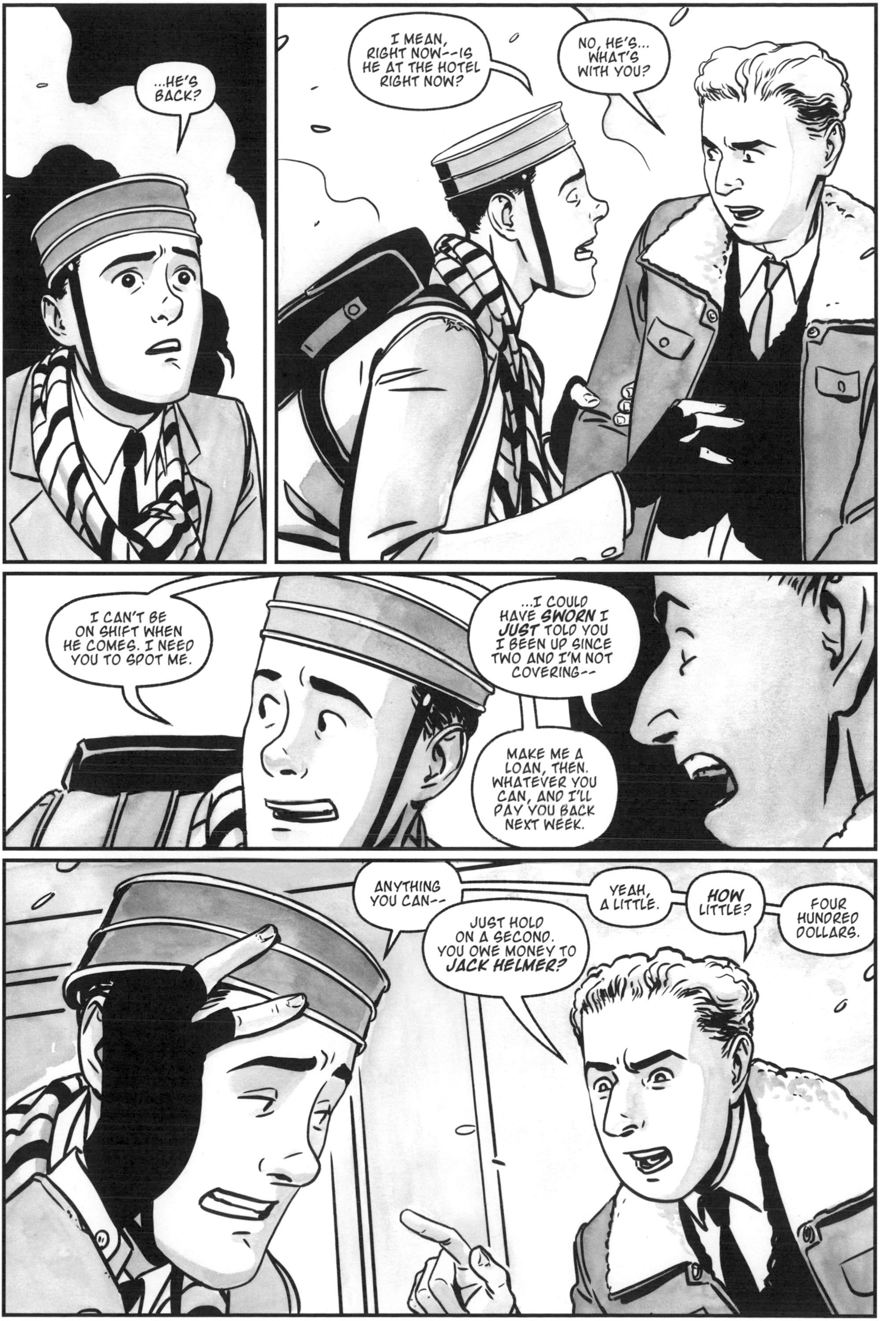
...HE'S BACK?
I MEAN, RIGHT NOW--IS HE AT THE HOTEL RIGHT NOW?
NO, HE'S... WHAT'S WITH YOU?
I CAN'T BE ON SHIFT WHEN HE COMES. I NEED YOU TO SPOT ME.
...I COULD HAVE SWORN I JUST TOLD YOU I BEEN UP SINCE TWO AND I'M NOT COVERING--
MAKE ME A LOAN, THEN. WHATEVER YOU CAN, AND I'LL PAY YOU BACK NEXT WEEK.
ANYTHING YOU CAN--
JUST HOLD ON A SECOND. YOU OWE MONEY TO JACK HELMER?
YEAH, A LITTLE.
HOW LITTLE?
FOUR HUNDRED DOLLARS.

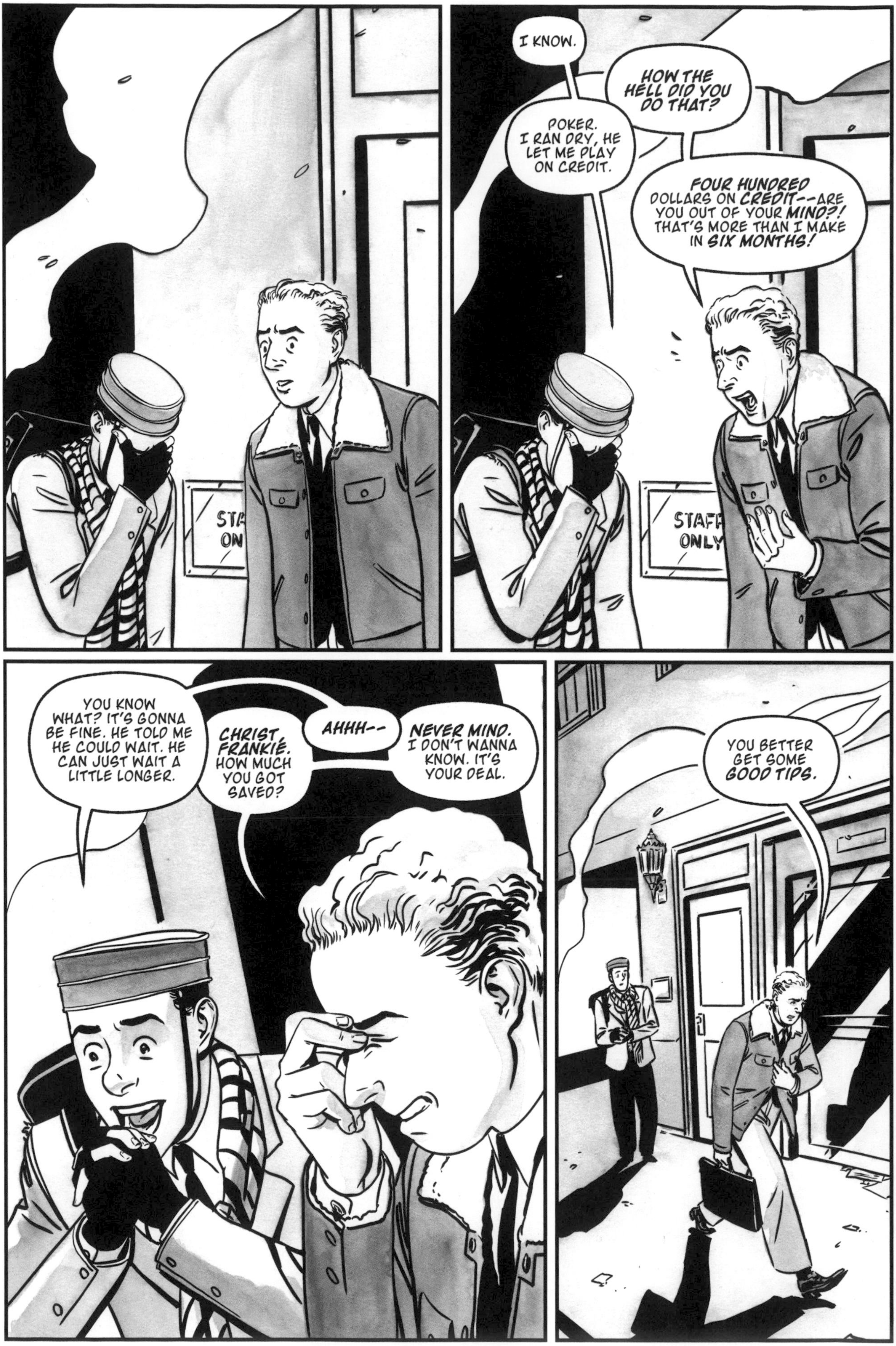
I KNOW.
HOW THE HELL DID YOU DO THAT?
POKER. I RAN DRY, HE LET ME PLAY ON CREDIT.
FOUR HUNDRED DOLLARS ON CREDIT--ARE YOU OUT OF YOUR MIND?! THAT'S MORE THAN I MAKE IN SIX MONTHS!
CHRIST, FRANKIE. HOW MUCH YOU GOT SAVED?
AHHH--
NEVER MIND. I DON'T WANNA KNOW. IT'S YOUR DEAL.
YOU KNOW WHAT? IT'S GONNA BE FINE. HE TOLD ME HE COULD WAIT. HE CAN JUST WAIT A LITTLE LONGER.
YOU BETTER GET SOME GOOD TIPS.

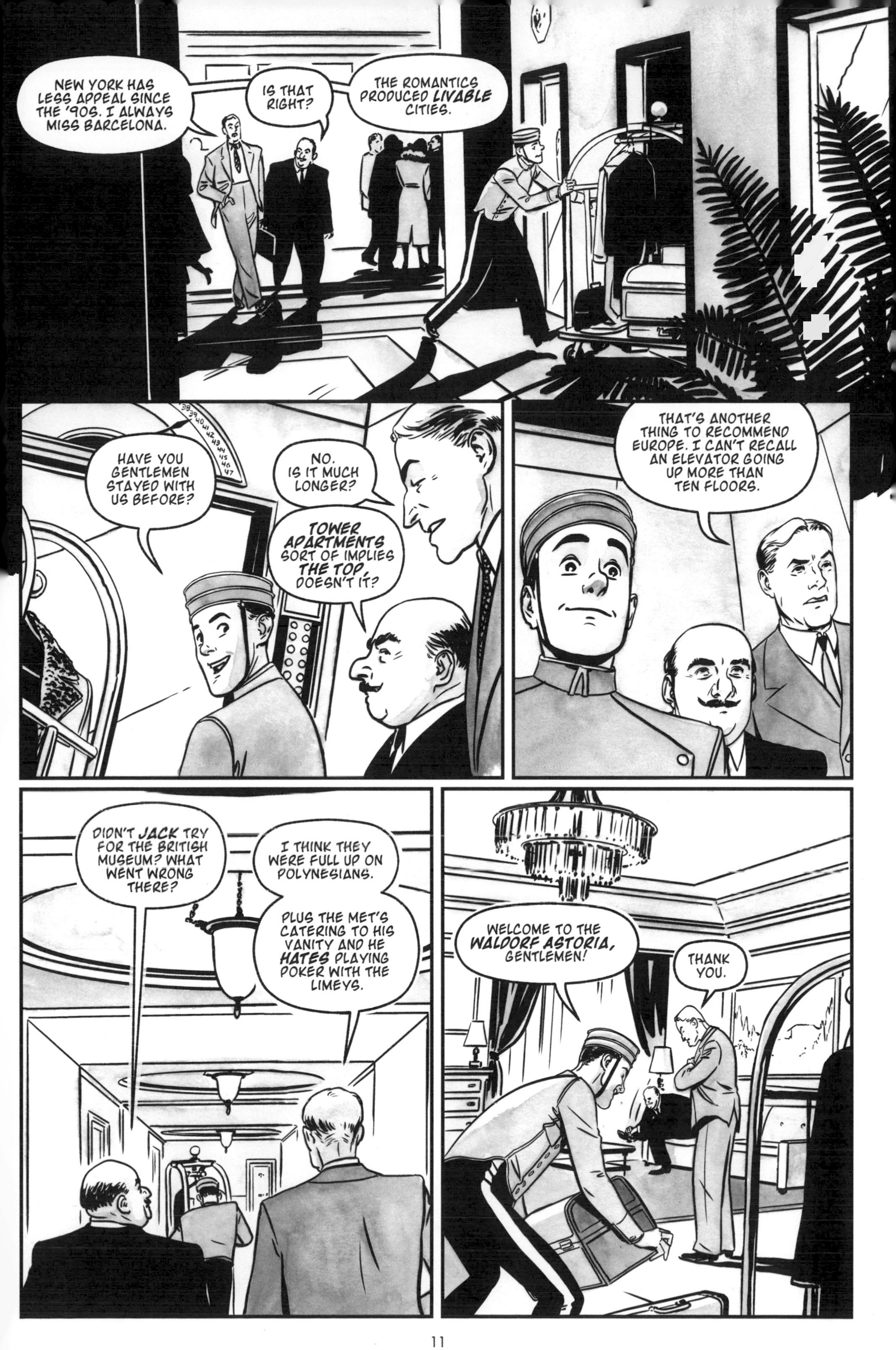
NEW YORK HAS LESS APPEAL SINCE THE '90S. I ALWAYS MISS BARCELONA.
IS THAT RIGHT?
THE ROMANTICS PRODUCED LIVABLE CITIES.
HAVE YOU GENTLEMEN STAYED WITH US BEFORE?
NO. IS IT MUCH LONGER?
TOWER APARTMENTS SORT OF IMPLIES THE TOP, DOESN'T IT?
THAT'S ANOTHER THING TO RECOMMEND EUROPE. I CAN'T RECALL AN ELEVATOR GOING UP MORE THAN TEN FLOORS.
DIDN'T JACK TRY FOR THE BRITISH MUSEUM? WHAT WENT WRONG THERE?
I THINK THEY WERE FULL UP ON POLYNESIANS.
PLUS THE MET'S CATERING TO HIS VANITY AND HE HATES PLAYING POKER WITH THE LIMEYS.
WELCOME TO THE WALDORF ASTORIA, GENTLEMEN!
THANK YOU.

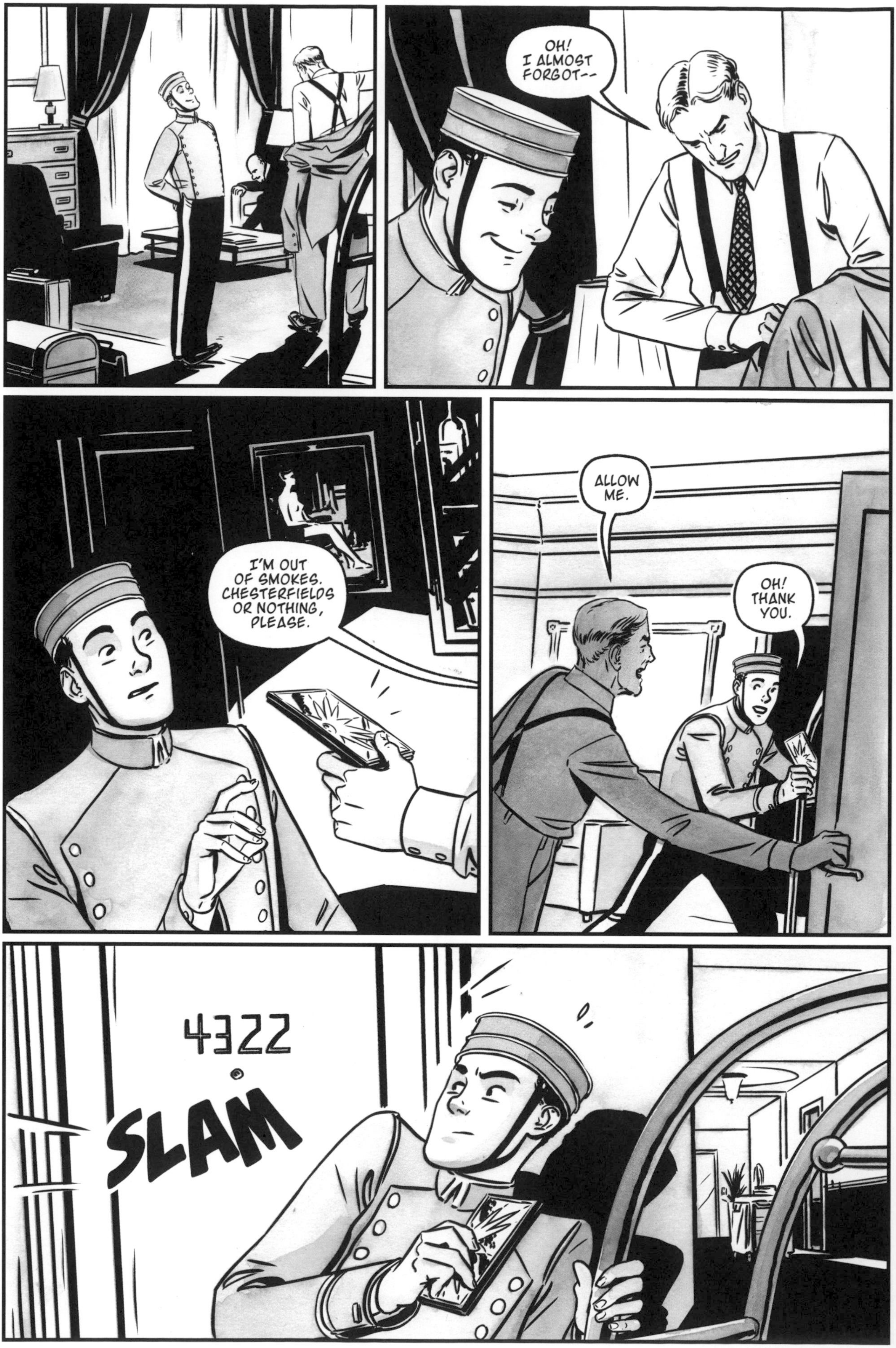
OH! I ALMOST FORGOT--
I'M OUT OF SMOKES. CHESTERFIELDS OR NOTHING, PLEASE.
ALLOW ME.
OH! THANK YOU.
4322
SLAM

OH...
RIGHT AWAY, SIR!
OF COURSE, SIR!
JUST THE PLEASURE OF SERVING YOU...
HELLO?
MR. O'MALLEY?
YEAH, HEY!

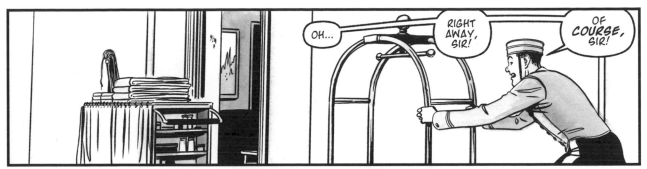

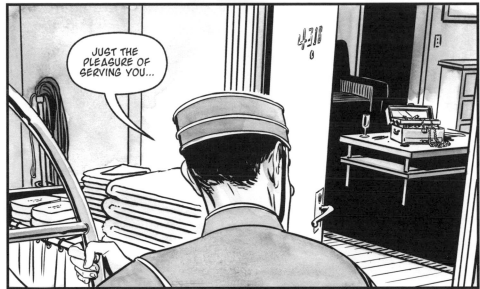

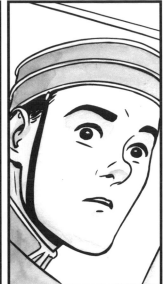

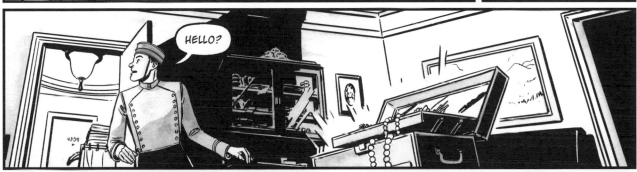

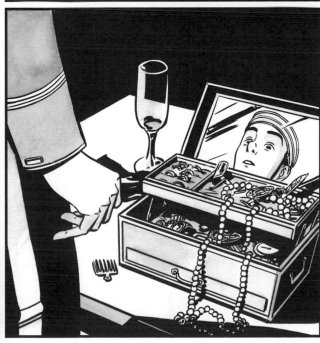

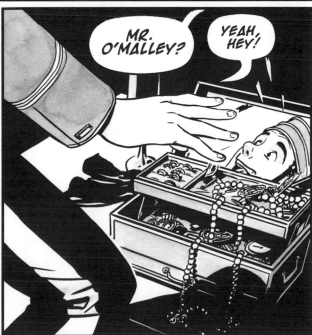

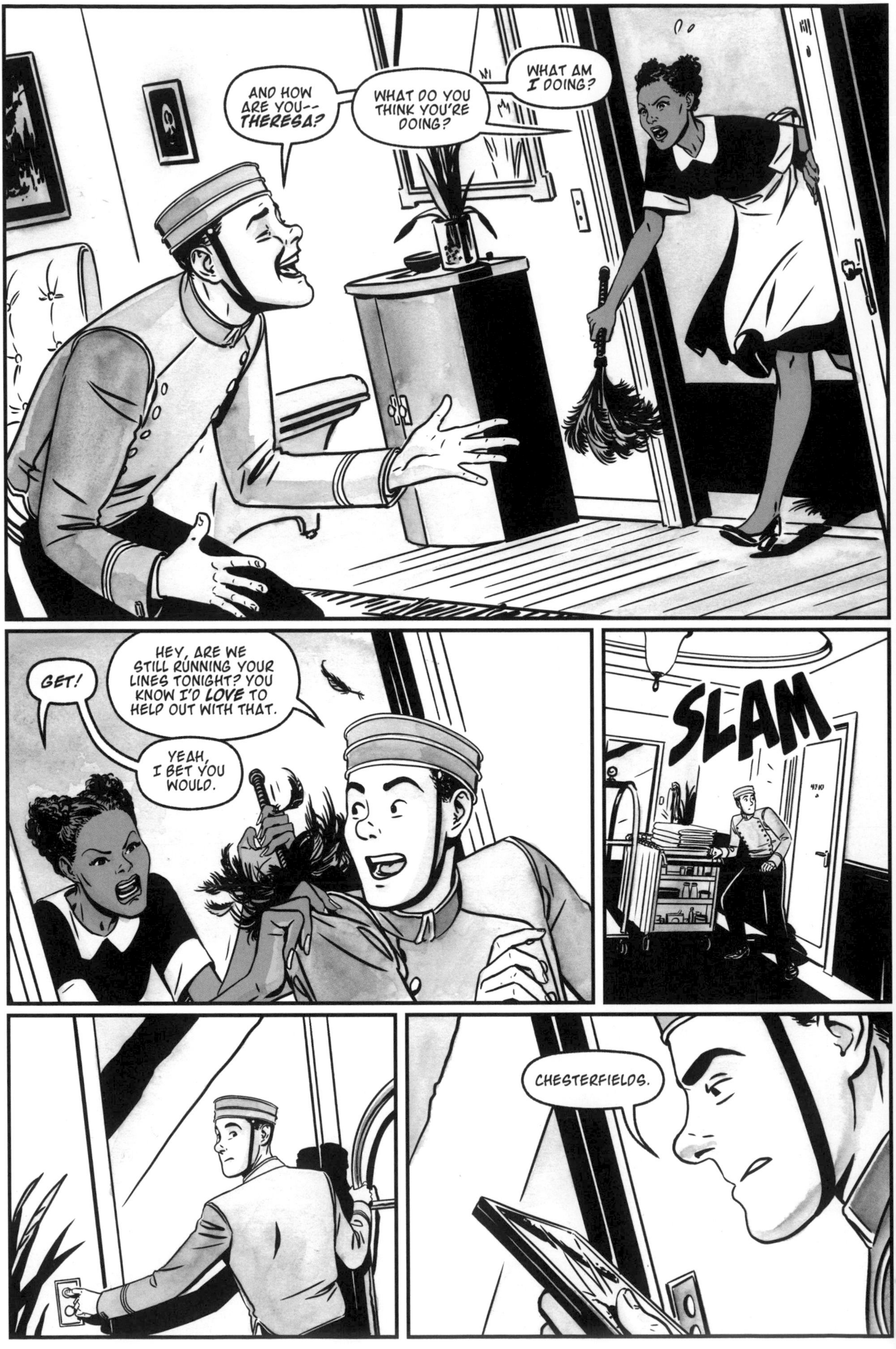
AND HOW ARE YOU-- THERESA?
WHAT DO YOU THINK YOU'RE DOING?
WHAT AM I DOING?
GET!
HEY, ARE WE STILL RUNNING YOUR LINES TONIGHT? YOU KNOW I'D LOVE TO HELP OUT WITH THAT.
YEAH, I BET YOU WOULD.
SLAM
CHESTERFIELDS.

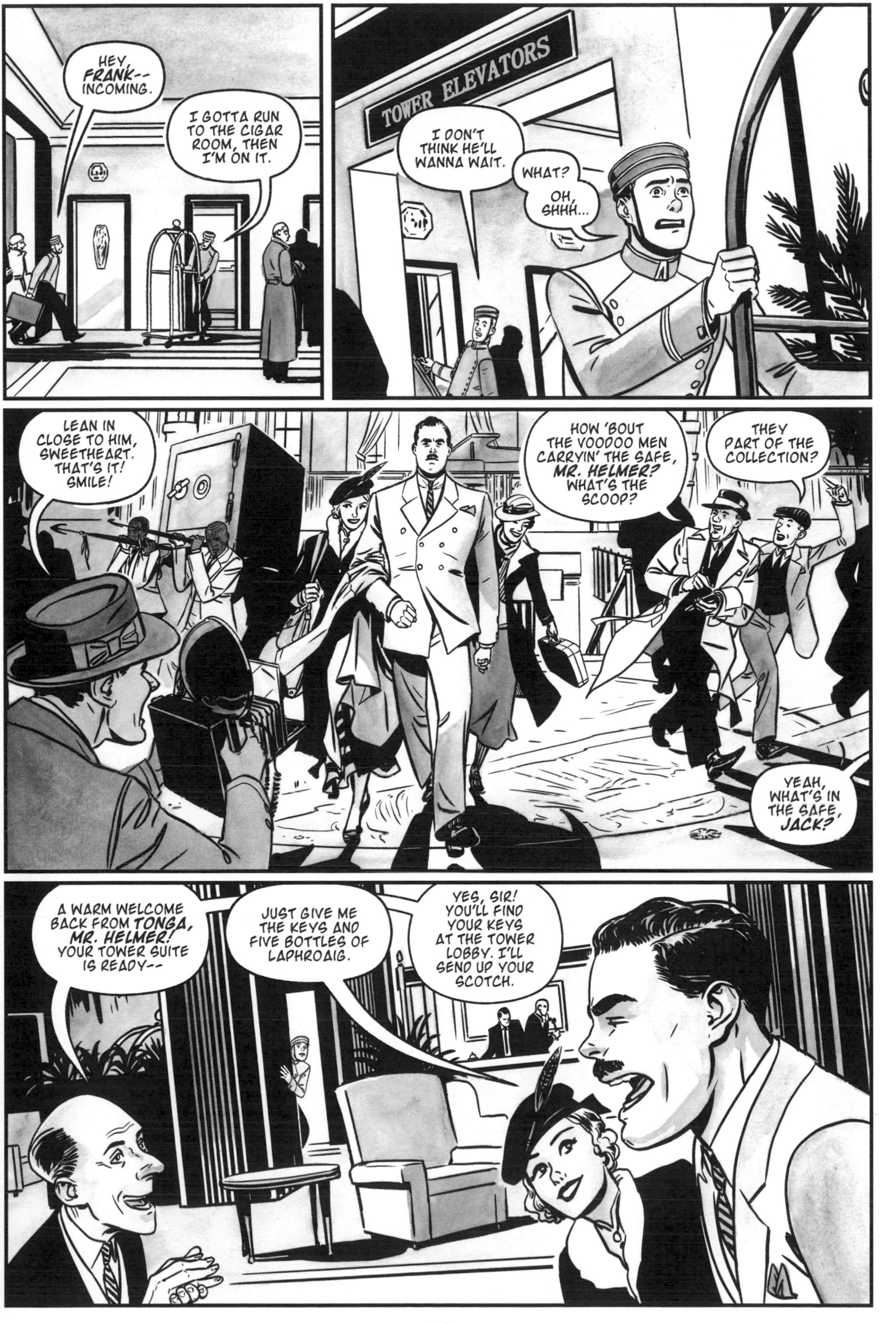
HEY, FRANK-- INCOMING.
I GOTTA RUN TO THE CIGAR ROOM, THEN I'M ON IT.
TOWER ELEVATORS
I DON'T THINK HE'LL WANNA WAIT.
WHAT? OH, SHHH...
LEAN IN CLOSE TO HIM, SWEETHEART. THAT'S IT! SMILE!
HOW 'BOUT THE VOODOO MEN CARRYIN' THE SAFE, MR. HELMER? WHAT'S THE SCOOP?
THEY PART OF THE COLLECTION?
YEAH, WHAT'S IN THE SAFE, JACK?
A WARM WELCOME BACK FROM TONGA, MR. HELMER! YOUR TOWER SUITE IS READY--
JUST GIVE ME THE KEYS AND FIVE BOTTLES OF LAPHROAIG.
YES, SIR! YOU'LL FIND YOUR KEYS AT THE TOWER LOBBY. I'LL SEND UP YOUR SCOTCH.

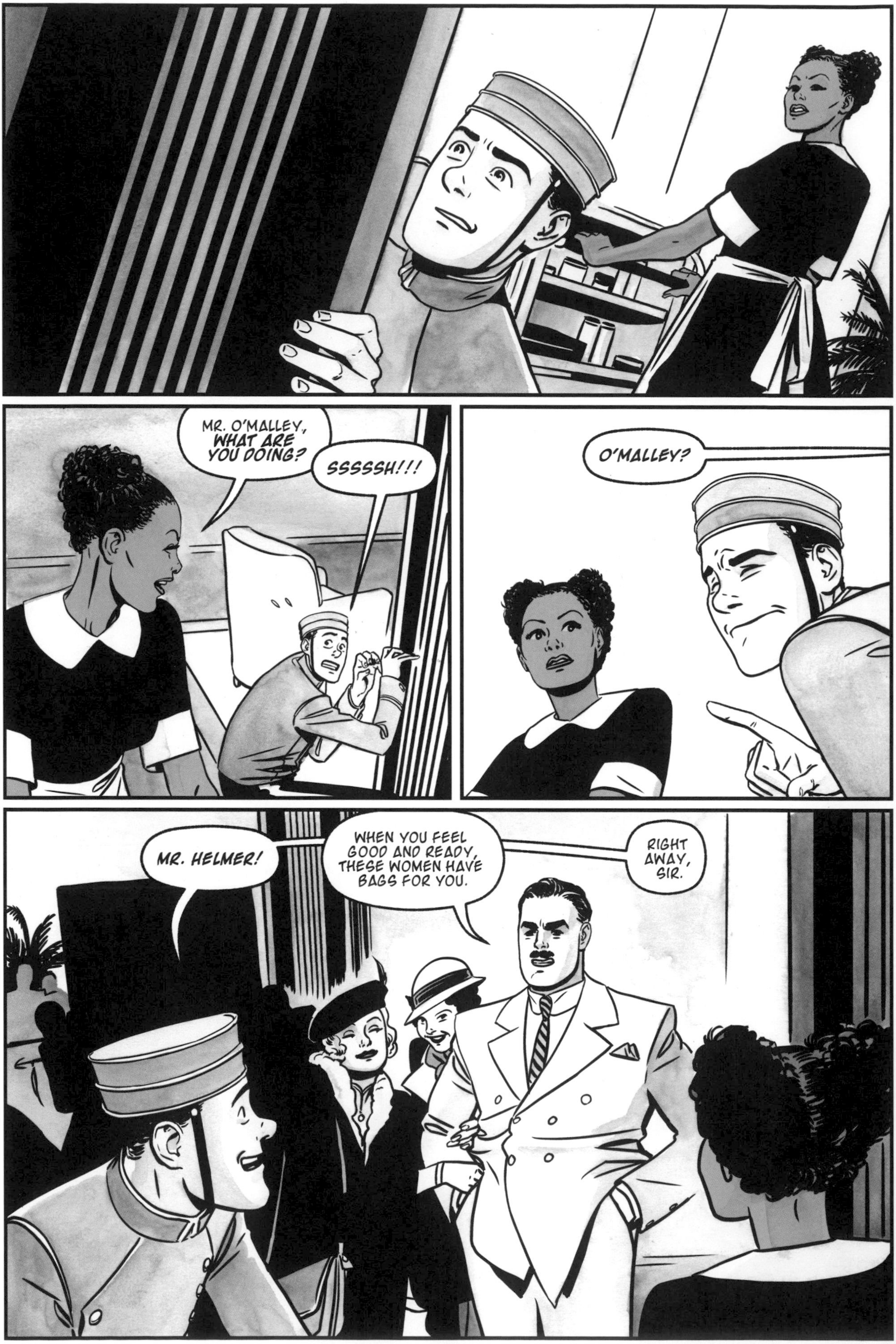
MR. O'MALLEY, WHAT ARE YOU DOING?
SSSSSH!!!
O'MALLEY?
MR. HELMER!
WHEN YOU FEEL GOOD AND READY, THESE WOMEN HAVE BAGS FOR YOU.
RIGHT AWAY, SIR.

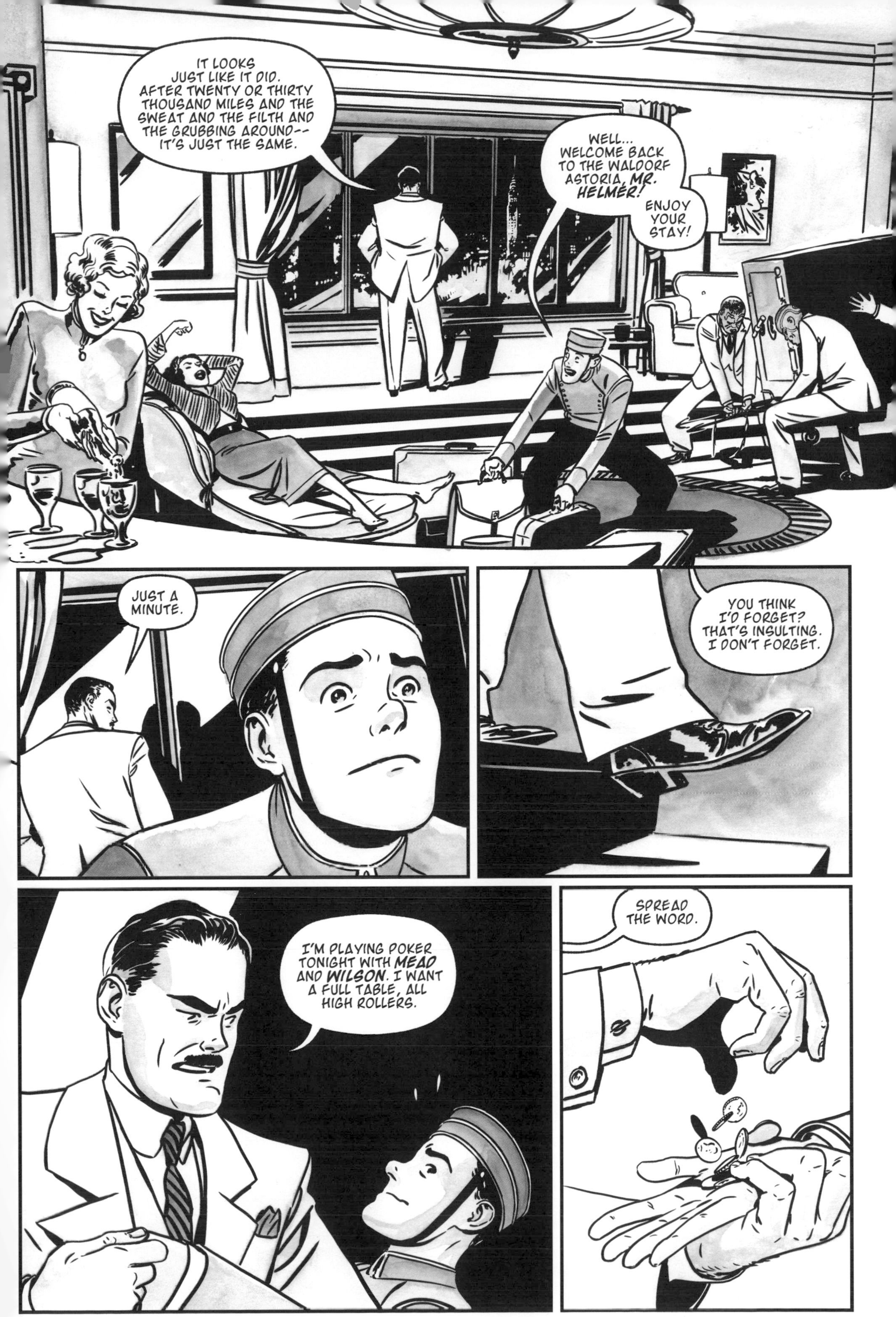
IT LOOKS JUST LIKE IT DID. AFTER TWENTY OR THIRTY THOUSAND MILES AND THE SWEAT AND THE FILTH AND THE GRUBBING AROUND-- IT'S JUST THE SAME.
WELL... WELCOME BACK TO THE WALDORF ASTORIA, MR. HELMÉR!
ENJOY YOUR STAY!
JUST A MINUTE.
YOU THINK I'D FORGET? THAT'S INSULTING. I DON'T FORGET.
I'M PLAYING POKER TONIGHT WITH MEAD AND WILSON. I WANT A FULL TABLE, ALL HIGH ROLLERS.
SPREAD THE WORD.

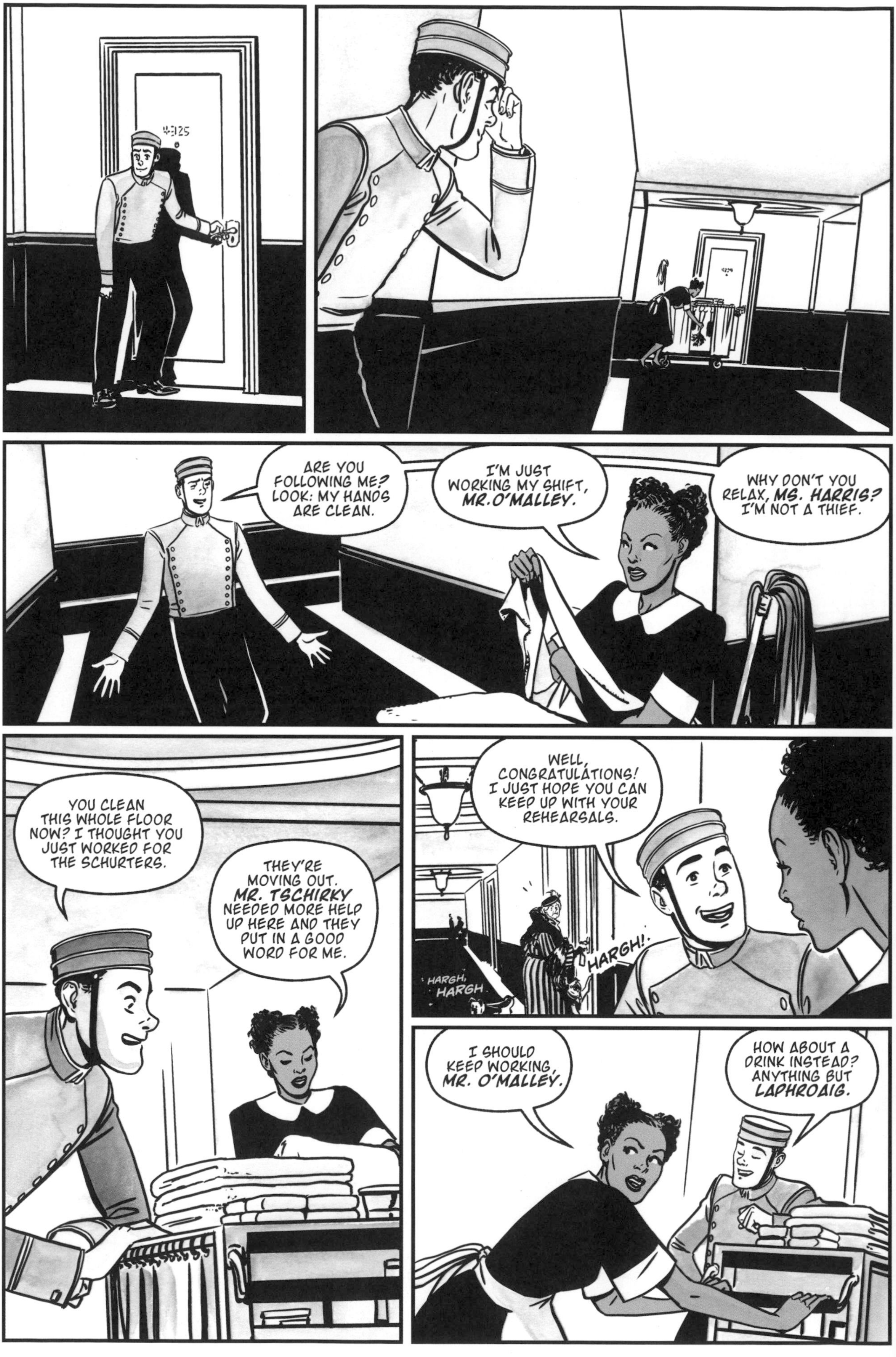
4125
ARE YOU FOLLOWING ME? LOOK: MY HANDS ARE CLEAN.
I'M JUST WORKING MY SHIFT, MR. O'MALLEY.
WHY DON'T YOU RELAX, MS. HARRIS? I'M NOT A THIEF.
YOU CLEAN THIS WHOLE FLOOR NOW? I THOUGHT YOU JUST WORKED FOR THE SCHURTERS.
THEY'RE MOVING OUT. MR. TSCHIRKY NEEDED MORE HELP UP HERE AND THEY PUT IN A GOOD WORD FOR ME.
WELL, CONGRATULATIONS! I JUST HOPE YOU CAN KEEP UP WITH YOUR REHEARSALS.
HARGH, HARGH
HARGH!
I SHOULD KEEP WORKING, MR. O'MALLEY.
HOW ABOUT A DRINK INSTEAD? ANYTHING BUT LAPHROAIG.

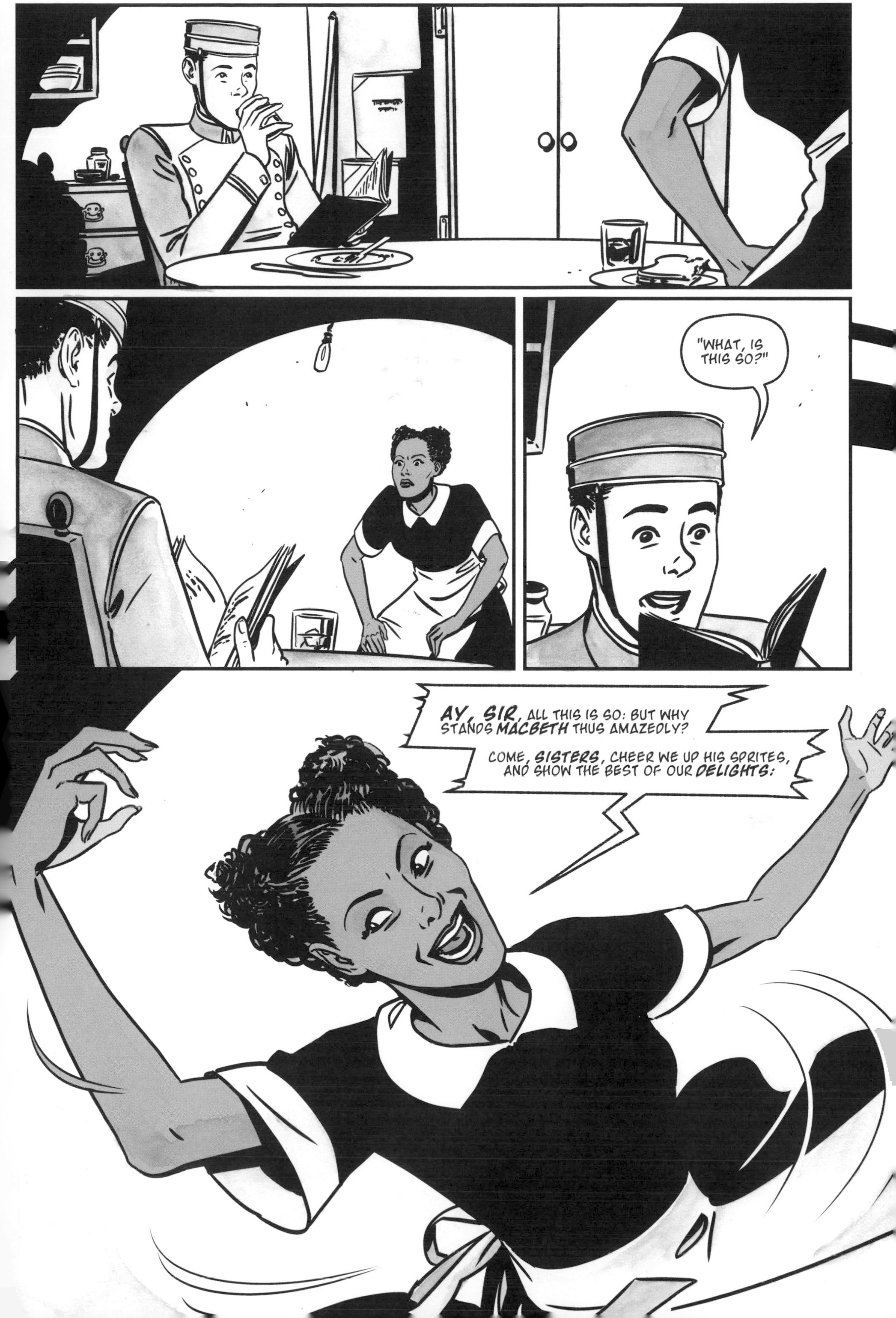
"WHAT, IS THIS SO?"
AY, SIR, ALL THIS IS SO: BUT WHY STANDS MACBETH THUS AMAZEDLY?
COME, SISTERS, CHEER WE UP HIS SPRITES, AND SHOW THE BEST OF OUR DELIGHTS:

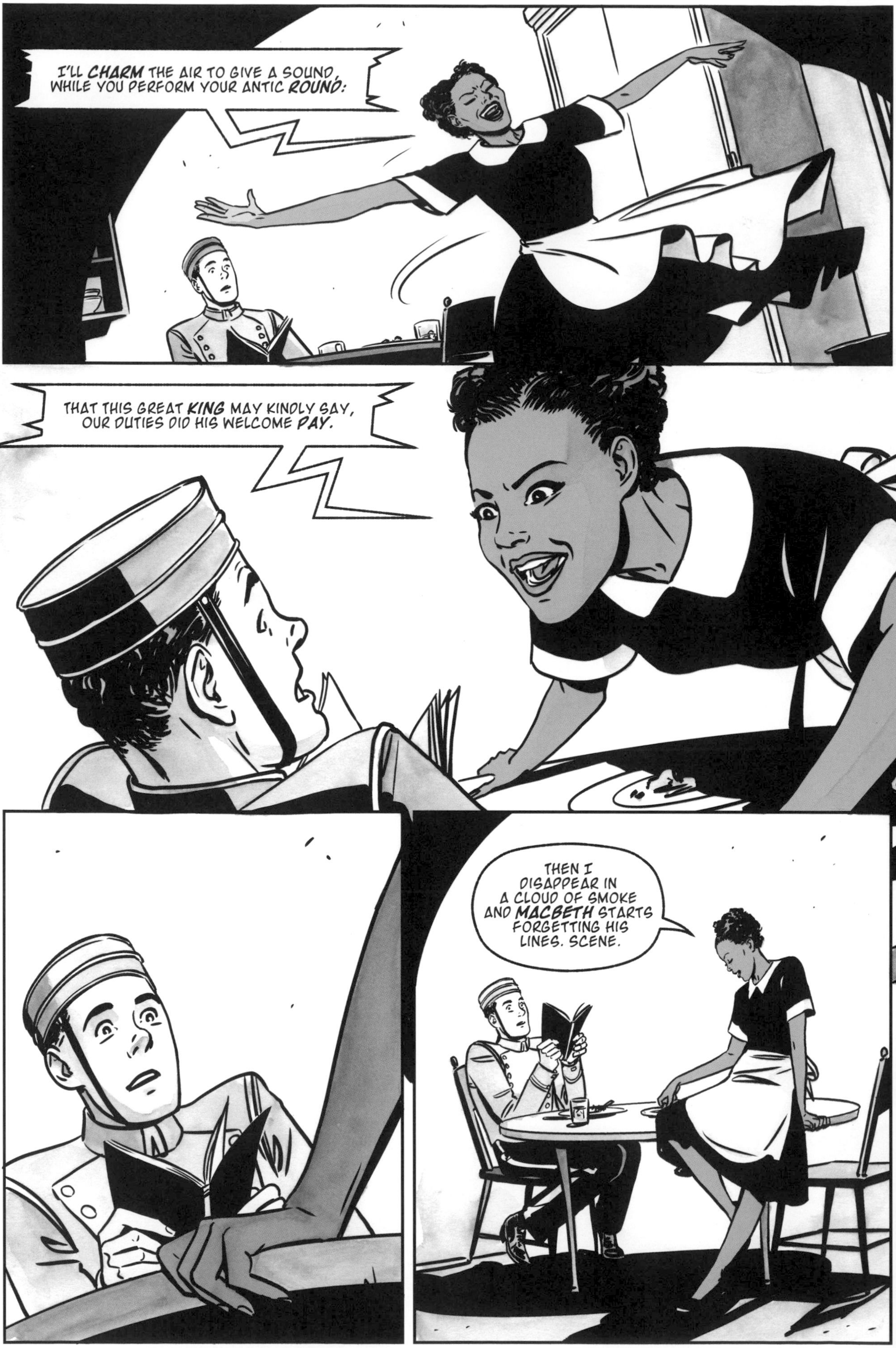
I'LL CHARM THE AIR TO GIVE A SOUND, WHILE YOU PERFORM YOUR ANTIC ROUND:
THAT THIS GREAT KING MAY KINDLY SAY, OUR DUTIES DID HIS WELCOME PAY.
THEN I DISAPPEAR IN A CLOUD OF SMOKE AND MACBETH STARTS FORGETTING HIS LINES. SCENE.

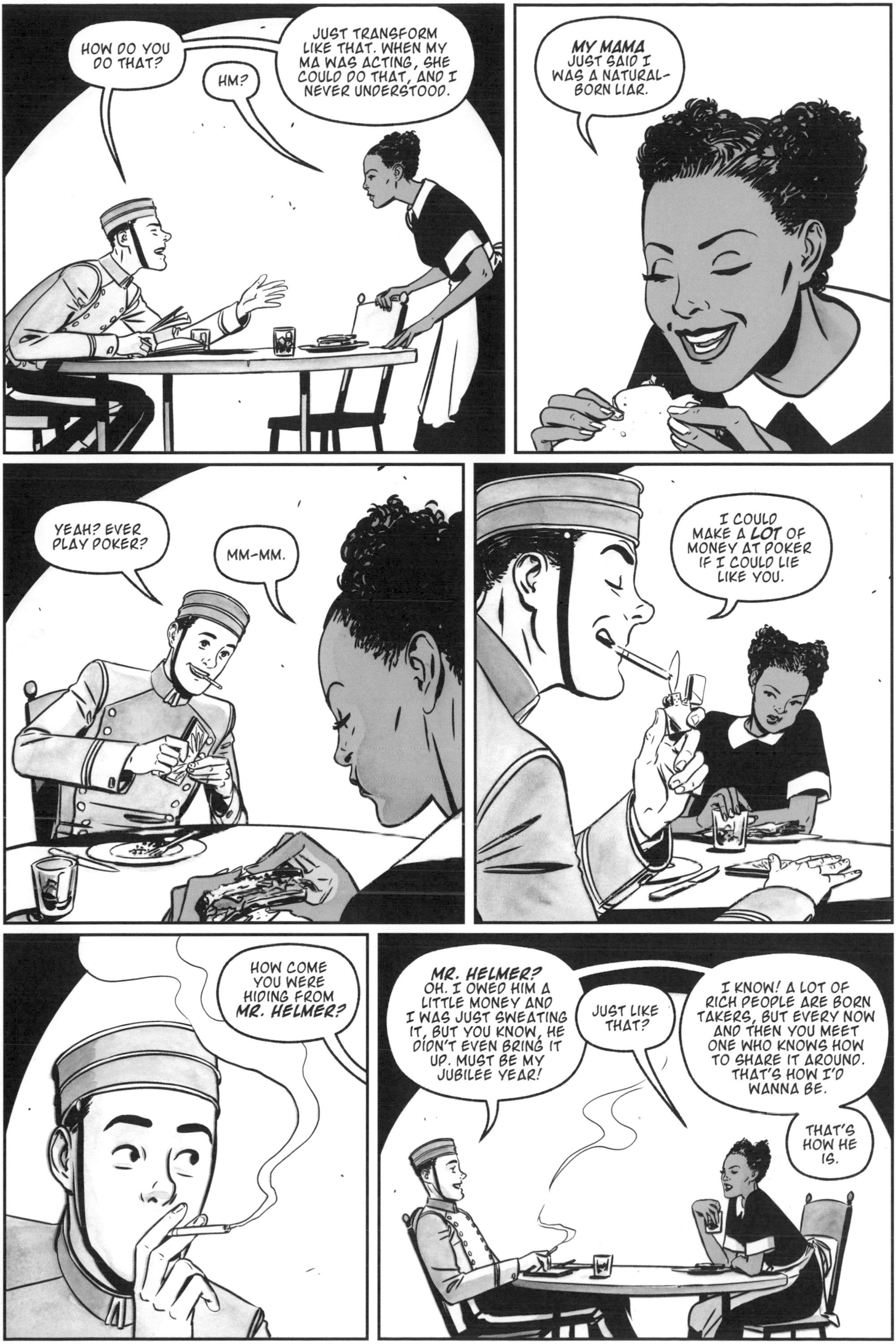
HOW DO YOU DO THAT?
HM?
JUST TRANSFORM LIKE THAT. WHEN MY MA WAS ACTING, SHE COULD DO THAT, AND I NEVER UNDERSTOOD.
MY MAMA JUST SAID I WAS A NATURAL-BORN LIAR.
YEAH? EVER PLAY POKER?
MM-MM.
I COULD MAKE A LOT OF MONEY AT POKER IF I COULD LIE LIKE YOU.
HOW COME YOU WERE HIDING FROM MR. HELMER?
MR. HELMER? OH. I OWED HIM A LITTLE MONEY AND I WAS JUST SWEATING IT, BUT YOU KNOW, HE DIDN'T EVEN BRING IT UP. MUST BE MY JUBILEE YEAR!
JUST LIKE THAT?
I KNOW! A LOT OF RICH PEOPLE ARE BORN TAKERS, BUT EVERY NOW AND THEN YOU MEET ONE WHO KNOWS HOW TO SHARE IT AROUND. THAT'S HOW I'D WANNA BE.
THAT'S HOW HE IS.

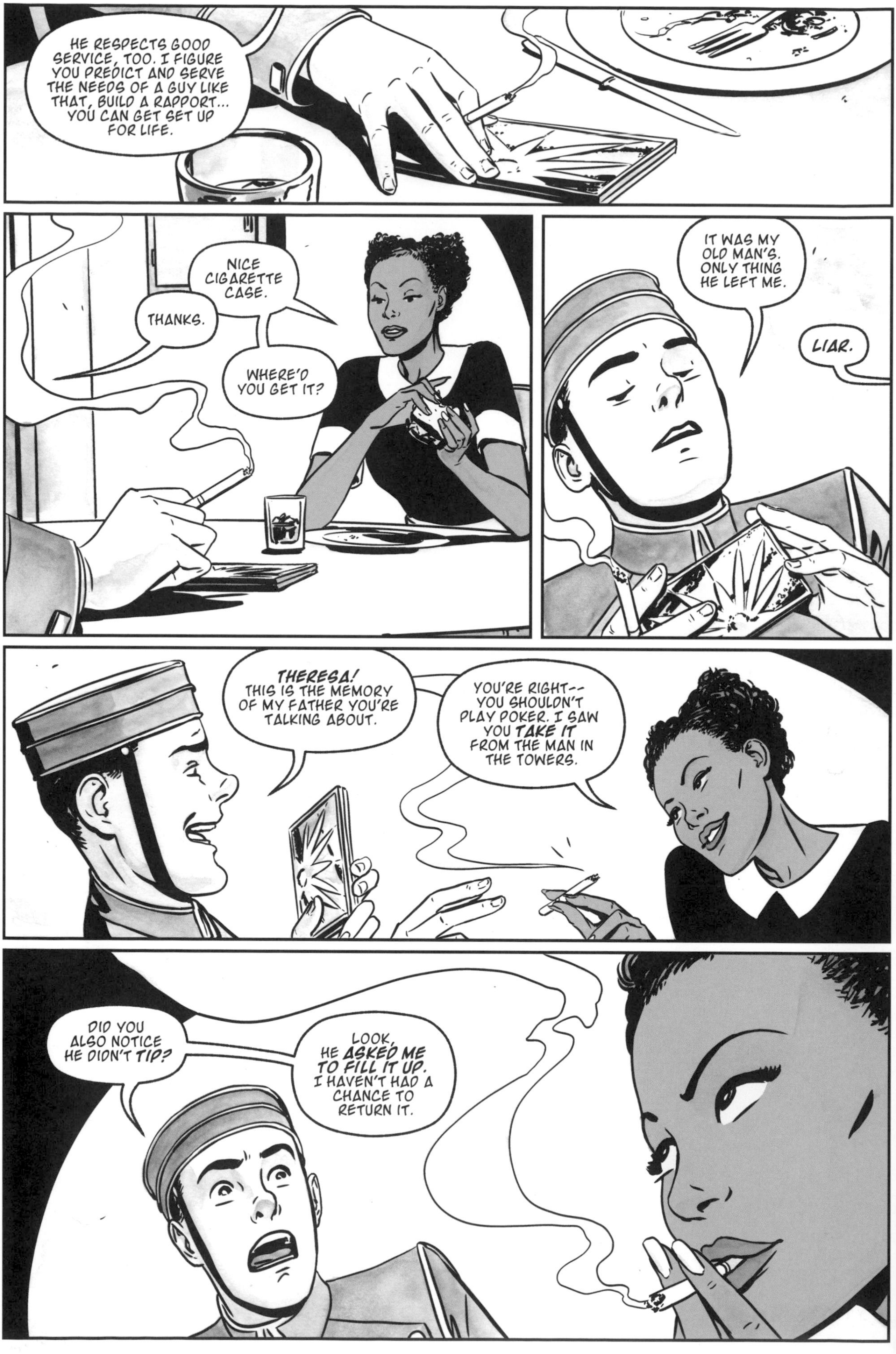
HE RESPECTS GOOD SERVICE, TOO. I FIGURE YOU PREDICT AND SERVE THE NEEDS OF A GUY LIKE THAT, BUILD A RAPPORT... YOU CAN GET SET UP FOR LIFE.
NICE CIGARETTE CASE.
THANKS.
WHERE'D YOU GET IT?
IT WAS MY OLD MAN'S. ONLY THING HE LEFT ME.
LIAR.
THERESA! THIS IS THE MEMORY OF MY FATHER YOU'RE TALKING ABOUT.
YOU'RE RIGHT-- YOU SHOULDN'T PLAY POKER. I SAW YOU TAKE IT FROM THE MAN IN THE TOWERS.
DID YOU ALSO NOTICE HE DIDN'T TIP?
LOOK, HE ASKED ME TO FILL IT UP. I HAVEN'T HAD A CHANCE TO RETURN IT.

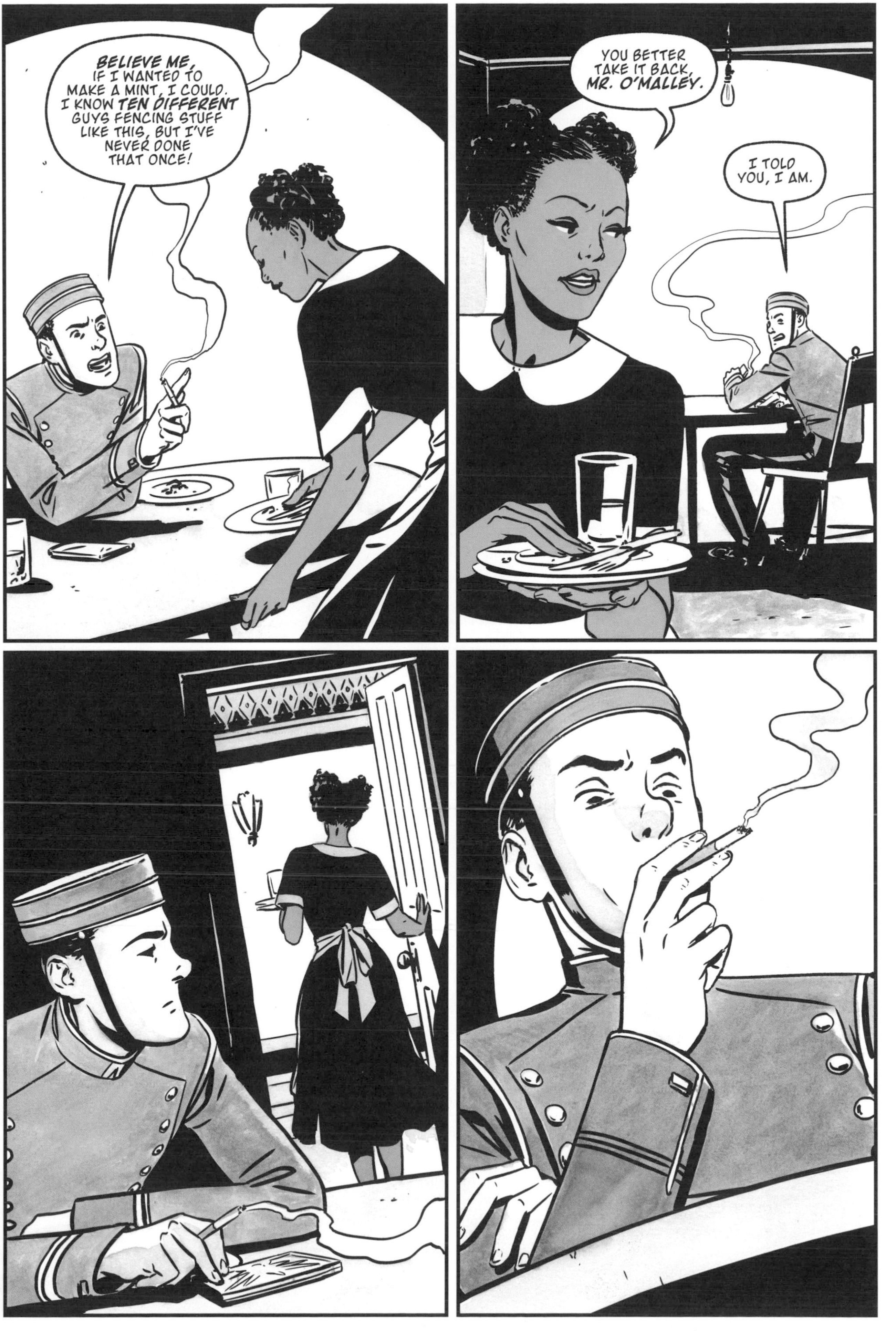
BELIEVE ME, IF I WANTED TO MAKE A MINT, I COULD. I KNOW TEN DIFFERENT GUYS FENCING STUFF LIKE THIS, BUT I'VE NEVER DONE THAT ONCE!
YOU BETTER TAKE IT BACK, MR. O'MALLEY.
I TOLD YOU, I AM.

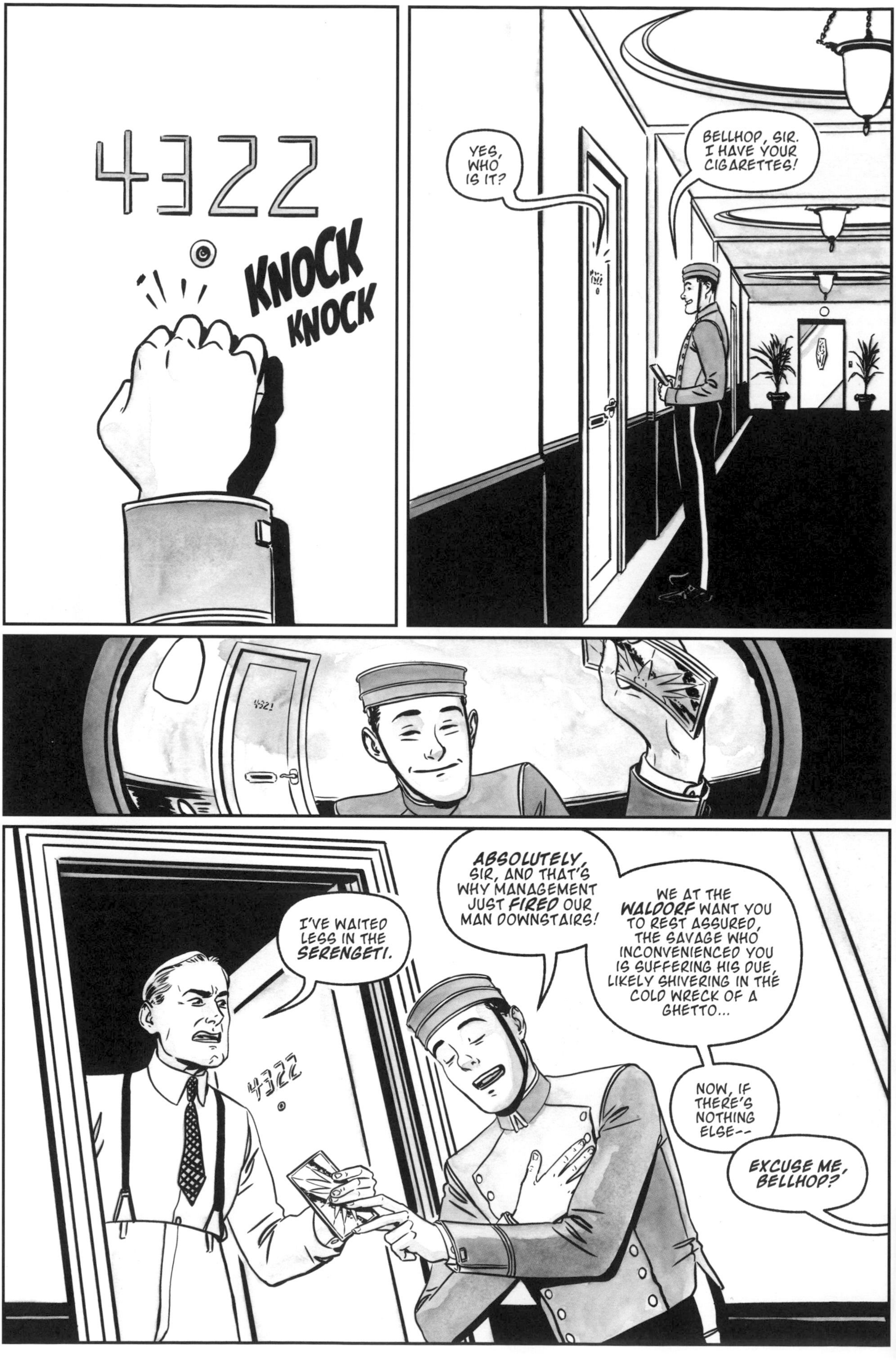
4322
KNOCK KNOCK
YES, WHO IS IT?
BELLHOP, SIR. I HAVE YOUR CIGARETTES!
I'VE WAITED LESS IN THE SERENGETI.
ABSOLUTELY, SIR, AND THAT'S WHY MANAGEMENT JUST FIRED OUR MAN DOWNSTAIRS!
WE AT THE WALDORF WANT YOU TO REST ASSURED, THE SAVAGE WHO INCONVENIENCED YOU IS SUFFERING HIS DUE, LIKELY SHIVERING IN THE COLD WRECK OF A GHETTO...
NOW, IF THERE'S NOTHING ELSE--
EXCUSE ME, BELLHOP?

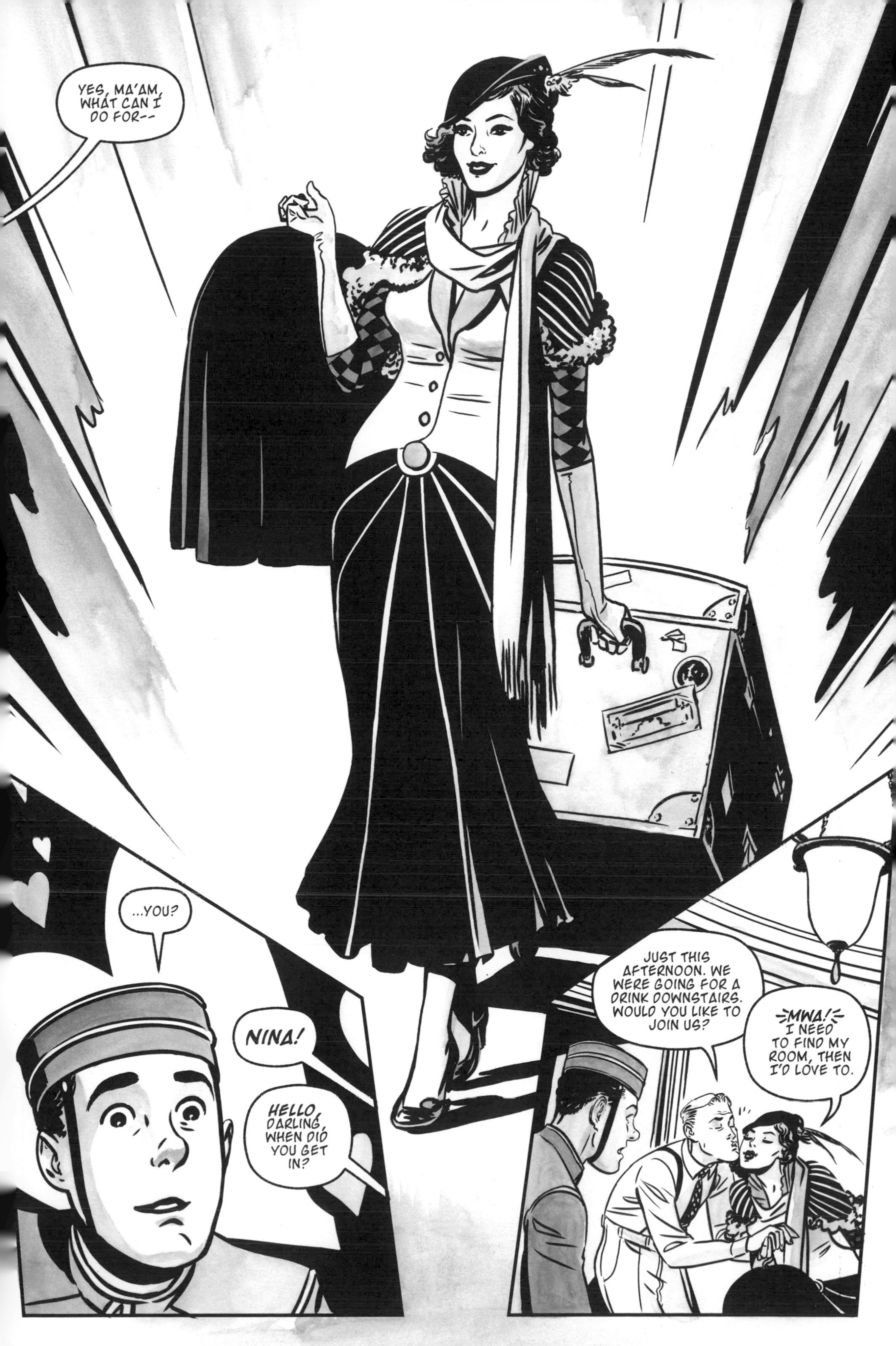
YES, MA'AM, WHAT CAN I DO FOR--
...YOU?
NINA!
HELLO, DARLING. WHEN DID YOU GET IN?
JUST THIS AFTERNOON. WE WERE GOING FOR A DRINK DOWNSTAIRS. WOULD YOU LIKE TO JOIN US?
MWA!
I NEED TO FIND MY ROOM, THEN I'D LOVE TO.

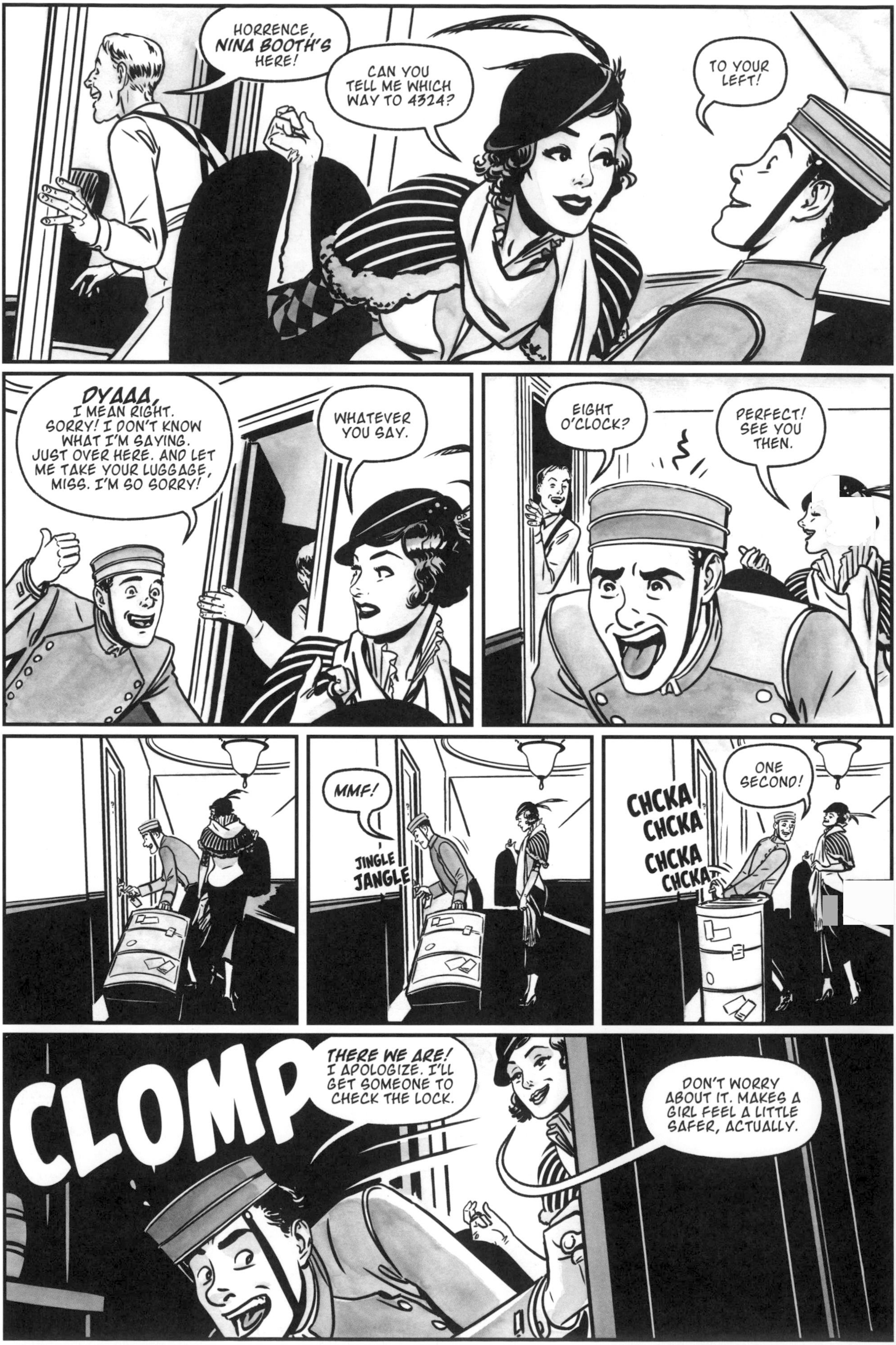
HORRENCE, NINA BOOTH'S HERE!
CAN YOU TELL ME WHICH WAY TO 4324?
TO YOUR LEFT!
DYAAA, I MEAN RIGHT. SORRY! I DON'T KNOW WHAT I'M SAYING. JUST OVER HERE. AND LET ME TAKE YOUR LUGGAGE, MISS. I'M SO SORRY!
WHATEVER YOU SAY.
EIGHT O'CLOCK?
PERFECT! SEE YOU THEN.
MMF!
JINGLE JANGLE
ONE SECOND!
CHCKA CHCKA CHCKA CHCKA
CLOMP
THERE WE ARE! I APOLOGIZE. I'LL GET SOMEONE TO CHECK THE LOCK.
DON'T WORRY ABOUT IT. MAKES A GIRL FEEL A LITTLE SAFER, ACTUALLY.

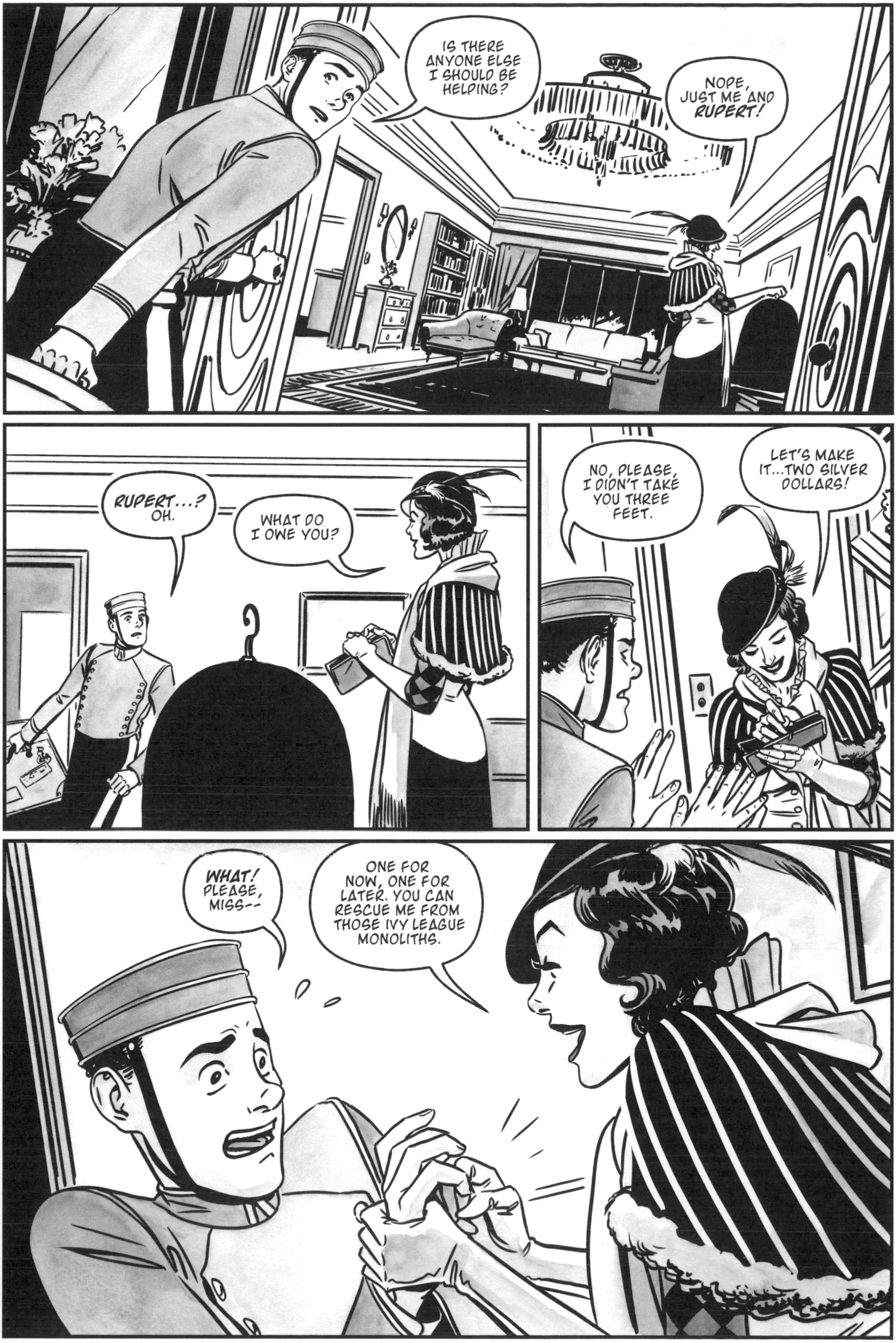
IS THERE ANYONE ELSE I SHOULD BE HELPING?
NOPE, JUST ME AND RUPERT!
RUPERT...? OH.
WHAT DO I OWE YOU?
NO, PLEASE, I DIDN'T TAKE YOU THREE FEET.
LET'S MAKE IT...TWO SILVER DOLLARS!
WHAT! PLEASE, MISS--
ONE FOR NOW, ONE FOR LATER. YOU CAN RESCUE ME FROM THOSE IVY LEAGUE MONOLITHS.

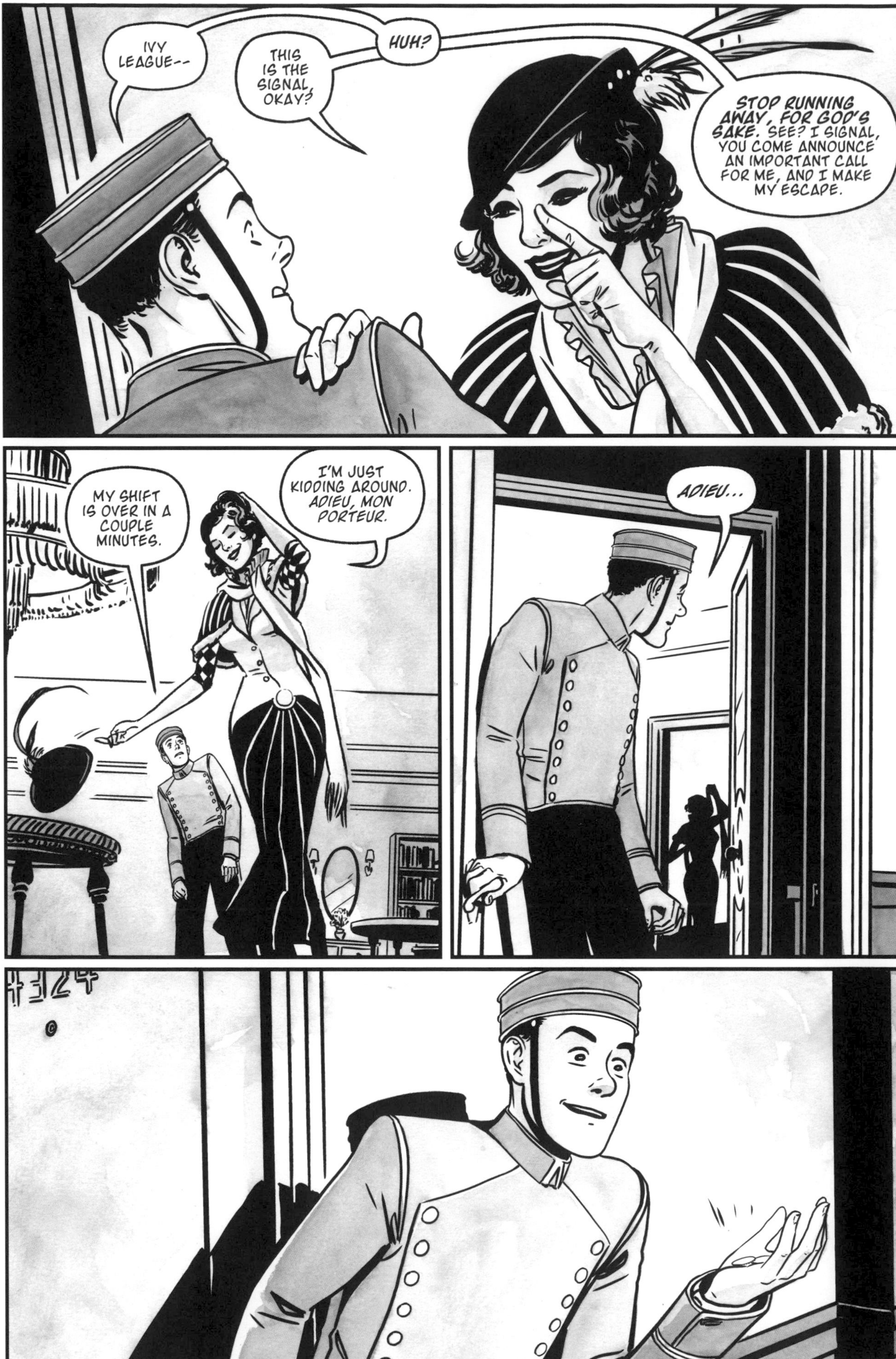
IVY LEAGUE--
THIS IS THE SIGNAL, OKAY?
HUH?
STOP RUNNING AWAY, FOR GOD'S SAKE. SEE? I SIGNAL, YOU COME ANNOUNCE AN IMPORTANT CALL FOR ME, AND I MAKE MY ESCAPE.
MY SHIFT IS OVER IN A COUPLE MINUTES.
I'M JUST KIDDING AROUND. ADIEU, MON PORTEUR.
ADIEU...
#324

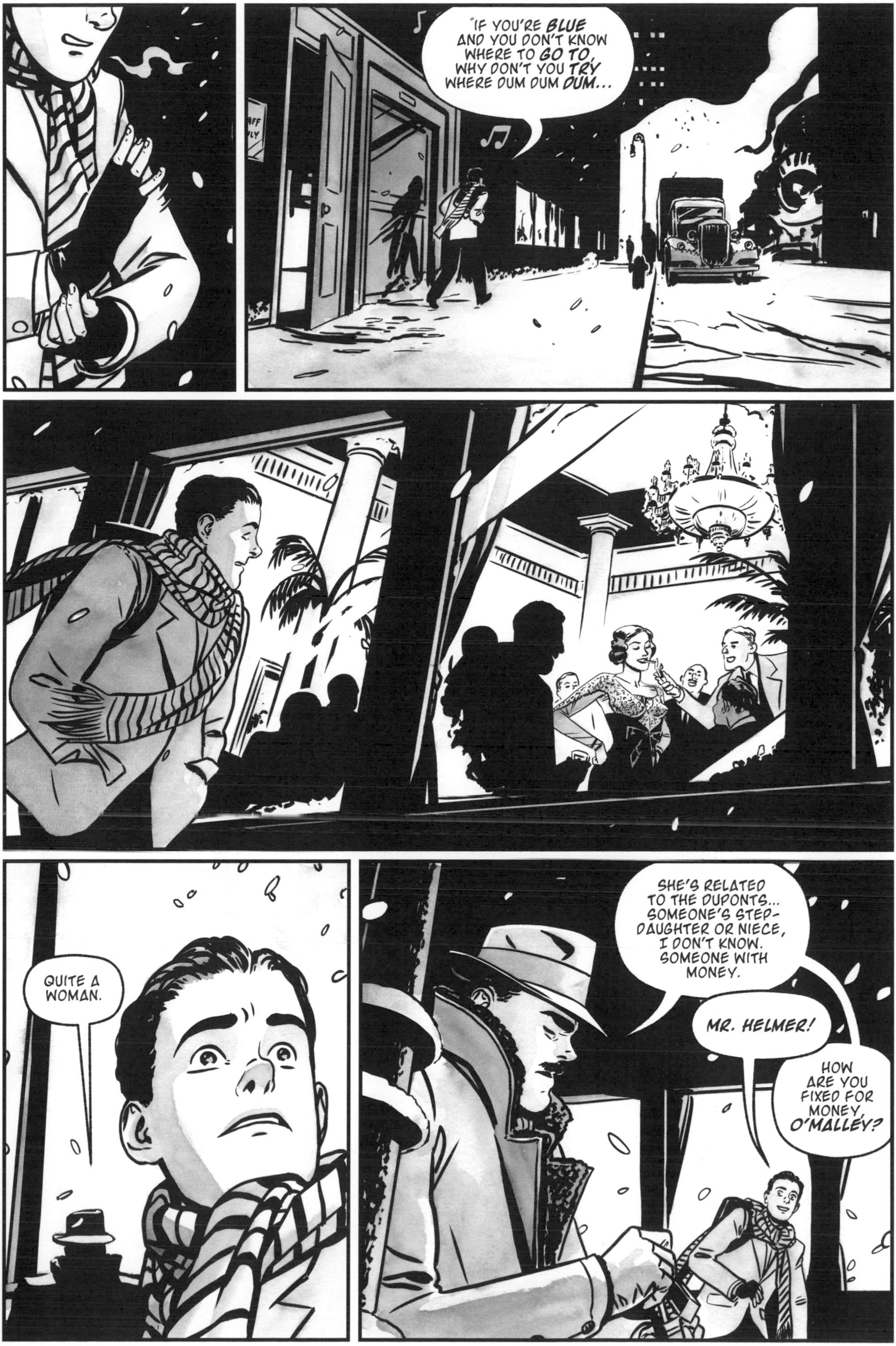
IF YOU'RE BLUE AND YOU DON'T KNOW WHERE TO GO TO, WHY DON'T YOU TRY WHERE DUM DUM DUM...
QUITE A WOMAN.
SHE'S RELATED TO THE DUPONTS... SOMEONE'S STEP-DAUGHTER OR NIECE, I DON'T KNOW. SOMEONE WITH MONEY.
MR. HELMER!
HOW ARE YOU FIXED FOR MONEY, O'MALLEY?

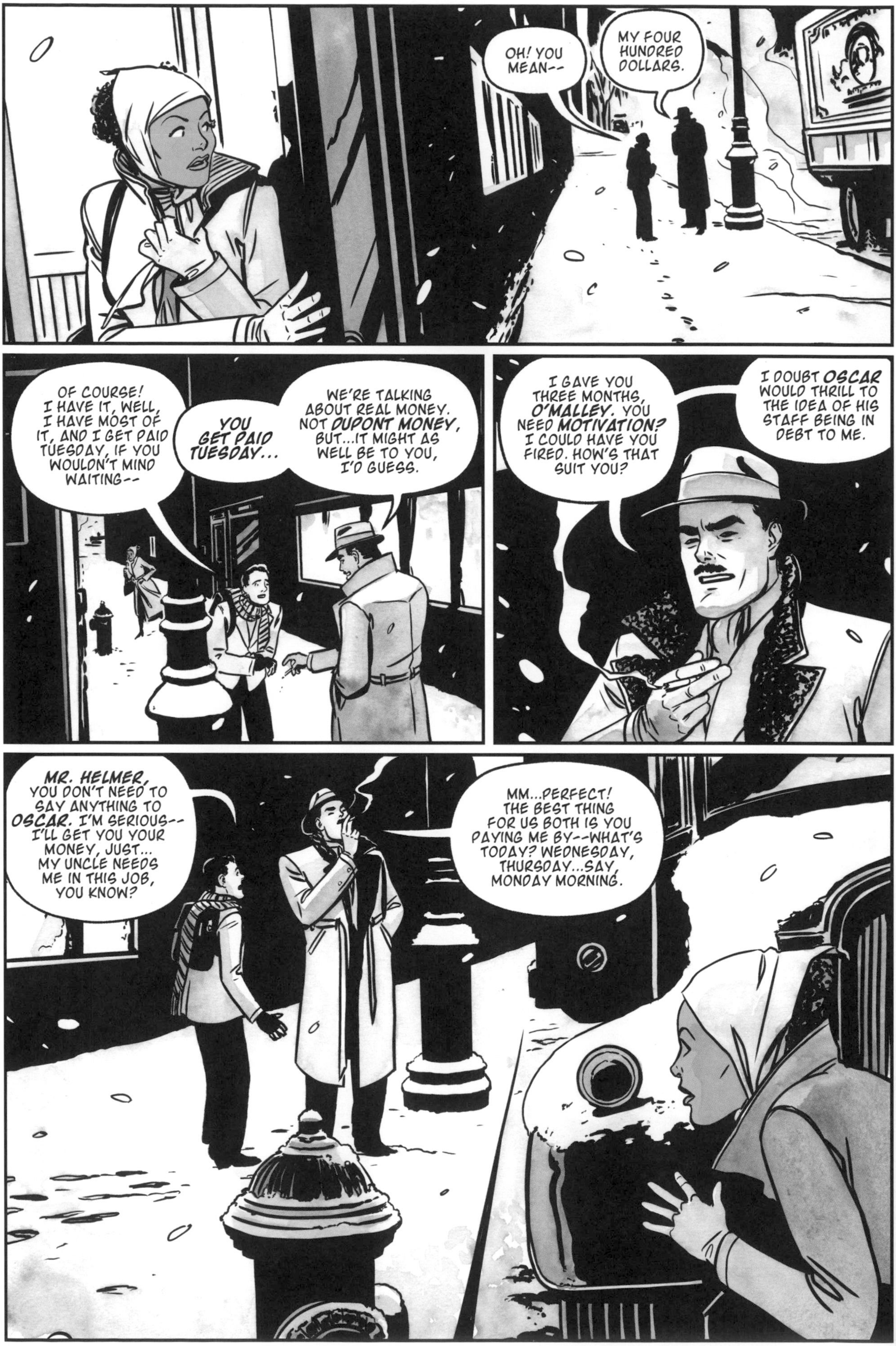
OH! YOU MEAN--
MY FOUR HUNDRED DOLLARS.
OF COURSE! I HAVE IT, WELL, I HAVE MOST OF IT, AND I GET PAID TUESDAY, IF YOU WOULDN'T MIND WAITING--
YOU GET PAID TUESDAY...
WE'RE TALKING ABOUT REAL MONEY. NOT DUPONT MONEY, BUT...IT MIGHT AS WELL BE TO YOU, I'D GUESS.
I GAVE YOU THREE MONTHS, O'MALLEY. YOU NEED MOTIVATION? I COULD HAVE YOU FIRED. HOW'S THAT SUIT YOU?
I DOUBT OSCAR WOULD THRILL TO THE IDEA OF HIS STAFF BEING IN DEBT TO ME.
MR. HELMER, YOU DON'T NEED TO SAY ANYTHING TO OSCAR. I'M SERIOUS-- I'LL GET YOU YOUR MONEY, JUST... MY UNCLE NEEDS ME IN THIS JOB, YOU KNOW?
MM...PERFECT! THE BEST THING FOR US BOTH IS YOU PAYING ME BY--WHAT'S TODAY? WEDNESDAY, THURSDAY...SAY, MONDAY MORNING.

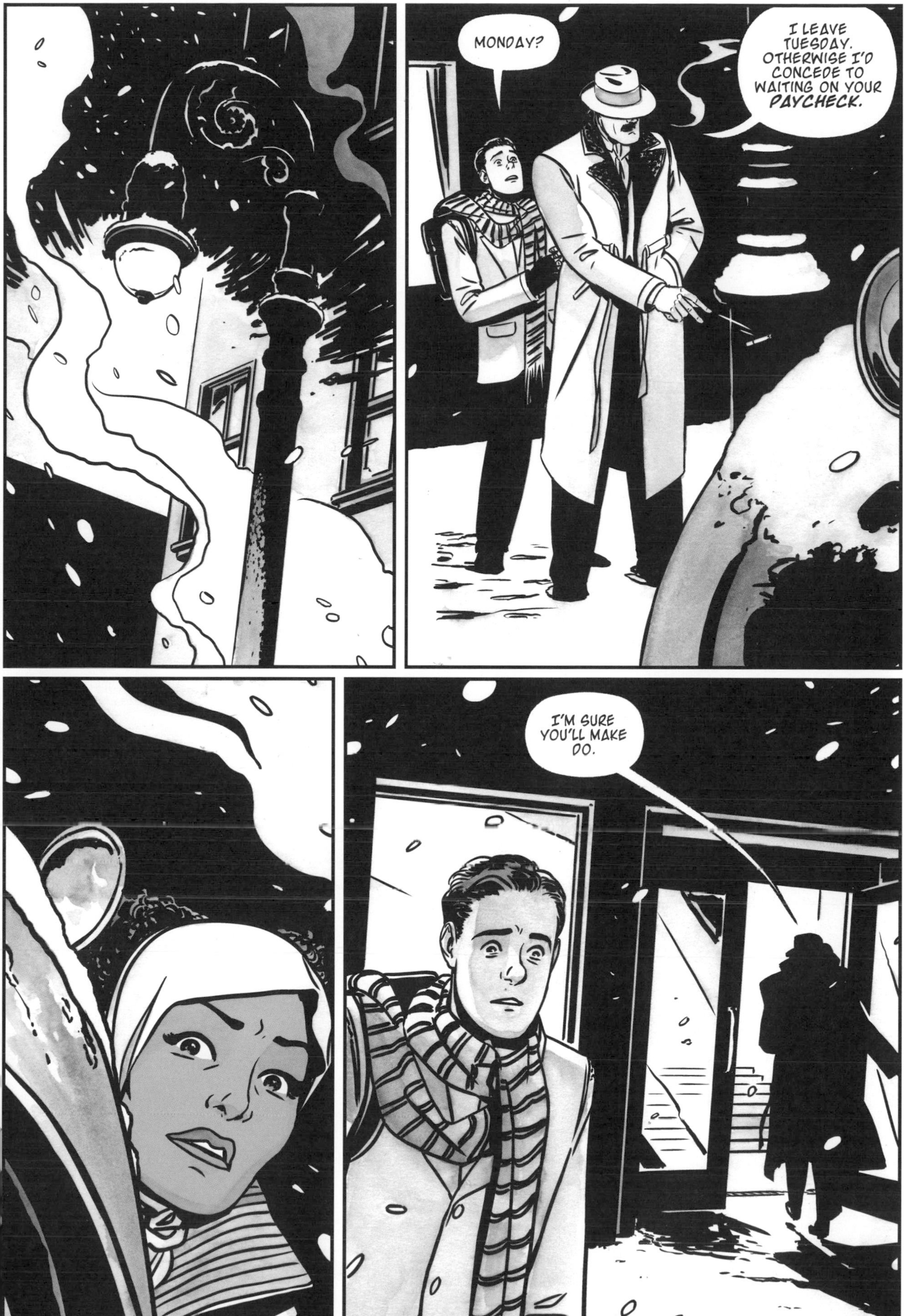
MONDAY?
I LEAVE TUESDAY. OTHERWISE I'D CONCEDE TO WAITING ON YOUR PAYCHECK.
I'M SURE YOU'LL MAKE DO.

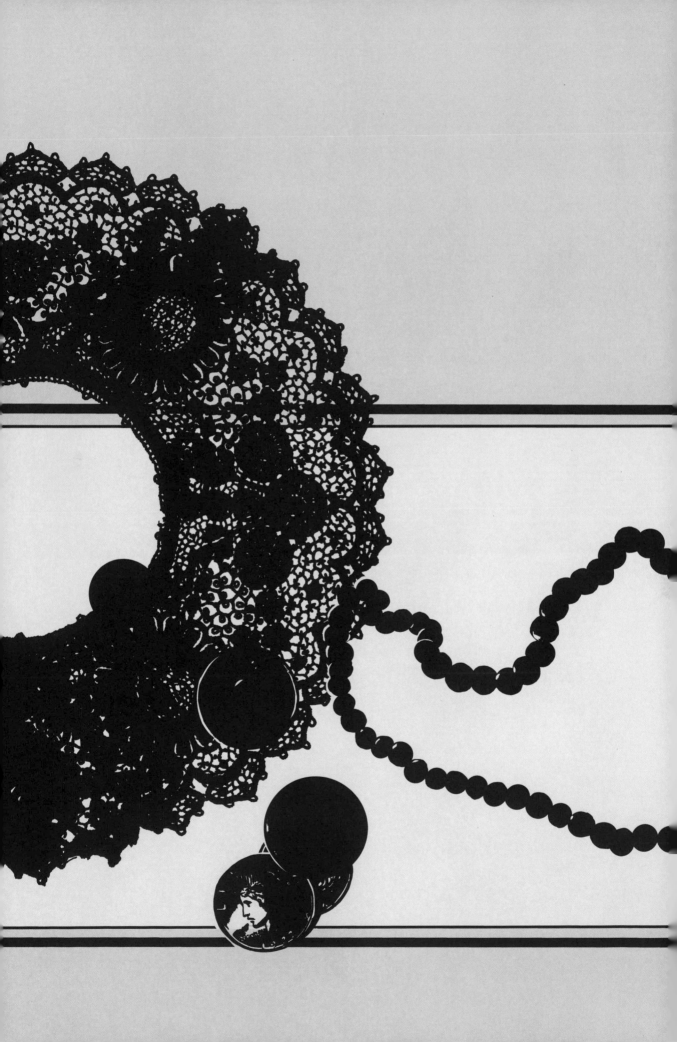

CHAPTER 2

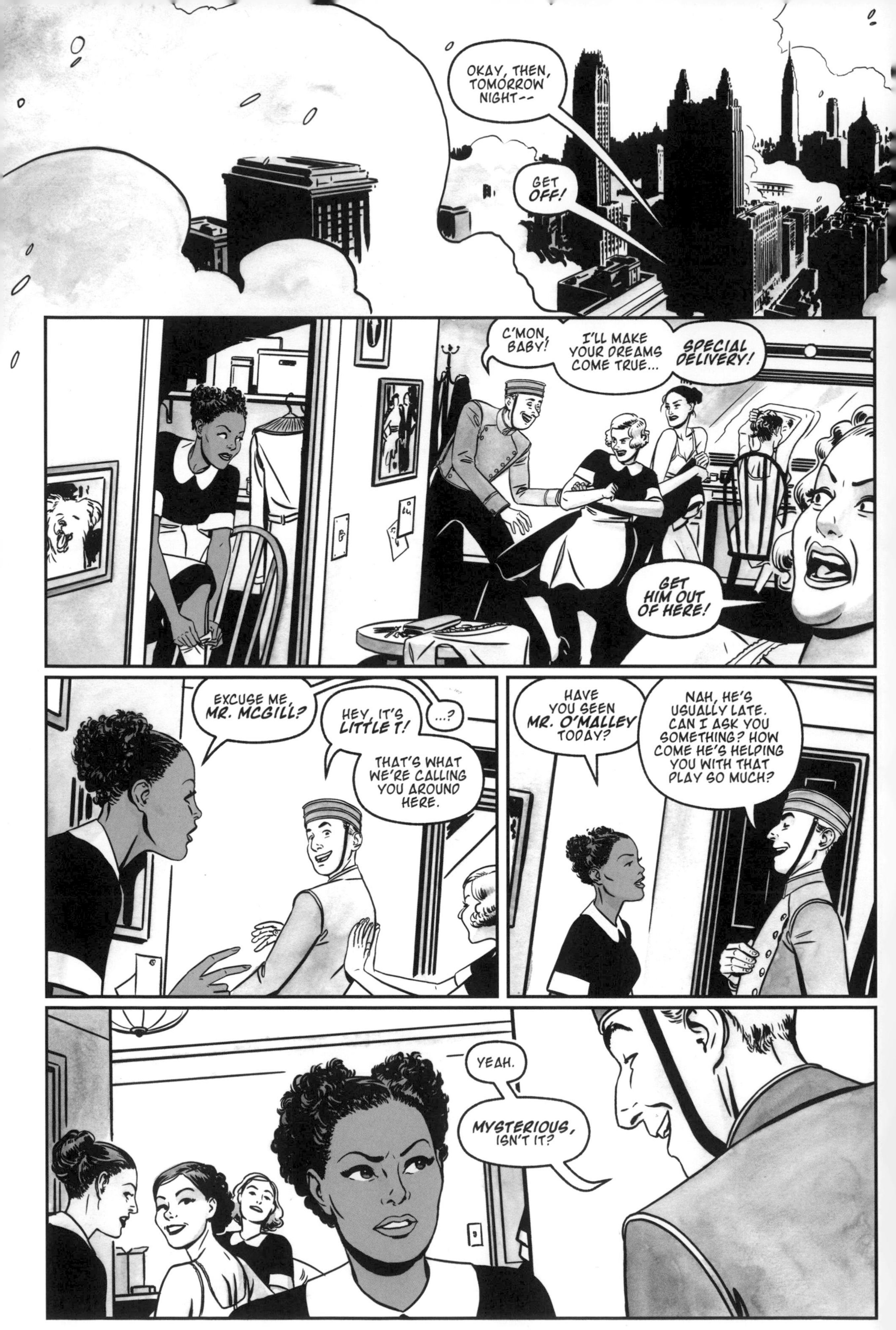
OKAY, THEN, TOMORROW NIGHT--
GET OFF!
C'MON, BABY!
I'LL MAKE YOUR DREAMS COME TRUE...
SPECIAL DELIVERY!
GET HIM OUT OF HERE!
EXCUSE ME, MR. MCGILL?
HEY, IT'S LITTLE T!
...?
THAT'S WHAT WE'RE CALLING YOU AROUND HERE.
HAVE YOU SEEN MR. O'MALLEY TODAY?
NAH, HE'S USUALLY LATE. CAN I ASK YOU SOMETHING? HOW COME HE'S HELPING YOU WITH THAT PLAY SO MUCH?
YEAH.
MYSTERIOUS, ISN'T IT?

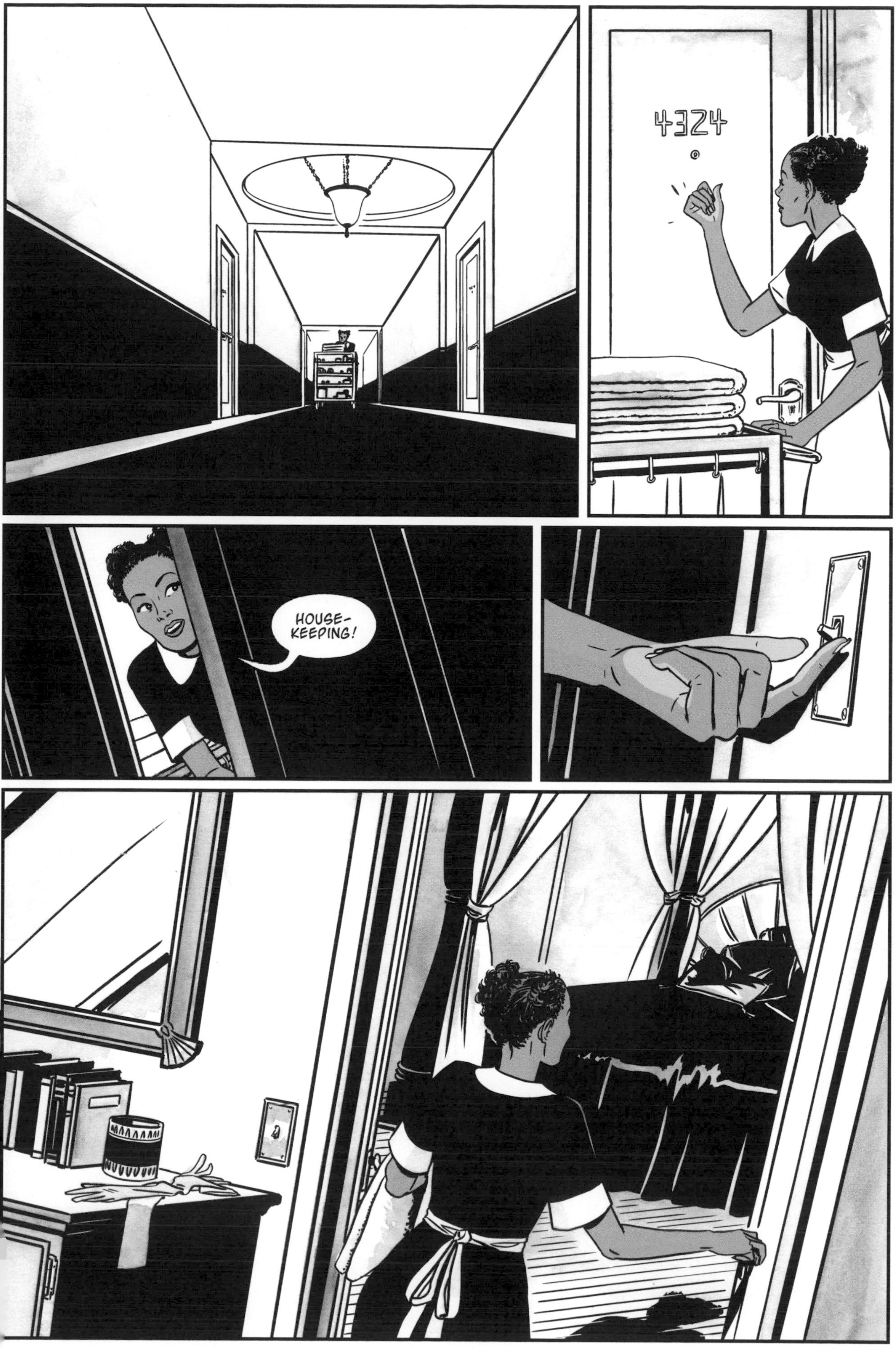
4324
HOUSE-KEEPING!

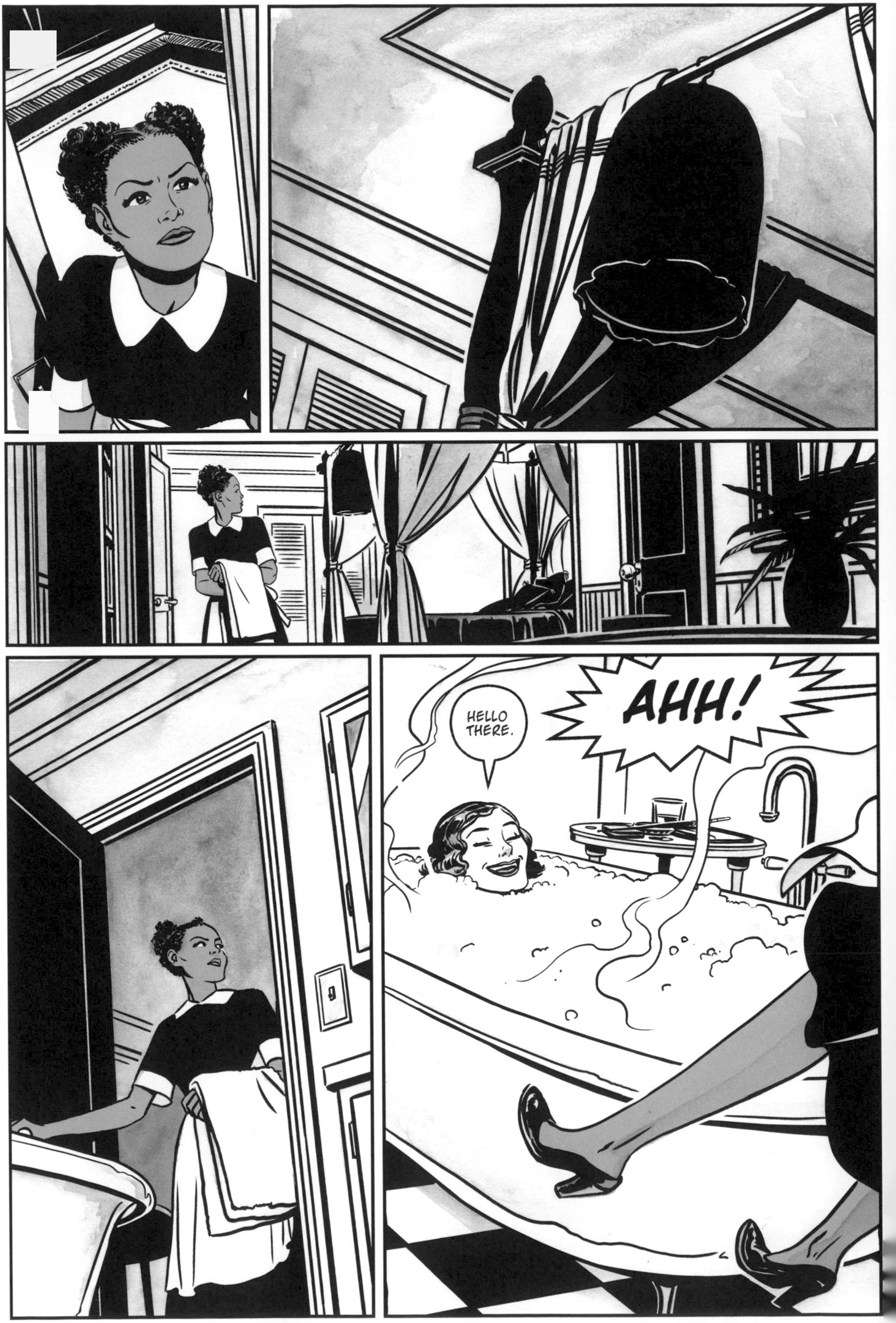
HELLO THERE.
AHH!

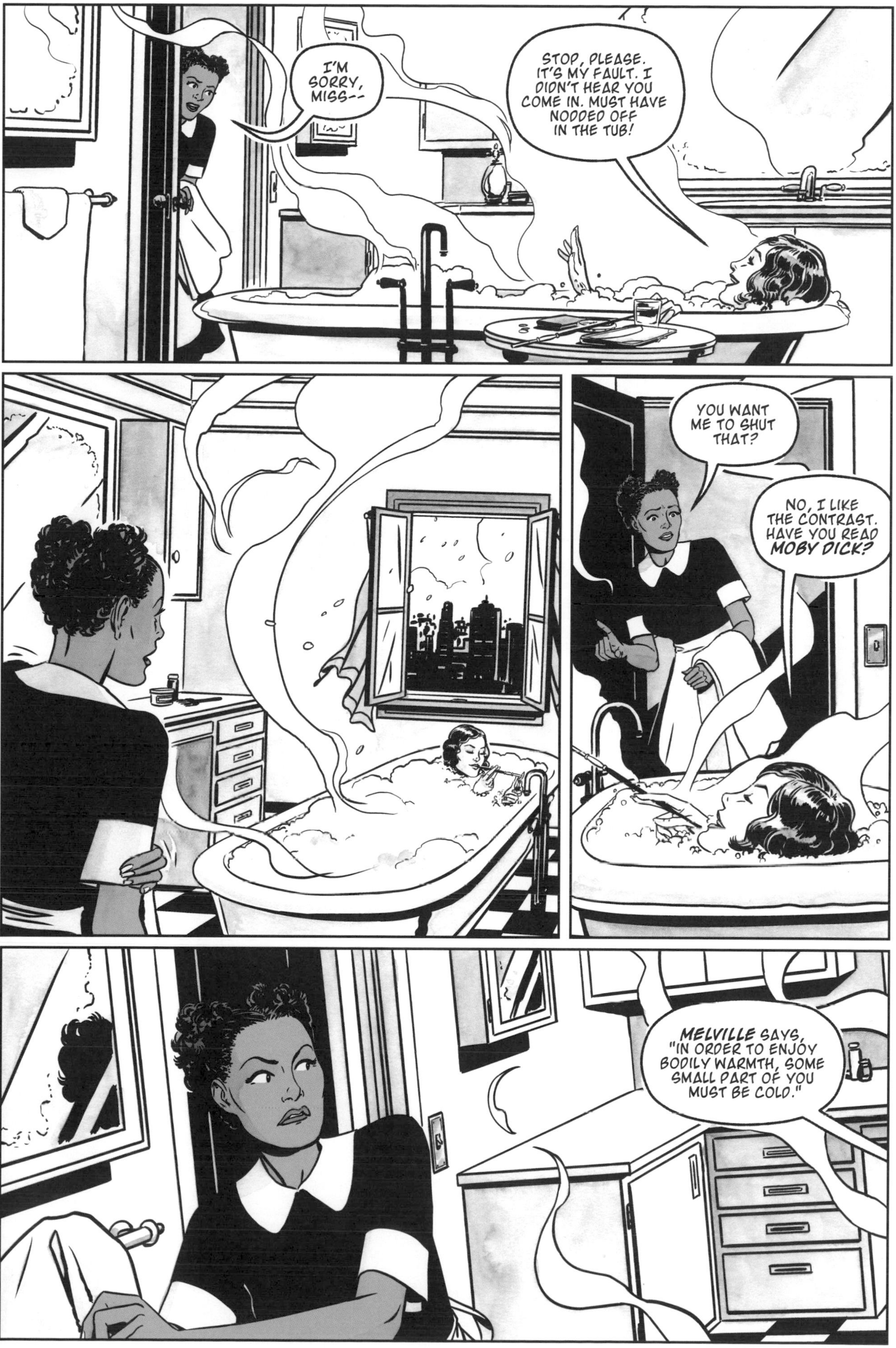
I'M SORRY, MISS--
STOP, PLEASE. IT'S MY FAULT. I DIDN'T HEAR YOU COME IN. MUST HAVE NODDED OFF IN THE TUB!
YOU WANT ME TO SHUT THAT?
NO, I LIKE THE CONTRAST. HAVE YOU READ MOBY DICK?
MELVILLE SAYS, "IN ORDER TO ENJOY BODILY WARMTH, SOME SMALL PART OF YOU MUST BE COLD."

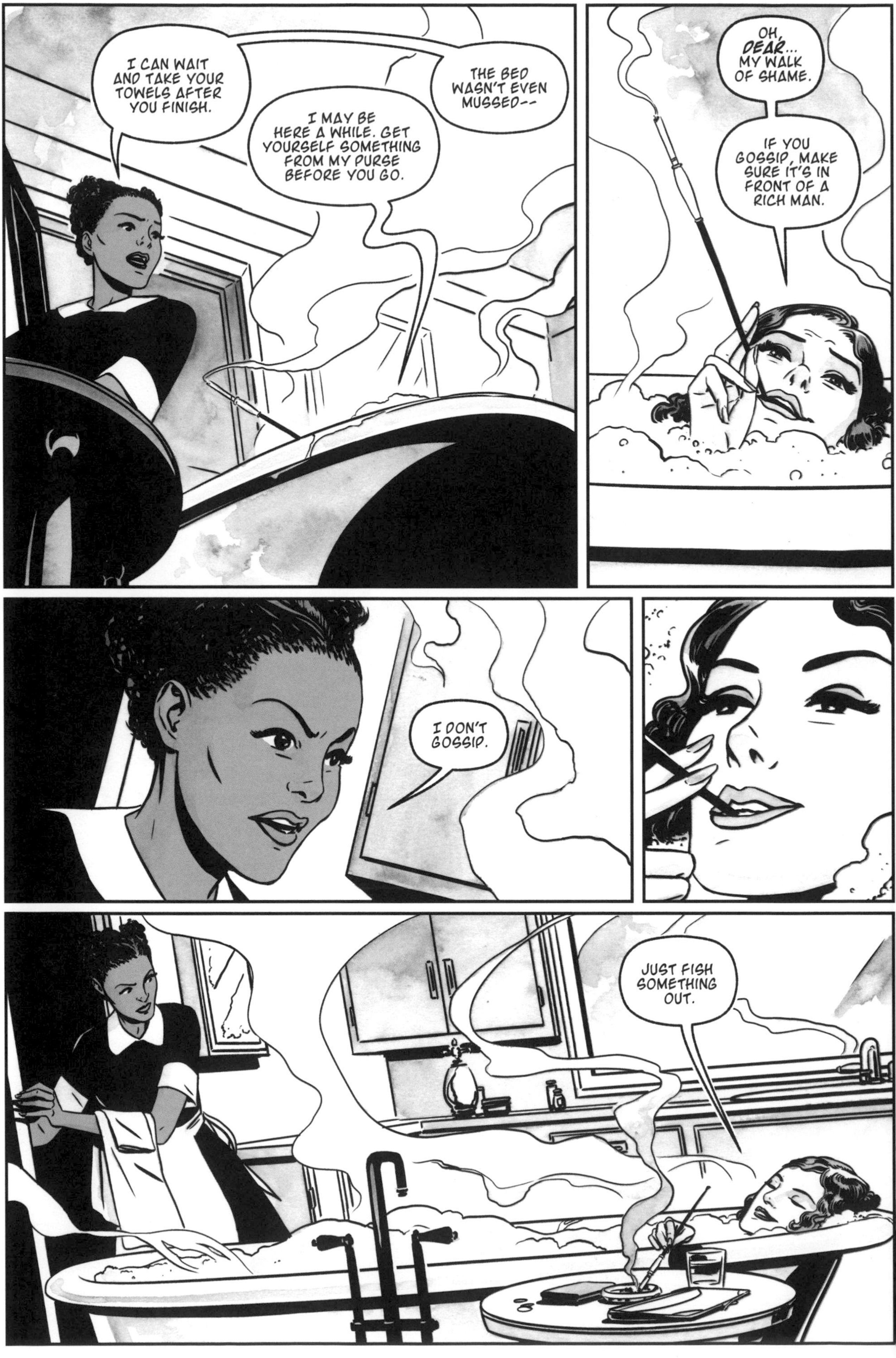
I CAN WAIT AND TAKE YOUR TOWELS AFTER YOU FINISH.
THE BED WASN'T EVEN MUSSED--
I MAY BE HERE A WHILE. GET YOURSELF SOMETHING FROM MY PURSE BEFORE YOU GO.
OH, DEAR... MY WALK OF SHAME.
IF YOU GOSSIP, MAKE SURE IT'S IN FRONT OF A RICH MAN.
I DON'T GOSSIP.
JUST FISH SOMETHING OUT.

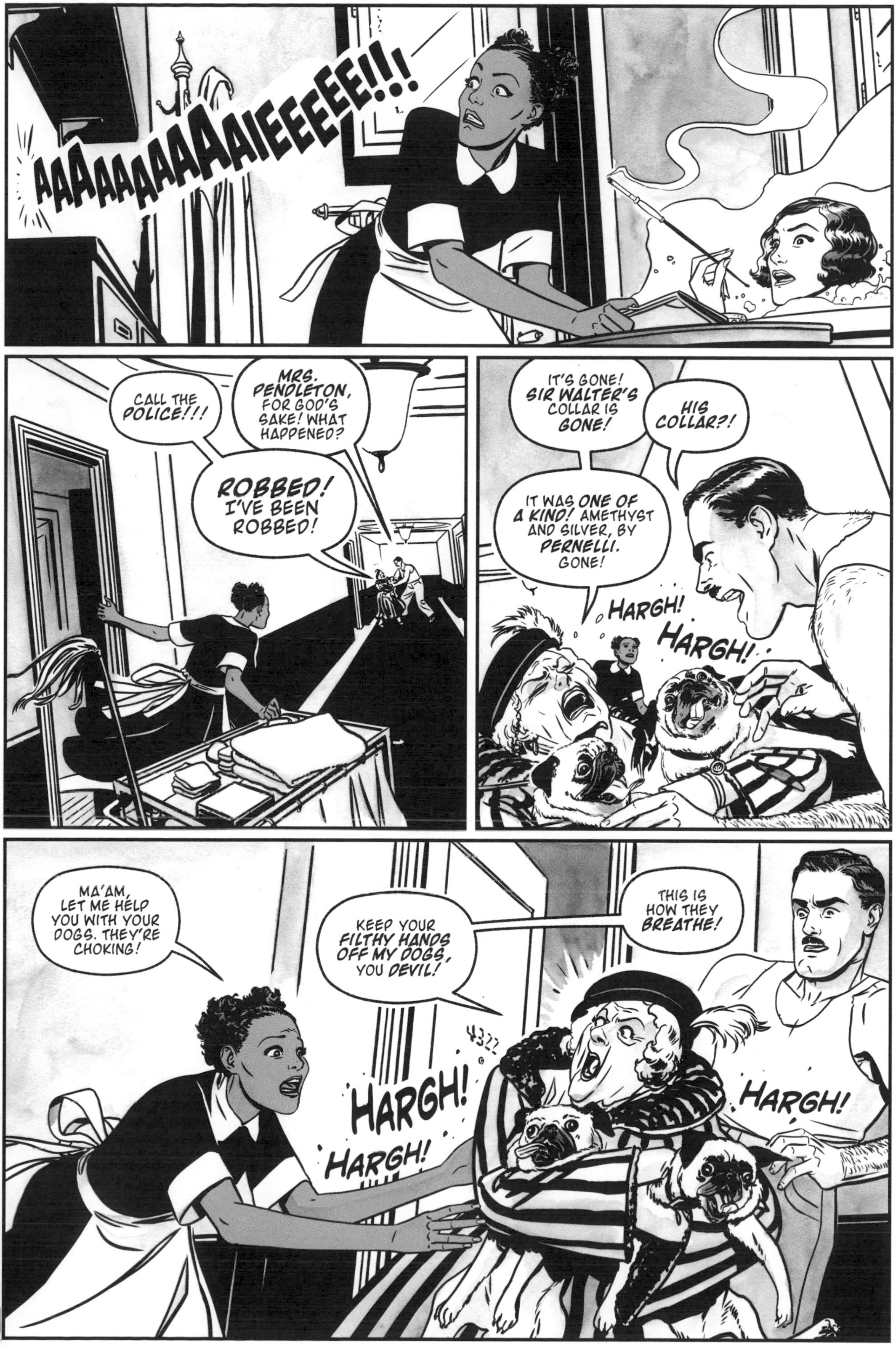
AAAAAAAAAAIEEEEEE!!!
CALL THE POLICE!!!
MRS. PENDLETON, FOR GOD'S SAKE! WHAT HAPPENED?
ROBBED! I'VE BEEN ROBBED!
IT'S GONE! SIR WALTER'S COLLAR IS GONE!
HIS COLLAR?!
IT WAS ONE OF A KIND! AMETHYST AND SILVER, BY PERNELLI. GONE!
HARGH!
HARGH!
MA'AM, LET ME HELP YOU WITH YOUR DOGS. THEY'RE CHOKING!
KEEP YOUR FILTHY HANDS OFF MY DOGS, YOU DEVIL!
THIS IS HOW THEY BREATHE!
HARGH!
HARGH!
HARGH!

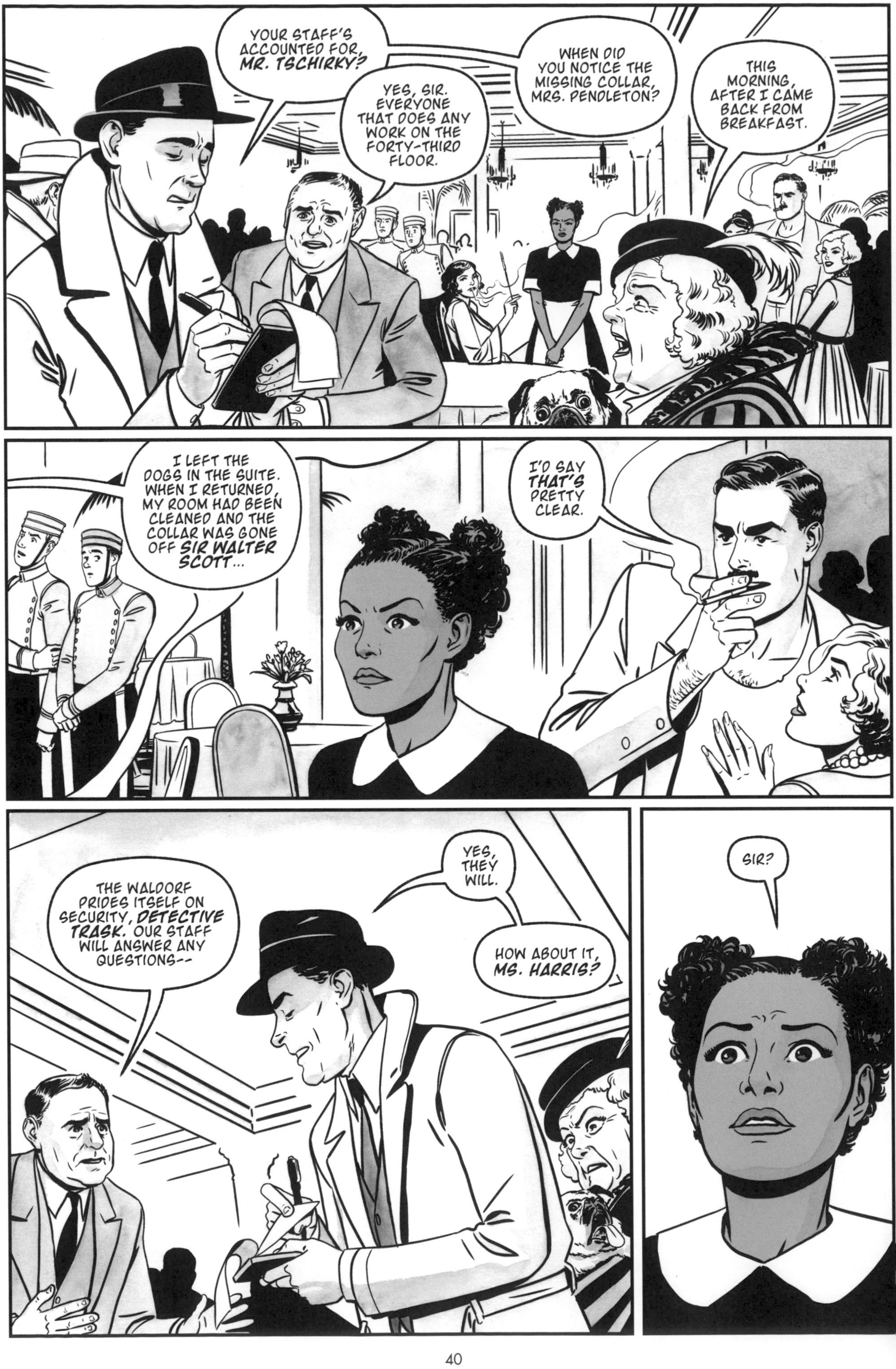
YOUR STAFF'S ACCOUNTED FOR, MR. TSCHIRKY?
YES, SIR. EVERYONE THAT DOES ANY WORK ON THE FORTY-THIRD FLOOR.
WHEN DID YOU NOTICE THE MISSING COLLAR, MRS. PENDLETON?
THIS MORNING, AFTER I CAME BACK FROM BREAKFAST.
I LEFT THE DOGS IN THE SUITE. WHEN I RETURNED, MY ROOM HAD BEEN CLEANED AND THE COLLAR WAS GONE OFF SIR WALTER SCOTT...
I'D SAY THAT'S PRETTY CLEAR.
THE WALDORF PRIDES ITSELF ON SECURITY, DETECTIVE TRASK. OUR STAFF WILL ANSWER ANY QUESTIONS--
YES, THEY WILL.
HOW ABOUT IT, MS. HARRIS?
SIR?

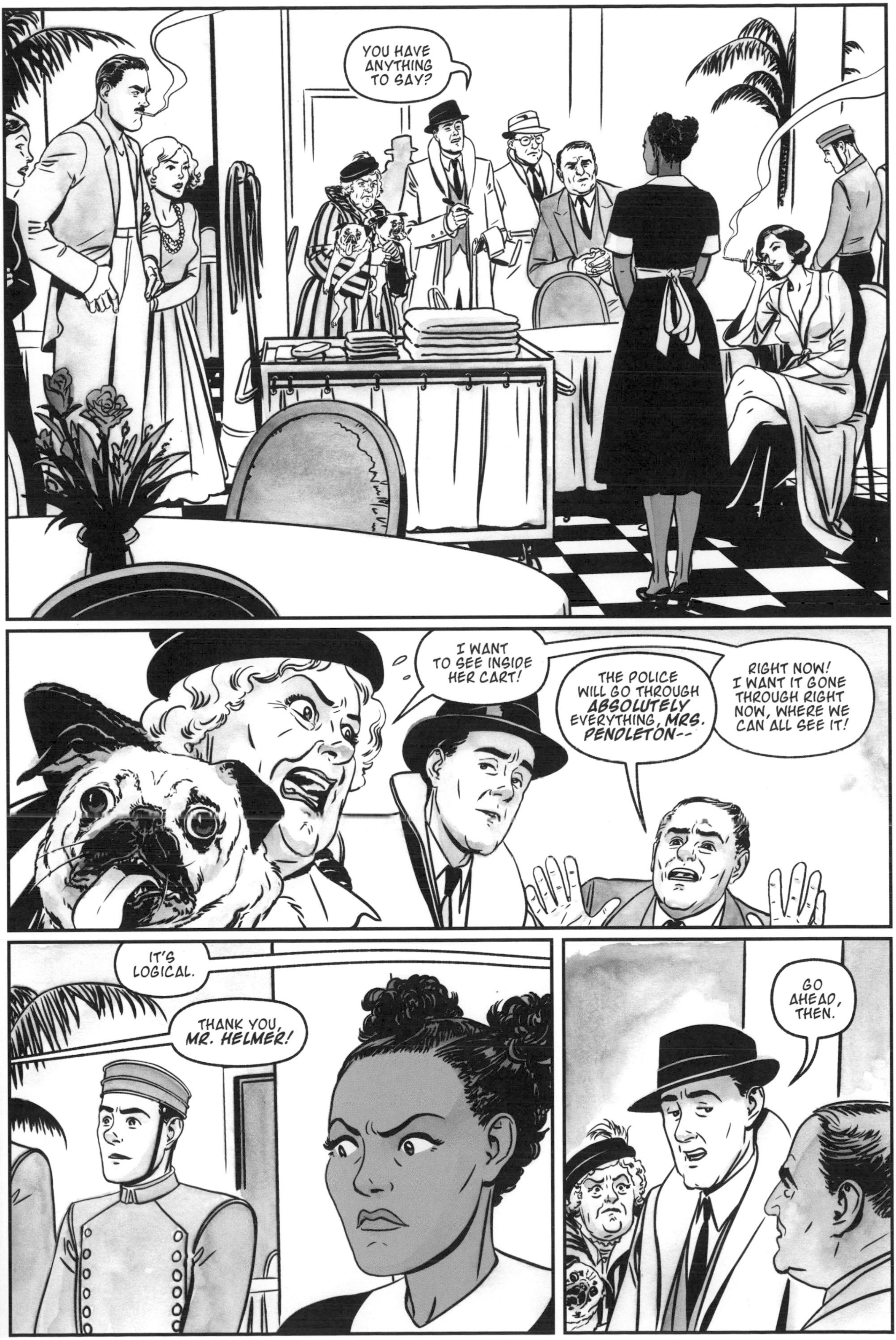
YOU HAVE ANYTHING TO SAY?
I WANT TO SEE INSIDE HER CART!
THE POLICE WILL GO THROUGH ABSOLUTELY EVERYTHING, MRS. PENDLETON--
RIGHT NOW! I WANT IT GONE THROUGH RIGHT NOW, WHERE WE CAN ALL SEE IT!
IT'S LOGICAL.
THANK YOU, MR. HELMER!
GO AHEAD, THEN.

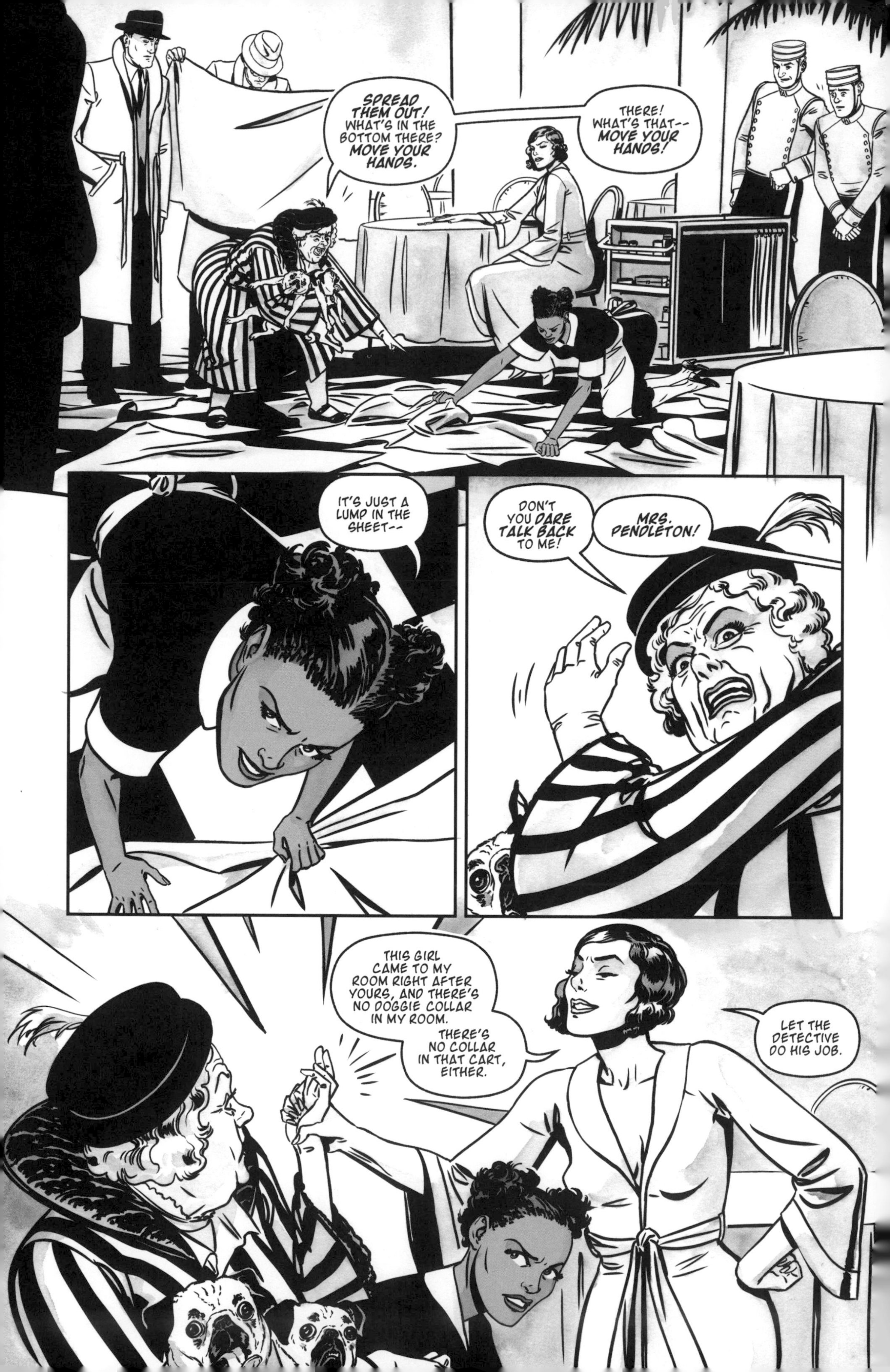
SPREAD THEM OUT! WHAT'S IN THE BOTTOM THERE? MOVE YOUR HANDS.
THERE! WHAT'S THAT-- MOVE YOUR HANDS!
IT'S JUST A LUMP IN THE SHEET--
DON'T YOU DARE TALK BACK TO ME!
MRS. PENDLETON!
THIS GIRL CAME TO MY ROOM RIGHT AFTER YOURS, AND THERE'S NO DOGGIE COLLAR IN MY ROOM.
THERE'S NO COLLAR IN THAT CART, EITHER.
LET THE DETECTIVE DO HIS JOB.

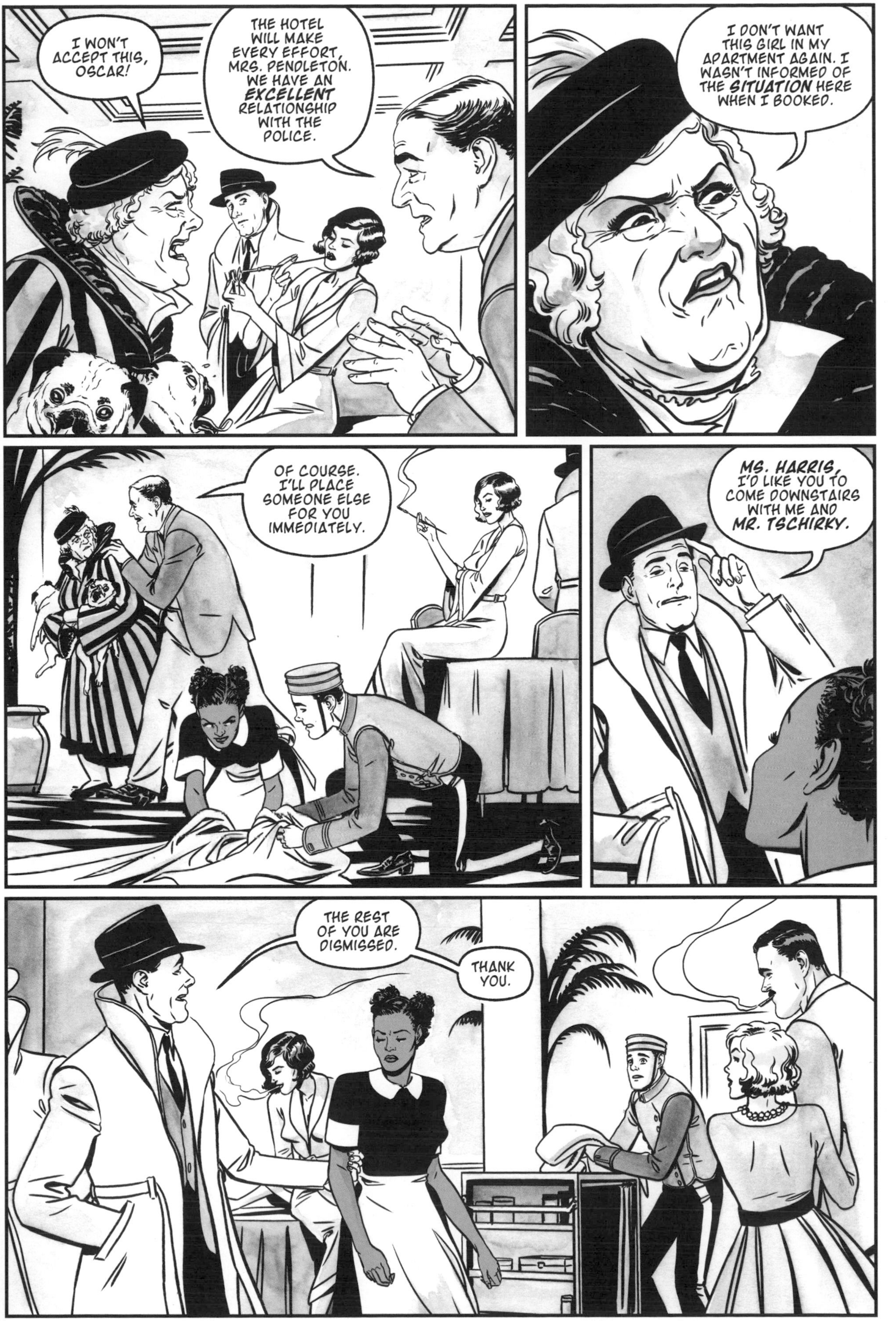
I WON'T ACCEPT THIS, OSCAR!
THE HOTEL WILL MAKE EVERY EFFORT, MRS. PENDLETON. WE HAVE AN EXCELLENT RELATIONSHIP WITH THE POLICE.
I DON'T WANT THIS GIRL IN MY APARTMENT AGAIN. I WASN'T INFORMED OF THE SITUATION HERE WHEN I BOOKED.
OF COURSE. I'LL PLACE SOMEONE ELSE FOR YOU IMMEDIATELY.
MS. HARRIS, I'D LIKE YOU TO COME DOWNSTAIRS WITH ME AND MR. TSCHIRKY.
THE REST OF YOU ARE DISMISSED.
THANK YOU.

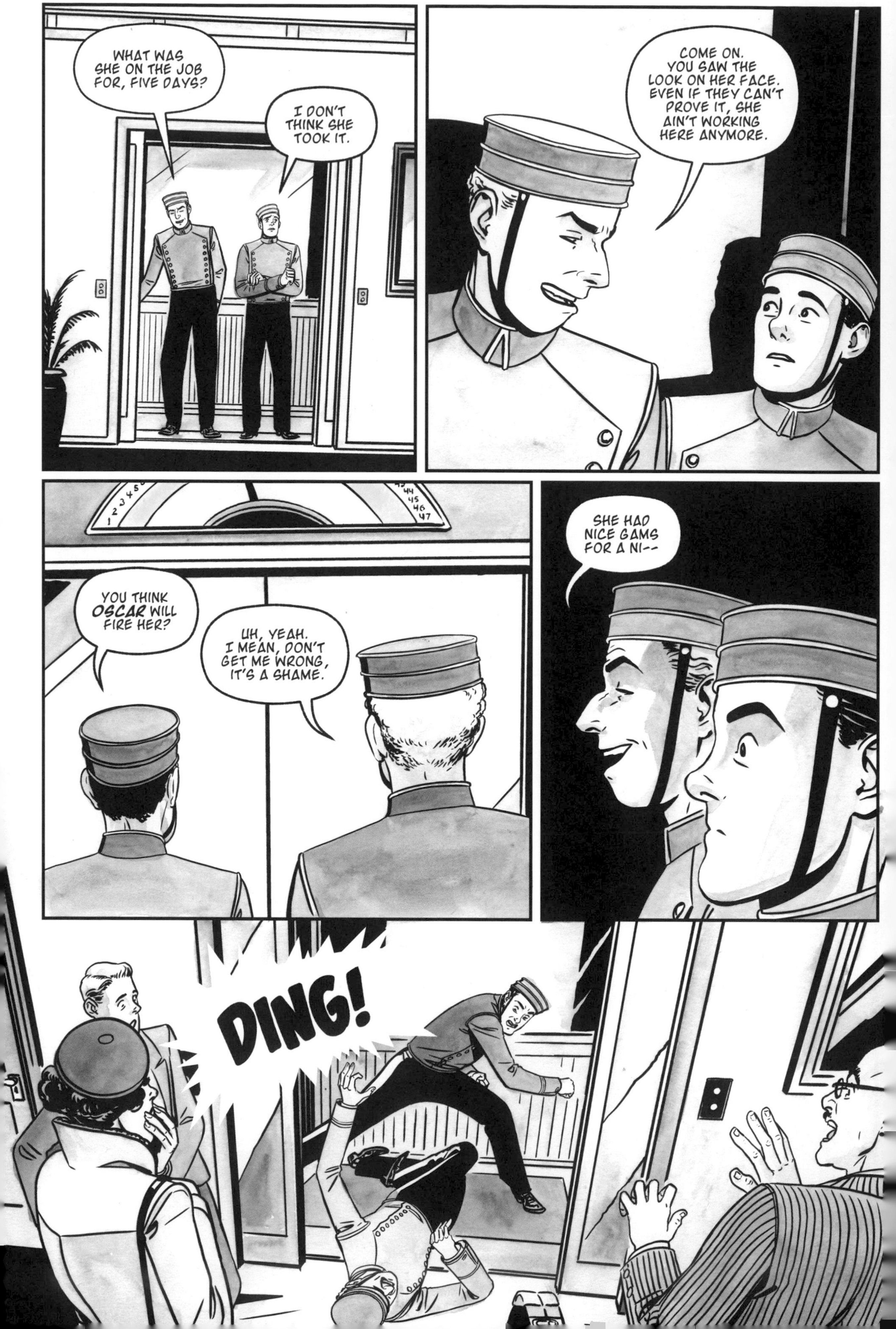
WHAT WAS SHE ON THE JOB FOR, FIVE DAYS?
I DON'T THINK SHE TOOK IT.
COME ON. YOU SAW THE LOOK ON HER FACE. EVEN IF THEY CAN'T PROVE IT, SHE AIN'T WORKING HERE ANYMORE.
YOU THINK OSCAR WILL FIRE HER?
UH, YEAH. I MEAN, DON'T GET ME WRONG, IT'S A SHAME.
SHE HAD NICE GAMS FOR A NI--
DING!

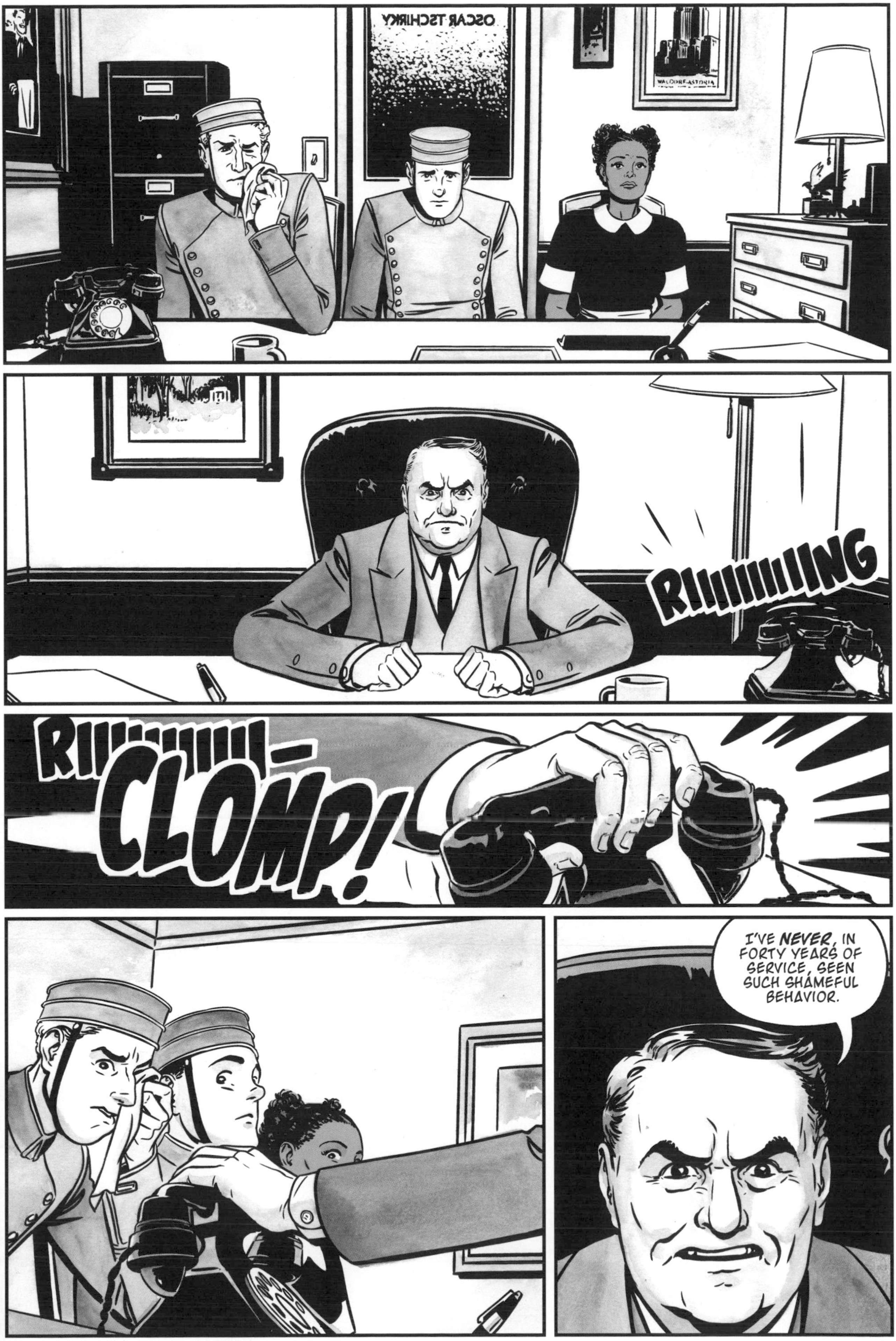
WALDORF-ASTORIA
RIIIIIIIIING
RIIIIIIIIIII-
CLOMP!
I'VE **NEVER**, IN FORTY YEARS OF SERVICE, SEEN SUCH SHAMEFUL BEHAVIOR.

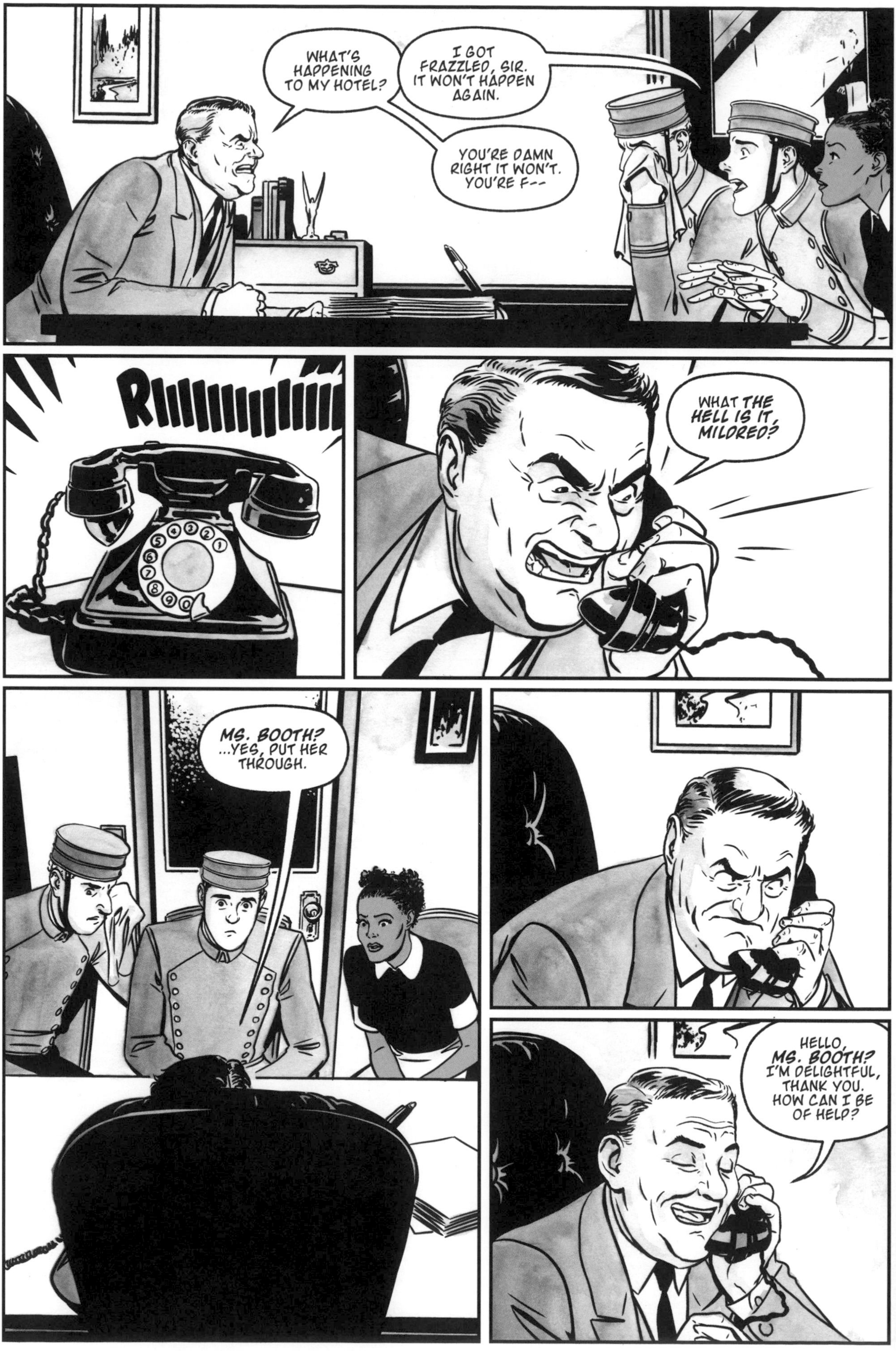
WHAT'S HAPPENING TO MY HOTEL?
I GOT FRAZZLED, SIR. IT WON'T HAPPEN AGAIN.
YOU'RE DAMN RIGHT IT WON'T. YOU'RE F--
RIIIIIIIIIIIIIII
WHAT THE HELL IS IT, MILDRED?
MS. BOOTH? ...YES, PUT HER THROUGH.
HELLO, MS. BOOTH? I'M DELIGHTFUL, THANK YOU. HOW CAN I BE OF HELP?

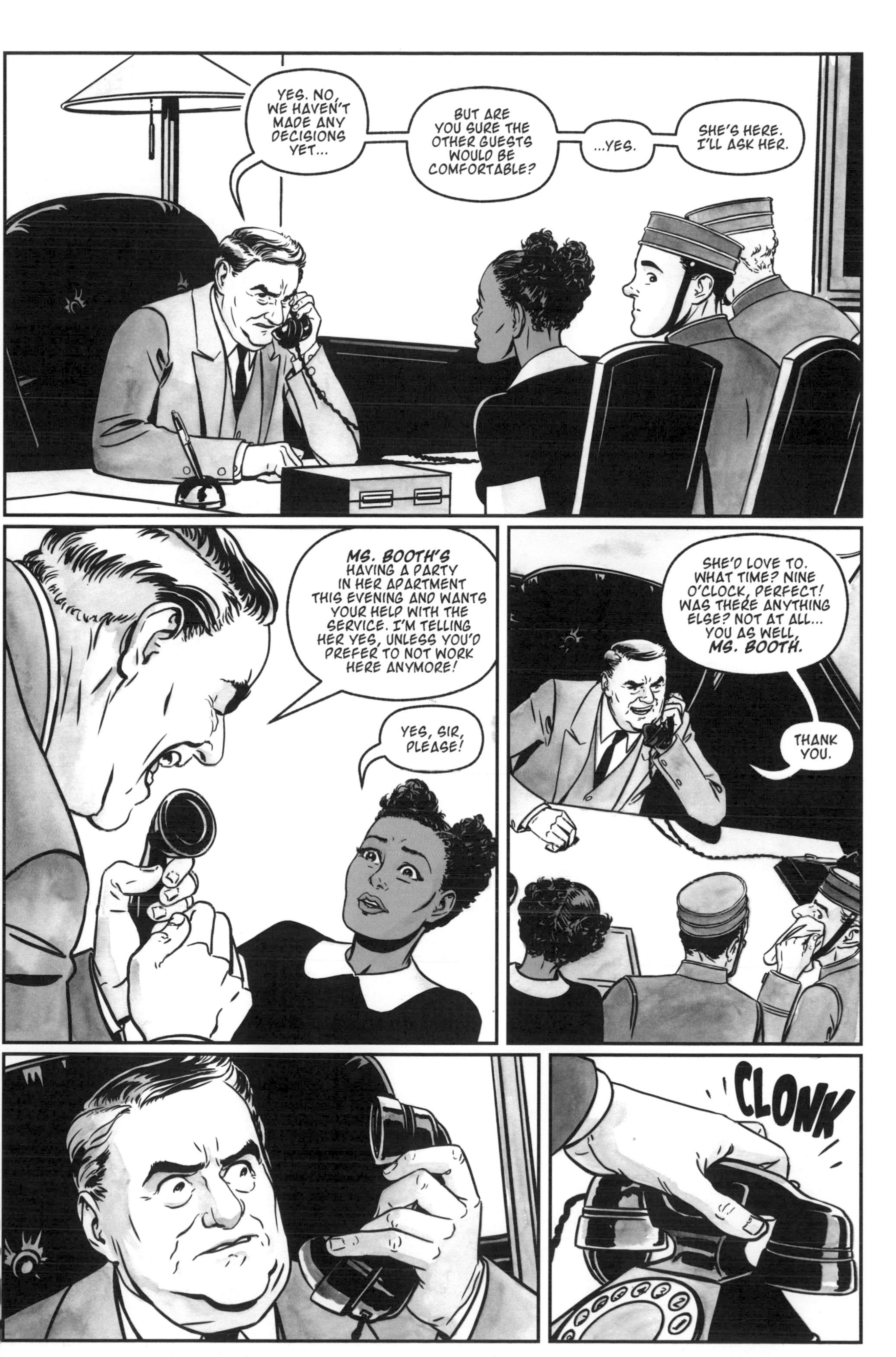
YES. NO, WE HAVEN'T MADE ANY DECISIONS YET...
BUT ARE YOU SURE THE OTHER GUESTS WOULD BE COMFORTABLE?
...YES.
SHE'S HERE. I'LL ASK HER.
MS. BOOTH'S HAVING A PARTY IN HER APARTMENT THIS EVENING AND WANTS YOUR HELP WITH THE SERVICE. I'M TELLING HER YES, UNLESS YOU'D PREFER TO NOT WORK HERE ANYMORE!
YES, SIR, PLEASE!
SHE'D LOVE TO. WHAT TIME? NINE O'CLOCK, PERFECT! WAS THERE ANYTHING ELSE? NOT AT ALL... YOU AS WELL, MS. BOOTH.
THANK YOU.
CLONK

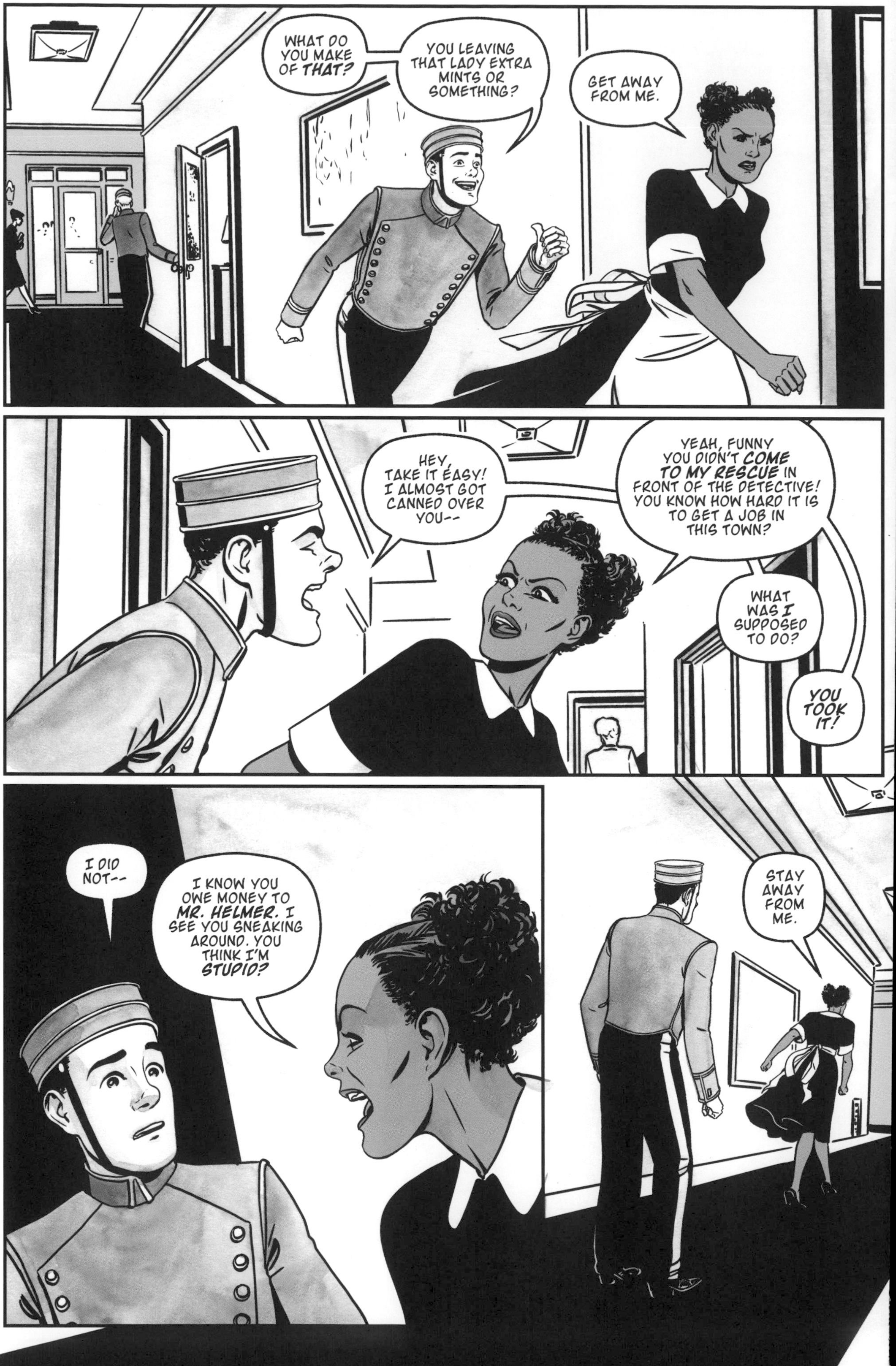
WHAT DO YOU MAKE OF THAT?
YOU LEAVING THAT LADY EXTRA MINTS OR SOMETHING?
GET AWAY FROM ME.
HEY, TAKE IT EASY! I ALMOST GOT CANNED OVER YOU--
YEAH, FUNNY YOU DIDN'T COME TO MY RESCUE IN FRONT OF THE DETECTIVE! YOU KNOW HOW HARD IT IS TO GET A JOB IN THIS TOWN?
WHAT WAS I SUPPOSED TO DO?
YOU TOOK IT!
I DID NOT--
I KNOW YOU OWE MONEY TO MR. HELMER. I SEE YOU SNEAKING AROUND. YOU THINK I'M STUPID?
STAY AWAY FROM ME.

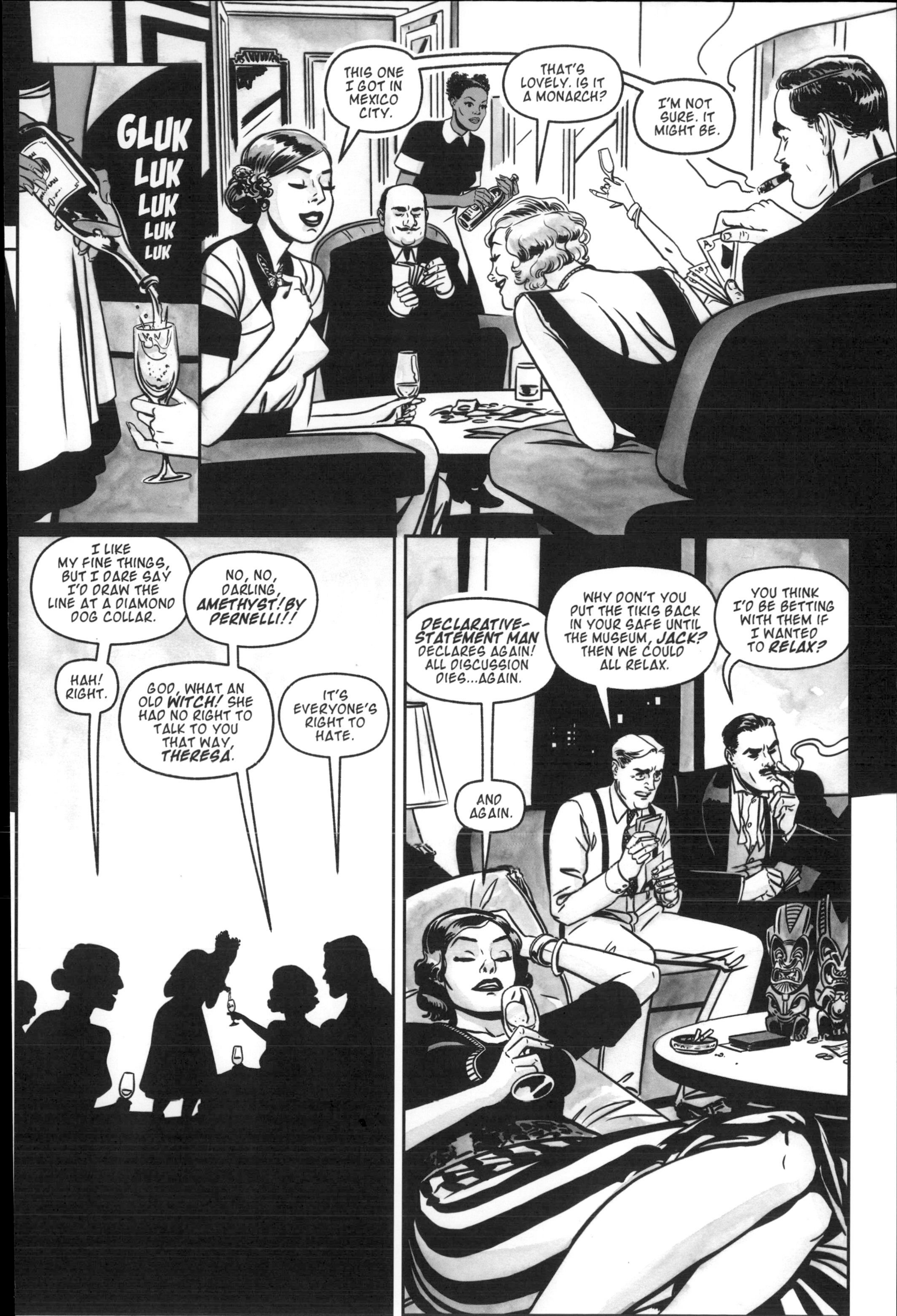
GLUK LUK LUK LUK LUK
THIS ONE I GOT IN MEXICO CITY.
THAT'S LOVELY. IS IT A MONARCH?
I'M NOT SURE. IT MIGHT BE.
I LIKE MY FINE THINGS, BUT I DARE SAY I'D DRAW THE LINE AT A DIAMOND DOG COLLAR.
HAH! RIGHT.
NO, NO, DARLING, AMETHYST! BY PERNELLI!!
GOD, WHAT AN OLD WITCH! SHE HAD NO RIGHT TO TALK TO YOU THAT WAY, THERESA.
IT'S EVERYONE'S RIGHT TO HATE.
DECLARATIVE-STATEMENT MAN DECLARES AGAIN! ALL DISCUSSION DIES...AGAIN.
AND AGAIN.
WHY DON'T YOU PUT THE TIKIS BACK IN YOUR SAFE UNTIL THE MUSEUM, JACK? THEN WE COULD ALL RELAX.
YOU THINK I'D BE BETTING WITH THEM IF I WANTED TO RELAX?

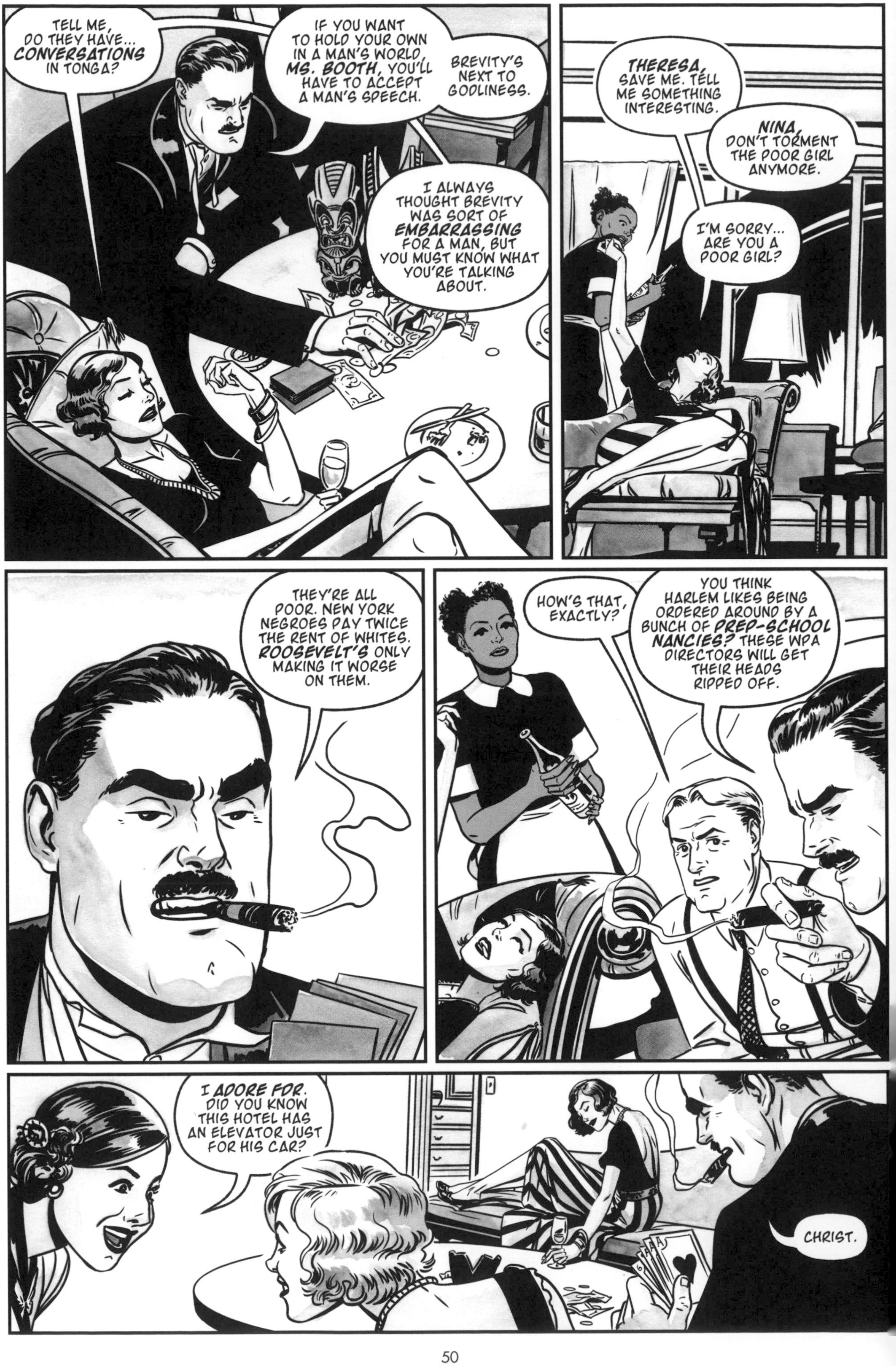
TELL ME, DO THEY HAVE... CONVERSATIONS IN TONGA?
IF YOU WANT TO HOLD YOUR OWN IN A MAN'S WORLD, MS. BOOTH, YOU'LL HAVE TO ACCEPT A MAN'S SPEECH.
BREVITY'S NEXT TO GODLINESS.
I ALWAYS THOUGHT BREVITY WAS SORT OF EMBARRASSING FOR A MAN, BUT YOU MUST KNOW WHAT YOU'RE TALKING ABOUT.
THERESA, SAVE ME. TELL ME SOMETHING INTERESTING.
NINA, DON'T TORMENT THE POOR GIRL ANYMORE.
I'M SORRY... ARE YOU A POOR GIRL?
THEY'RE ALL POOR. NEW YORK NEGROES PAY TWICE THE RENT OF WHITES. ROOSEVELT'S ONLY MAKING IT WORSE ON THEM.
HOW'S THAT, EXACTLY?
YOU THINK HARLEM LIKES BEING ORDERED AROUND BY A BUNCH OF PREP-SCHOOL NANCIES? THESE WPA DIRECTORS WILL GET THEIR HEADS RIPPED OFF.
I ADORE FDR. DID YOU KNOW THIS HOTEL HAS AN ELEVATOR JUST FOR HIS CAR?
CHRIST.

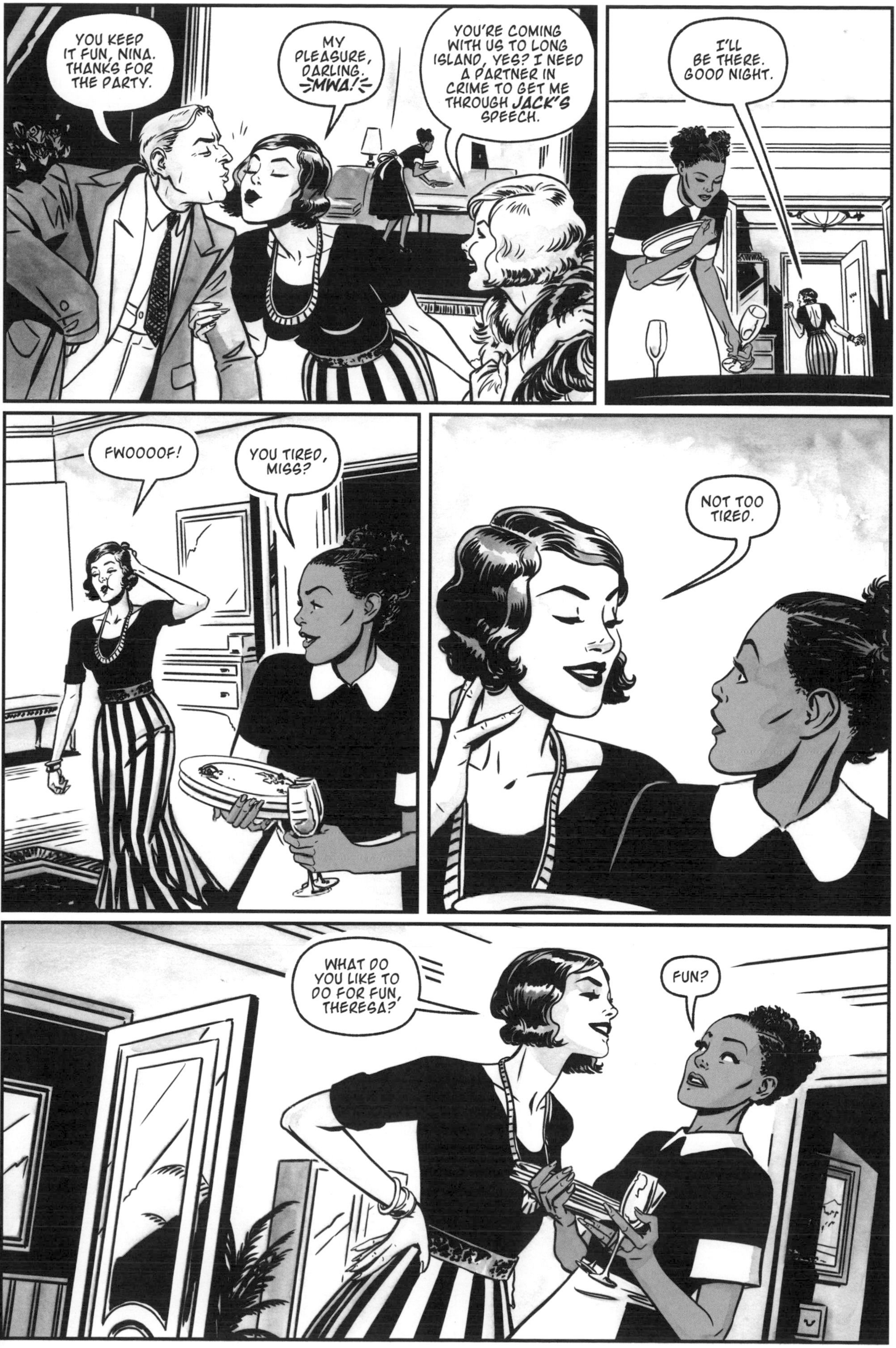
YOU KEEP IT FUN, NINA. THANKS FOR THE PARTY.
MY PLEASURE, DARLING. *MWA!*
YOU'RE COMING WITH US TO LONG ISLAND, YES? I NEED A PARTNER IN CRIME TO GET ME THROUGH **JACK'S** SPEECH.
I'LL BE THERE. GOOD NIGHT.
FWOOOOF!
YOU TIRED, MISS?
NOT TOO TIRED.
WHAT DO YOU LIKE TO DO FOR FUN, THERESA?
FUN?

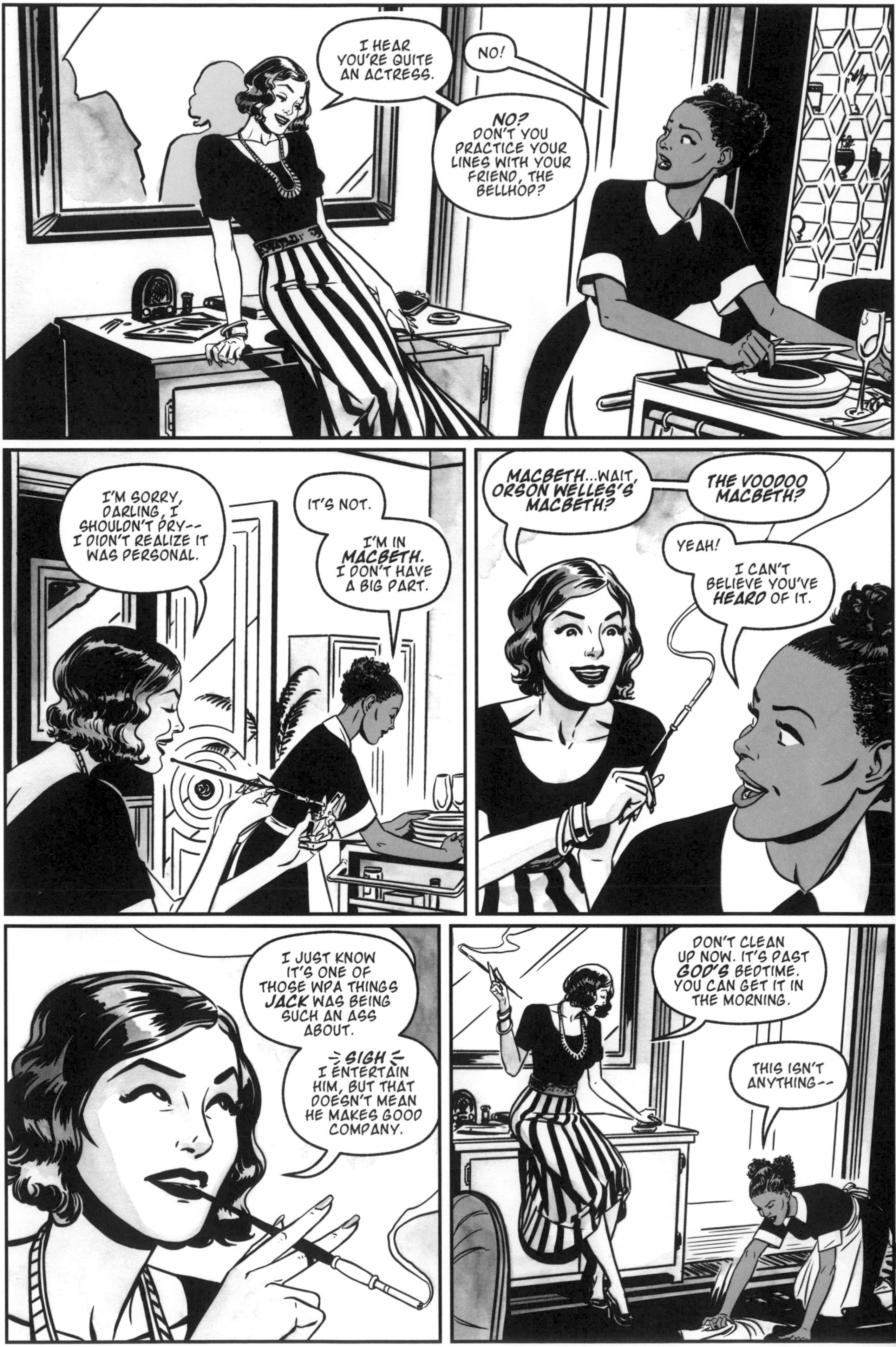
I HEAR YOU'RE QUITE AN ACTRESS.
NO!
NO? DON'T YOU PRACTICE YOUR LINES WITH YOUR FRIEND, THE BELLHOP?
I'M SORRY, DARLING, I SHOULDN'T PRY-- I DIDN'T REALIZE IT WAS PERSONAL.
IT'S NOT.
I'M IN MACBETH. I DON'T HAVE A BIG PART.
MACBETH...WAIT, ORSON WELLES'S MACBETH?
THE VOODOO MACBETH?
YEAH!
I CAN'T BELIEVE YOU'VE HEARD OF IT.
I JUST KNOW IT'S ONE OF THOSE WPA THINGS JACK WAS BEING SUCH AN ASS ABOUT.
SIGH
I ENTERTAIN HIM, BUT THAT DOESN'T MEAN HE MAKES GOOD COMPANY.
DON'T CLEAN UP NOW. IT'S PAST GOD'S BEDTIME. YOU CAN GET IT IN THE MORNING.
THIS ISN'T ANYTHING--

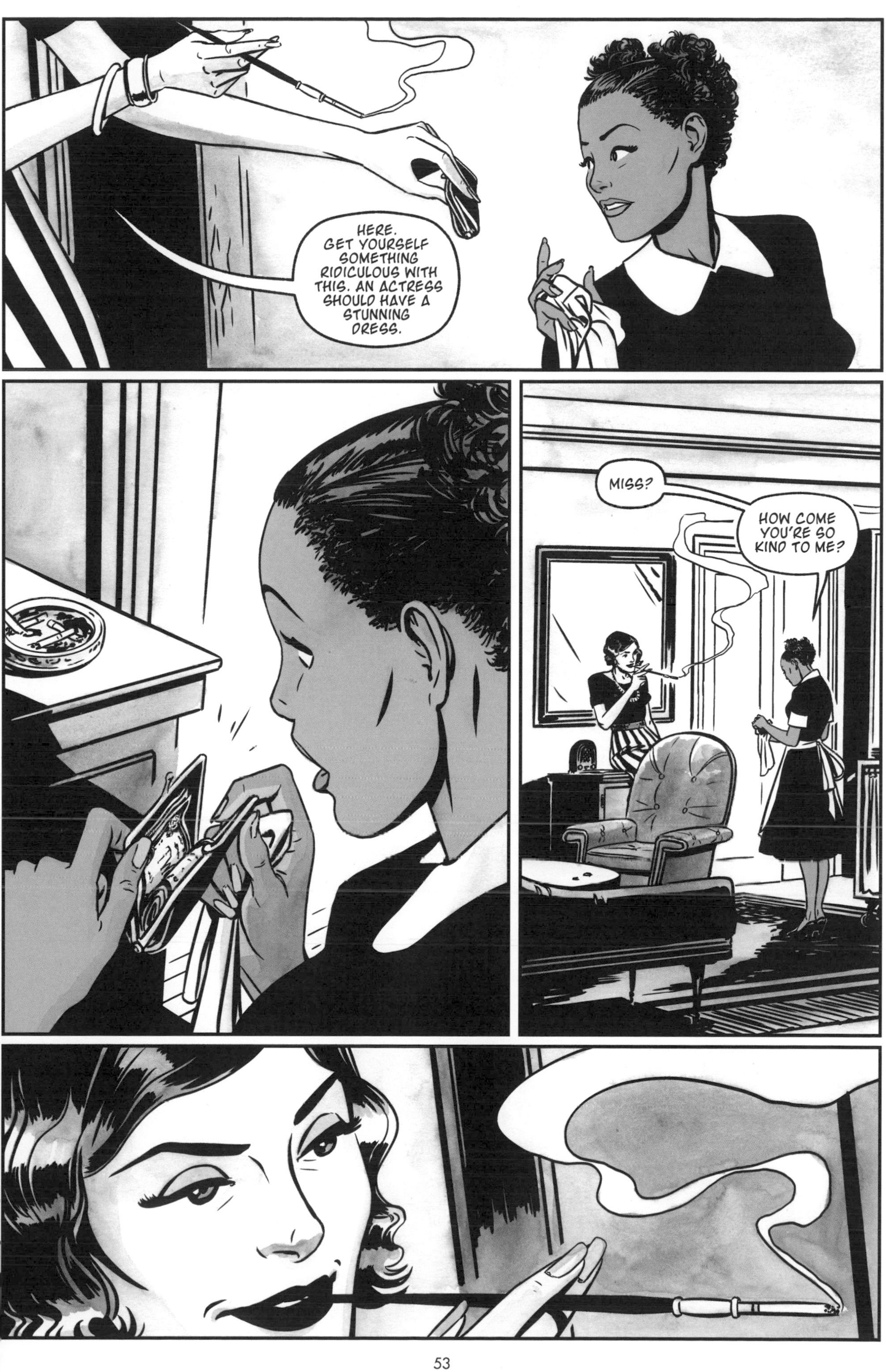
HERE. GET YOURSELF SOMETHING RIDICULOUS WITH THIS. AN ACTRESS SHOULD HAVE A STUNNING DRESS.
MISS?
HOW COME YOU'RE SO KIND TO ME?

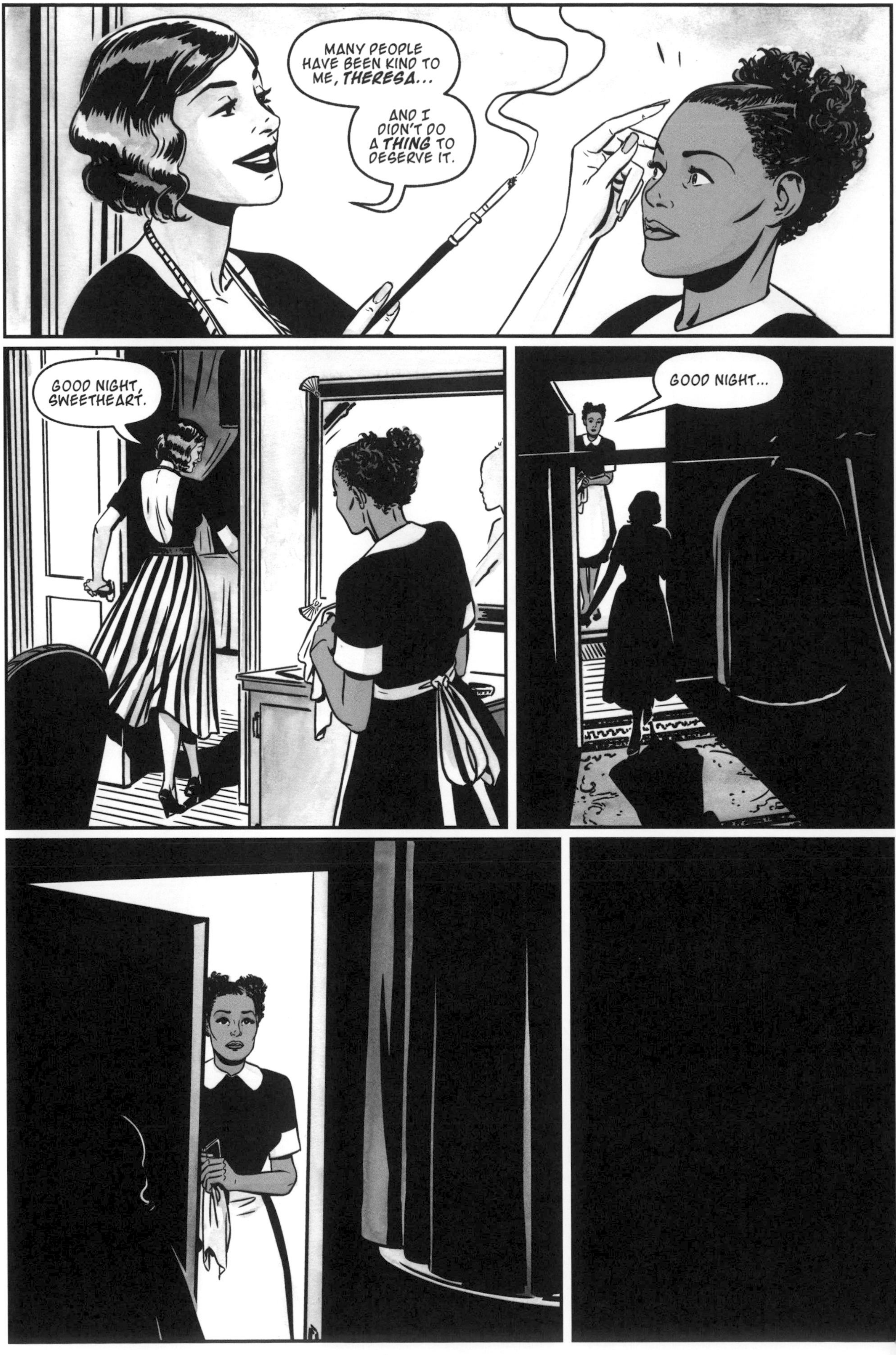
MANY PEOPLE HAVE BEEN KIND TO ME, THERESA...
AND I DIDN'T DO A THING TO DESERVE IT.
GOOD NIGHT, SWEETHEART.
GOOD NIGHT...

CHAPTER 3

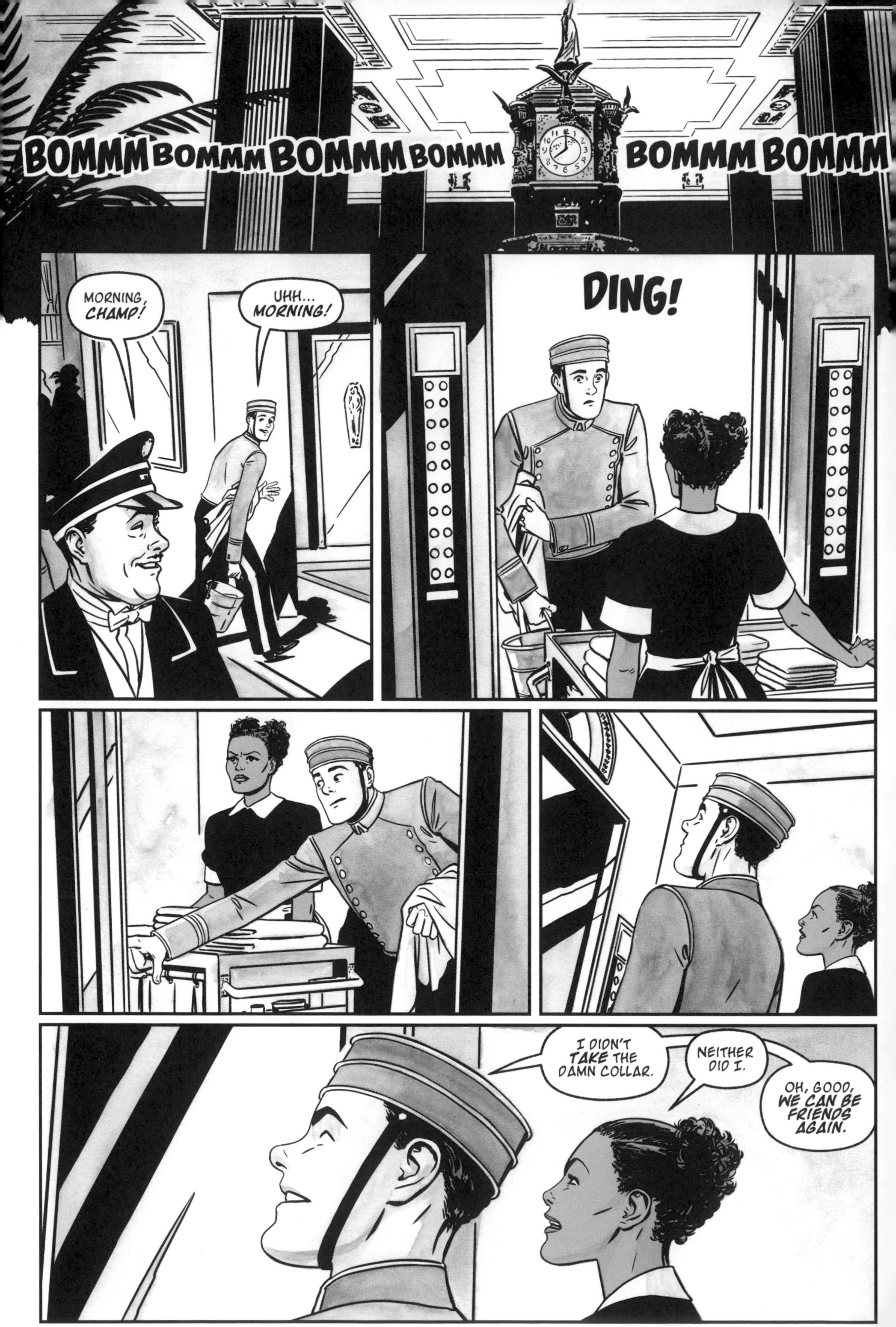
BOMMM BOMMM BOMMM BOMMM
BOMMM BOMMM
MORNING, CHAMP!
UHH... MORNING!
DING!
I DIDN'T TAKE THE DAMN COLLAR.
NEITHER DID I.
OH, GOOD, WE CAN BE FRIENDS AGAIN.

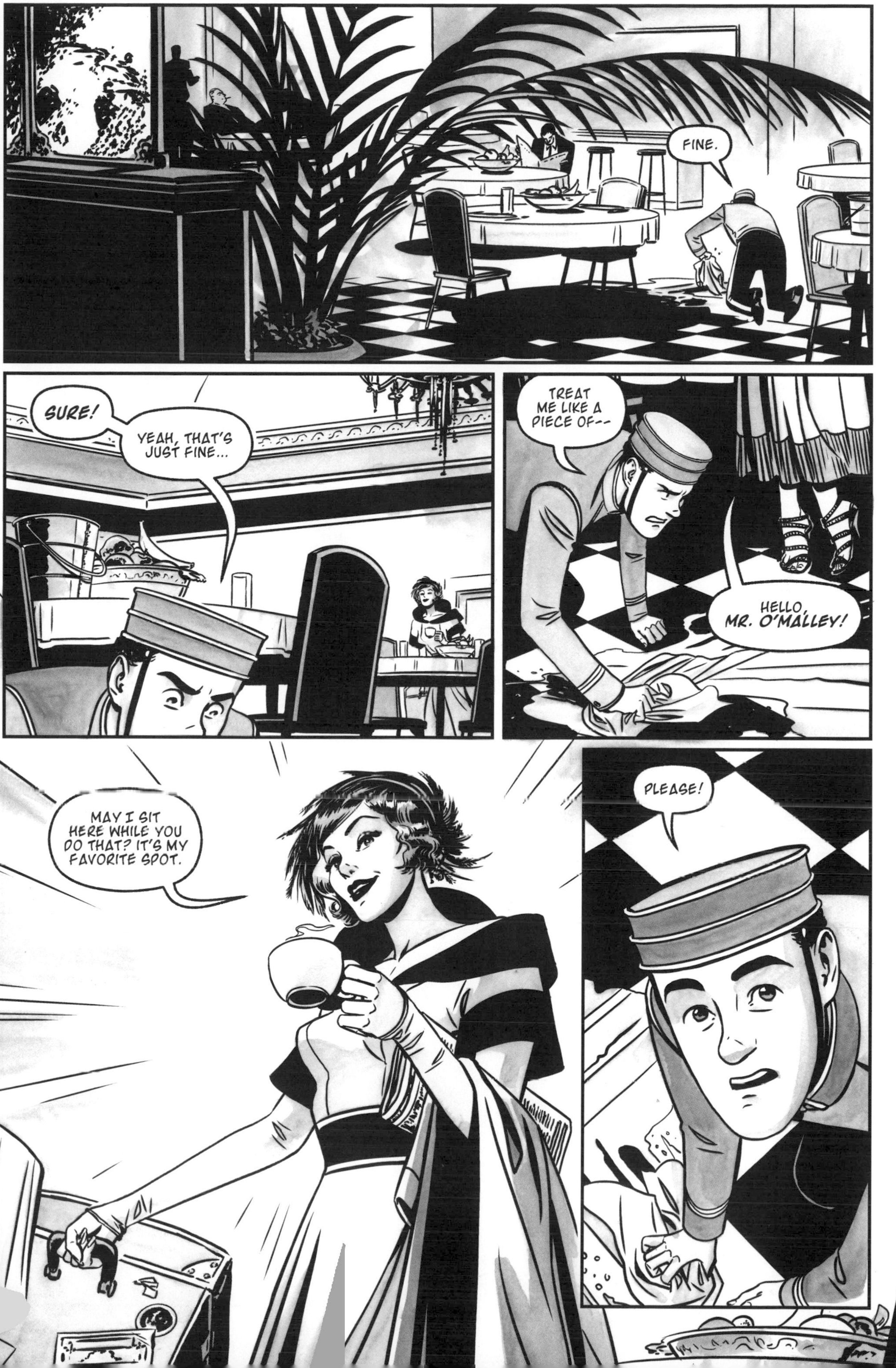
FINE.
SURE!
YEAH, THAT'S JUST FINE...
TREAT ME LIKE A PIECE OF--
HELLO, MR. O'MALLEY!
MAY I SIT HERE WHILE YOU DO THAT? IT'S MY FAVORITE SPOT.
PLEASE!

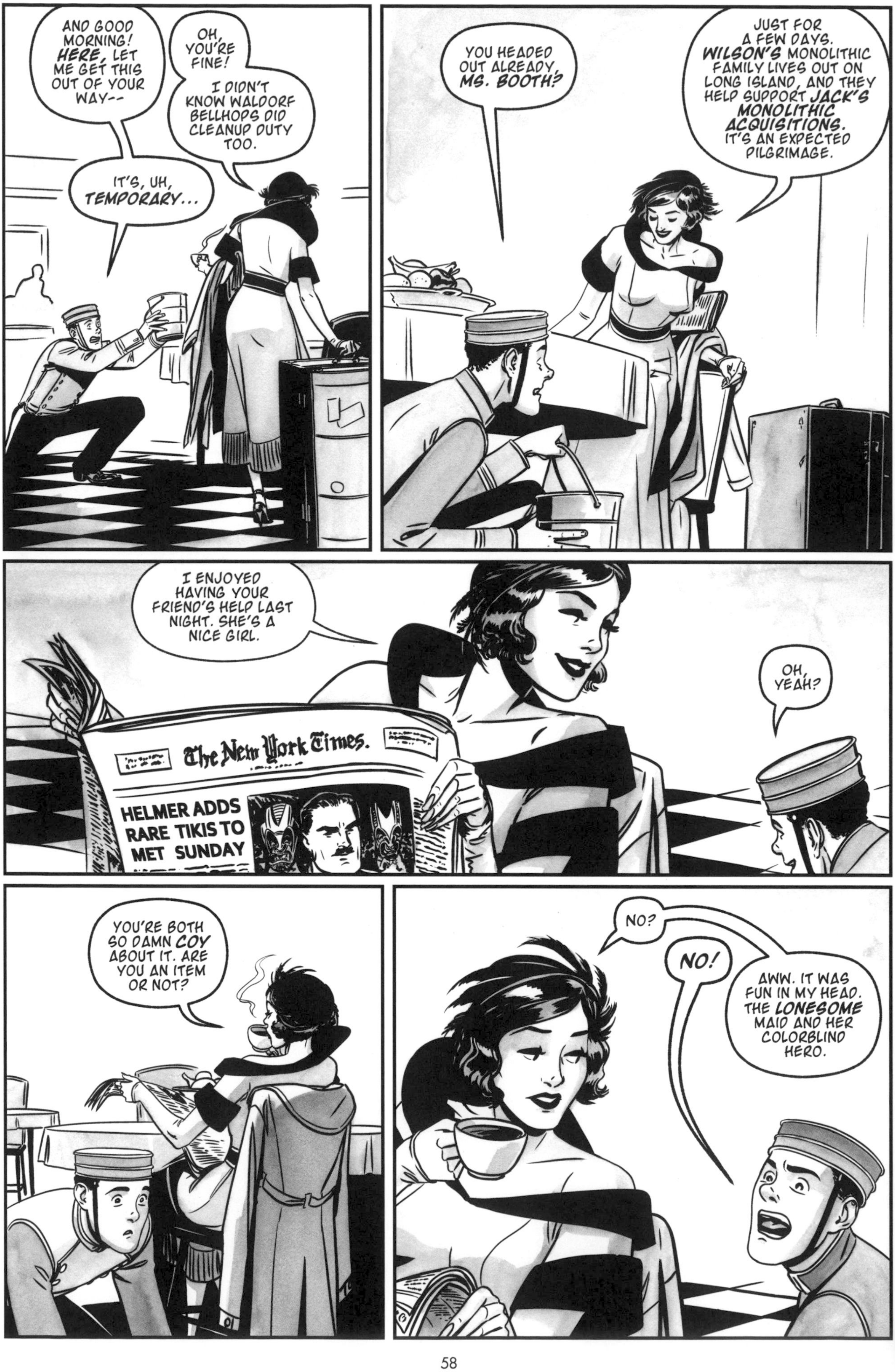
AND GOOD MORNING! HERE, LET ME GET THIS OUT OF YOUR WAY--
OH, YOU'RE FINE!
I DIDN'T KNOW WALDORF BELLHOPS DID CLEANUP DUTY TOO.
IT'S, UH, TEMPORARY...
YOU HEADED OUT ALREADY, MS. BOOTH?
JUST FOR A FEW DAYS. WILSON'S MONOLITHIC FAMILY LIVES OUT ON LONG ISLAND, AND THEY HELP SUPPORT JACK'S MONOLITHIC ACQUISITIONS. IT'S AN EXPECTED PILGRIMAGE.
I ENJOYED HAVING YOUR FRIEND'S HELP LAST NIGHT. SHE'S A NICE GIRL.
The New York Times.
HELMER ADDS RARE TIKIS TO MET SUNDAY
OH, YEAH?
YOU'RE BOTH SO DAMN COY ABOUT IT. ARE YOU AN ITEM OR NOT?
NO?
NO!
AWW. IT WAS FUN IN MY HEAD. THE LONESOME MAID AND HER COLORBLIND HERO.

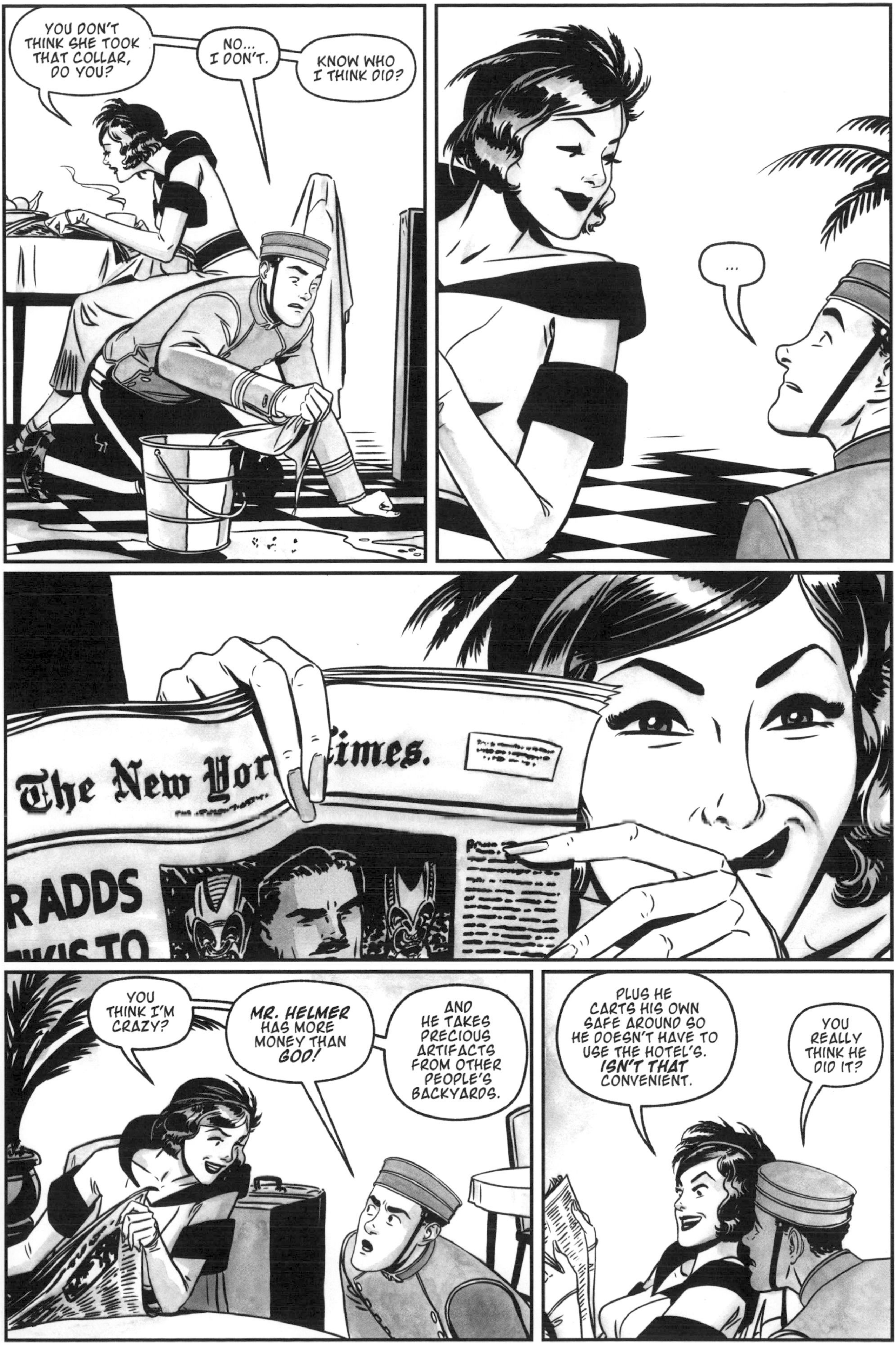
YOU DON'T THINK SHE TOOK THAT COLLAR, DO YOU?
NO... I DON'T.
KNOW WHO I THINK DID?
...
The New Yor
imes.
R ADDS
YOU THINK I'M CRAZY?
MR. HELMER HAS MORE MONEY THAN GOD!
AND HE TAKES PRECIOUS ARTIFACTS FROM OTHER PEOPLE'S BACKYARDS.
PLUS HE CARTS HIS OWN SAFE AROUND SO HE DOESN'T HAVE TO USE THE HOTEL'S. ISN'T THAT CONVENIENT.
YOU REALLY THINK HE DID IT?

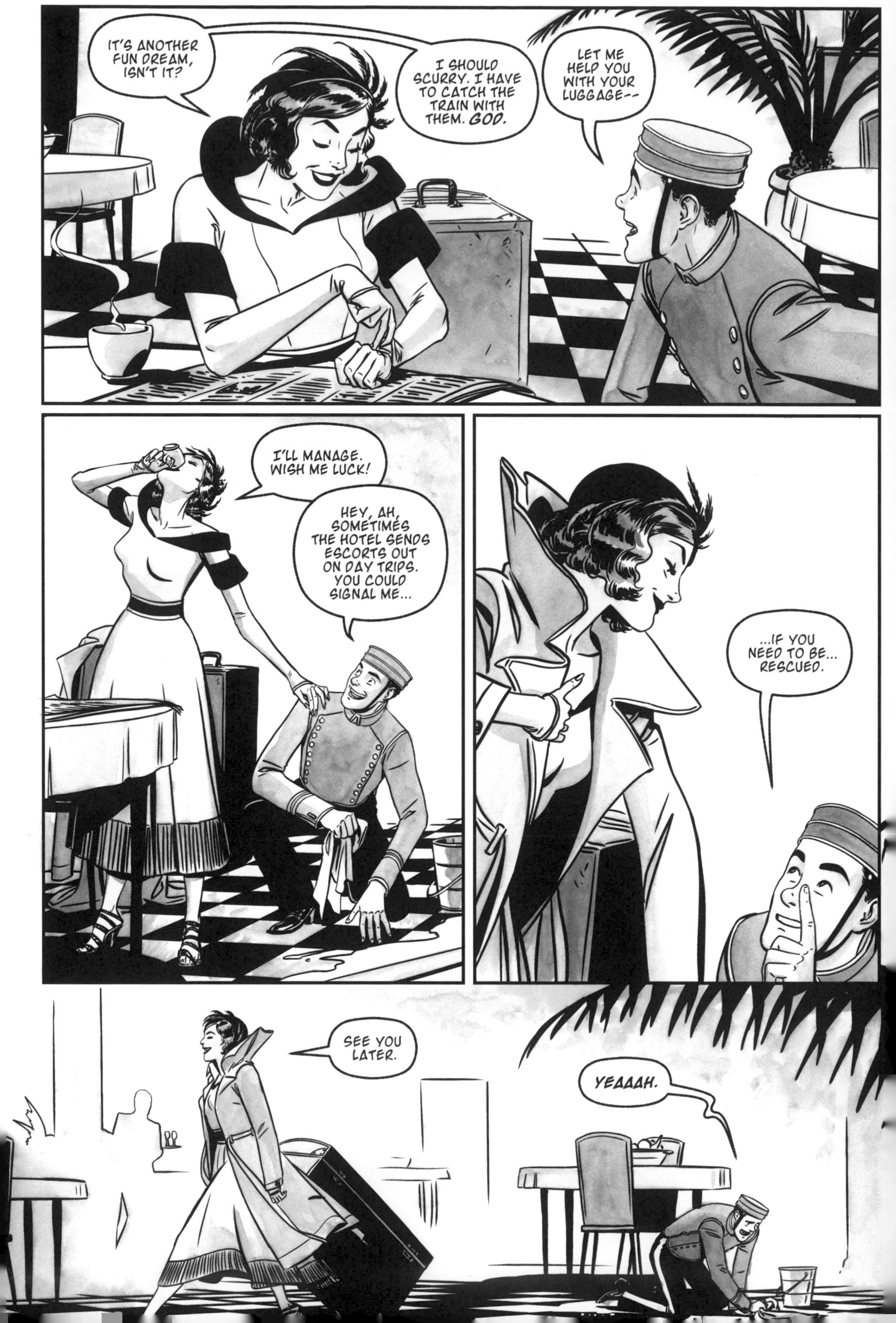
IT'S ANOTHER FUN DREAM, ISN'T IT?
I SHOULD SCURRY. I HAVE TO CATCH THE TRAIN WITH THEM. GOD.
LET ME HELP YOU WITH YOUR LUGGAGE--
I'LL MANAGE. WISH ME LUCK!
HEY, AH, SOMETIMES THE HOTEL SENDS ESCORTS OUT ON DAY TRIPS. YOU COULD SIGNAL ME...
...IF YOU NEED TO BE... RESCUED.
SEE YOU LATER.
YEAAAH.

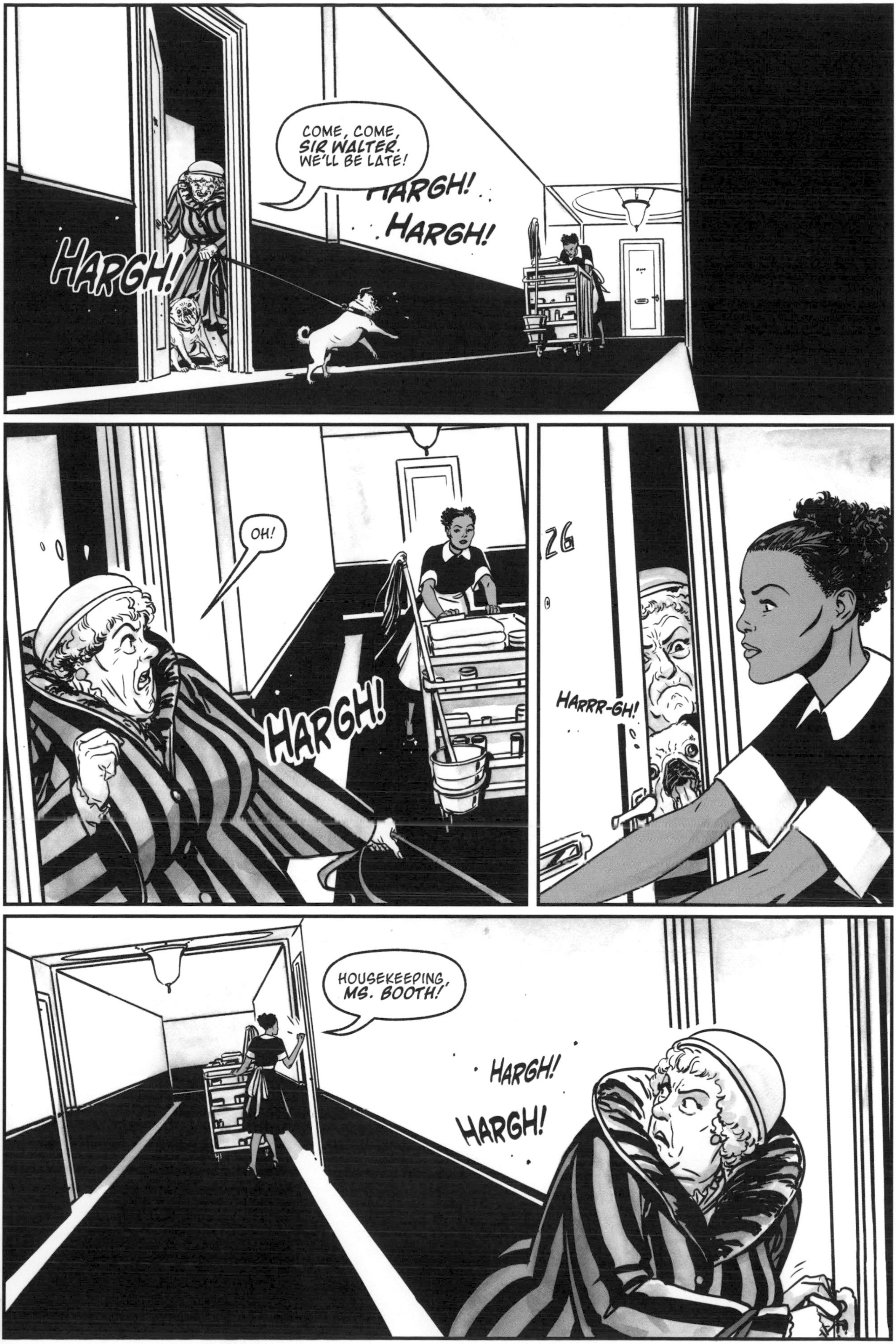
COME, COME, SIR WALTER. WE'LL BE LATE!
HARGH!
HARGH!
HARGH!
OH!
HARGH!
26
HARRR-GH!
HOUSEKEEPING, MS. BOOTH!
HARGH!
HARGH!

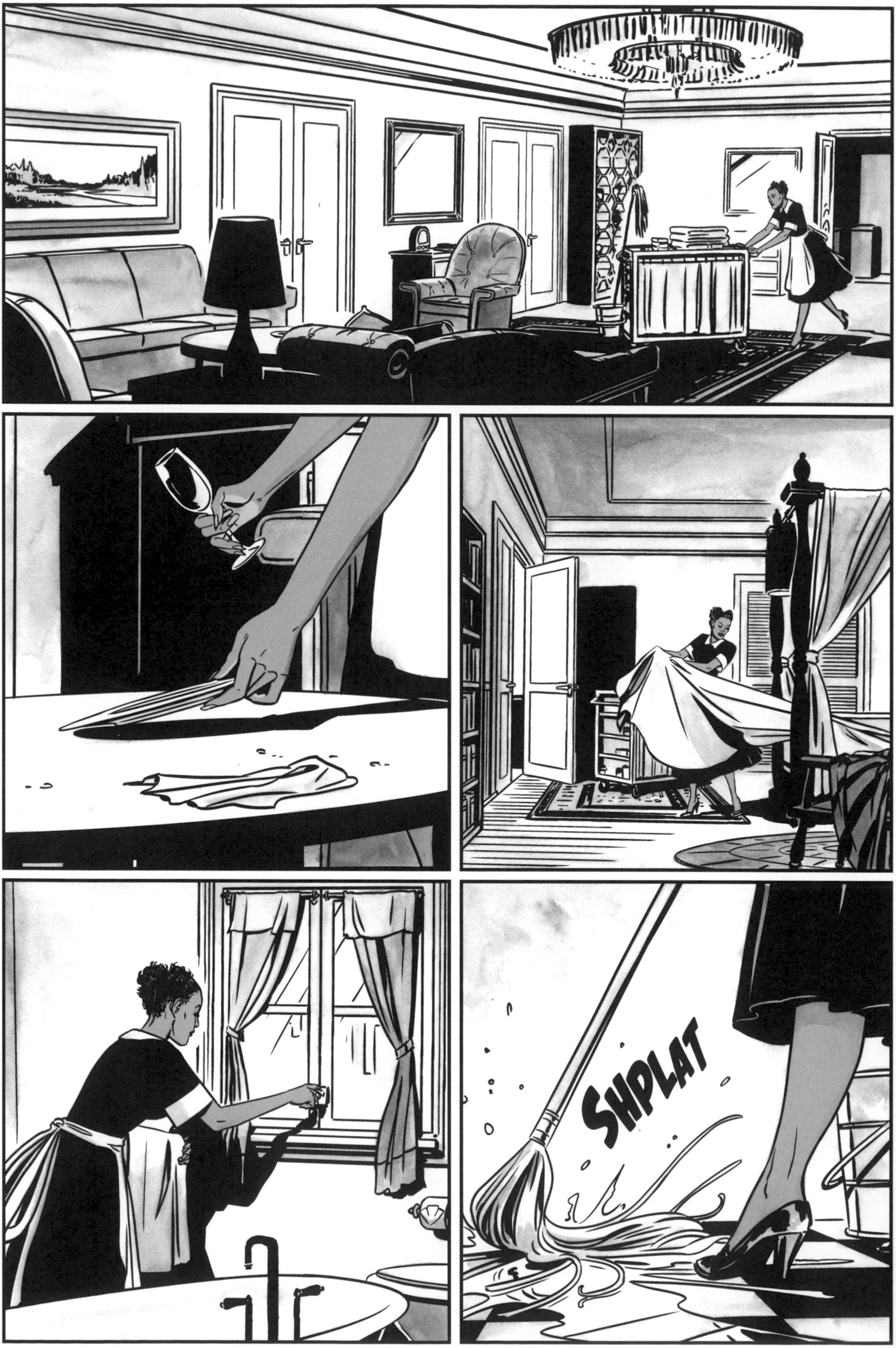
SHPLAT

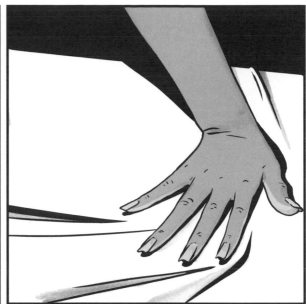

RSH
RSH
RSHH

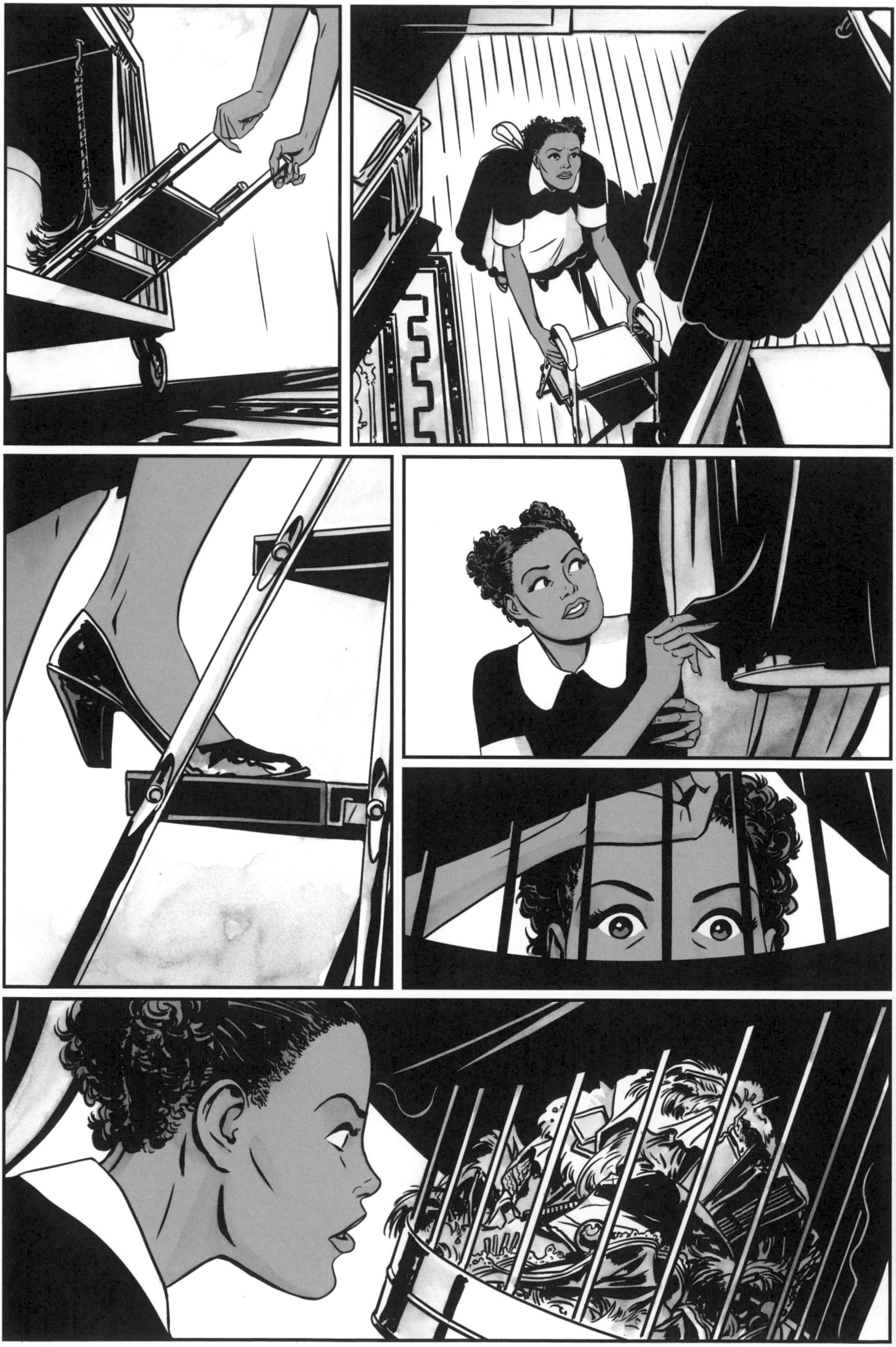

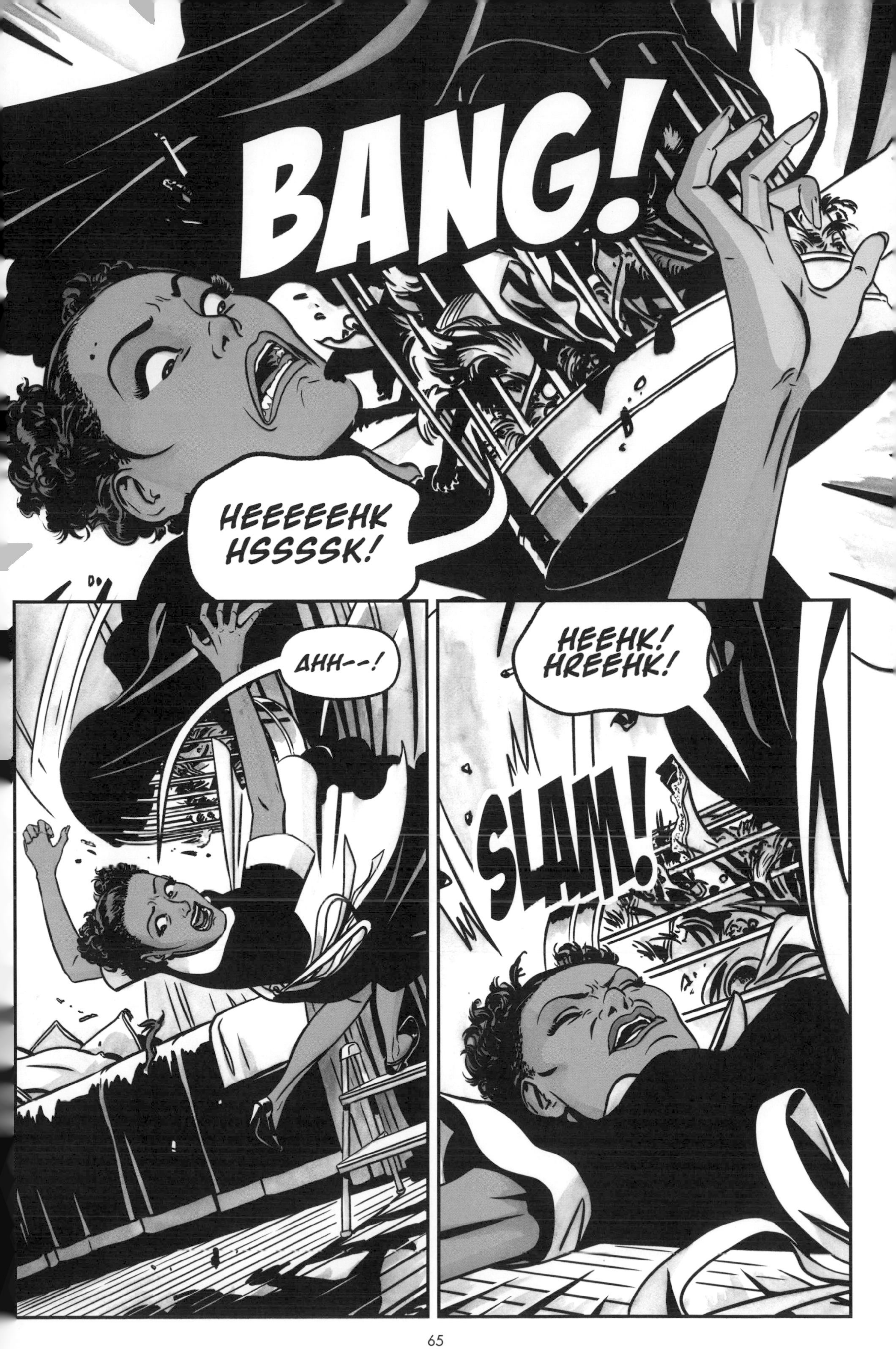
BANG!
HEEEEEEHK HSSSSK!
AHH--!
HEEHK! HREEHK!
SLAM!

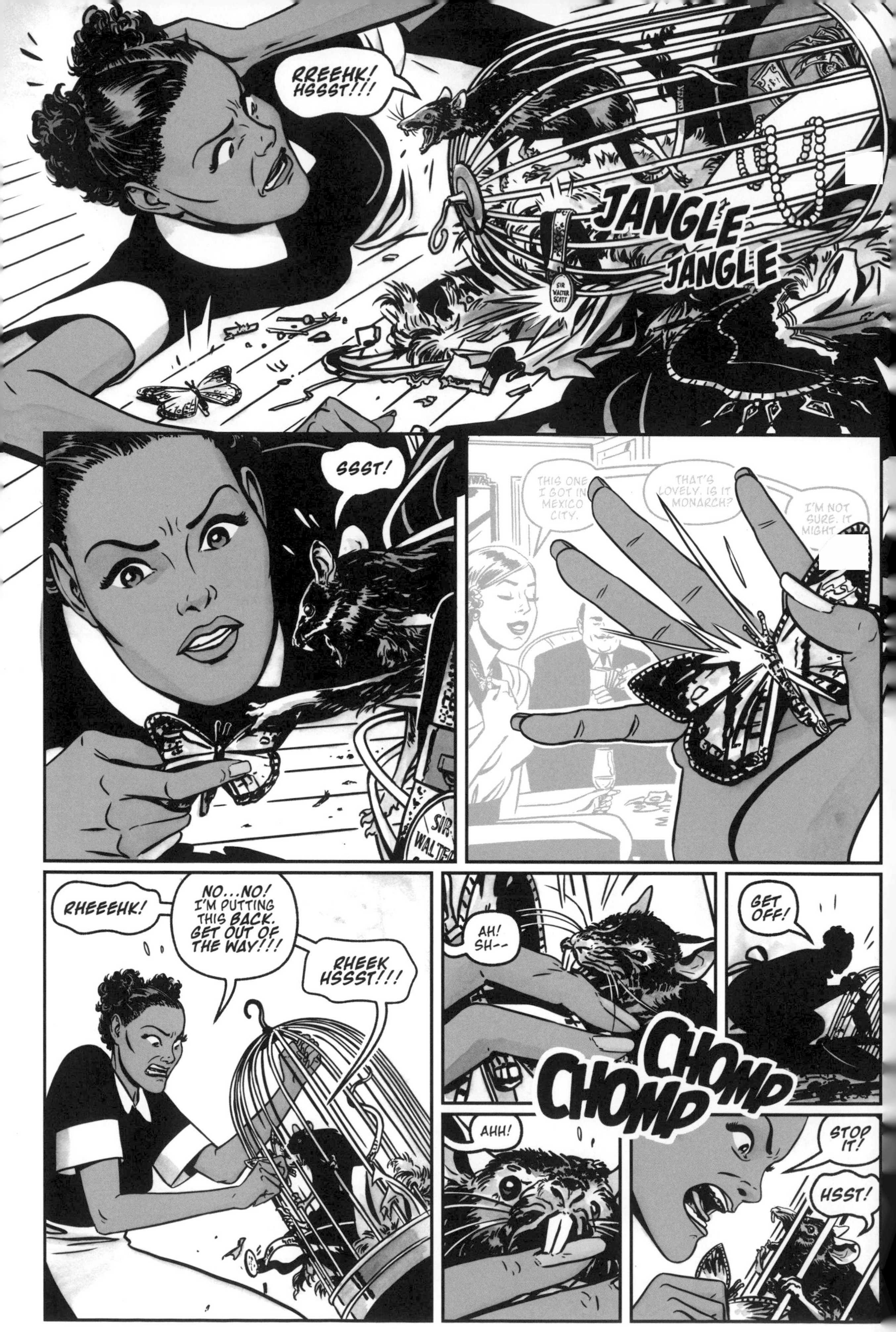
RREEHK! HSSST!!!
JANGLE
JANGLE
SIR WALTER SCOTT
SSST!
THIS ONE I GOT IN MEXICO CITY.
THAT'S LOVELY. IS IT MONARCH?
I'M NOT SURE. IT MIGHT
RHEEEHK!
NO...NO! I'M PUTTING THIS BACK. GET OUT OF THE WAY!!!
RHEEK HSSST!!!
AH! SH--
GET OFF!
CHOMP
CHOMP
AHH!
STOP IT!
HSST!

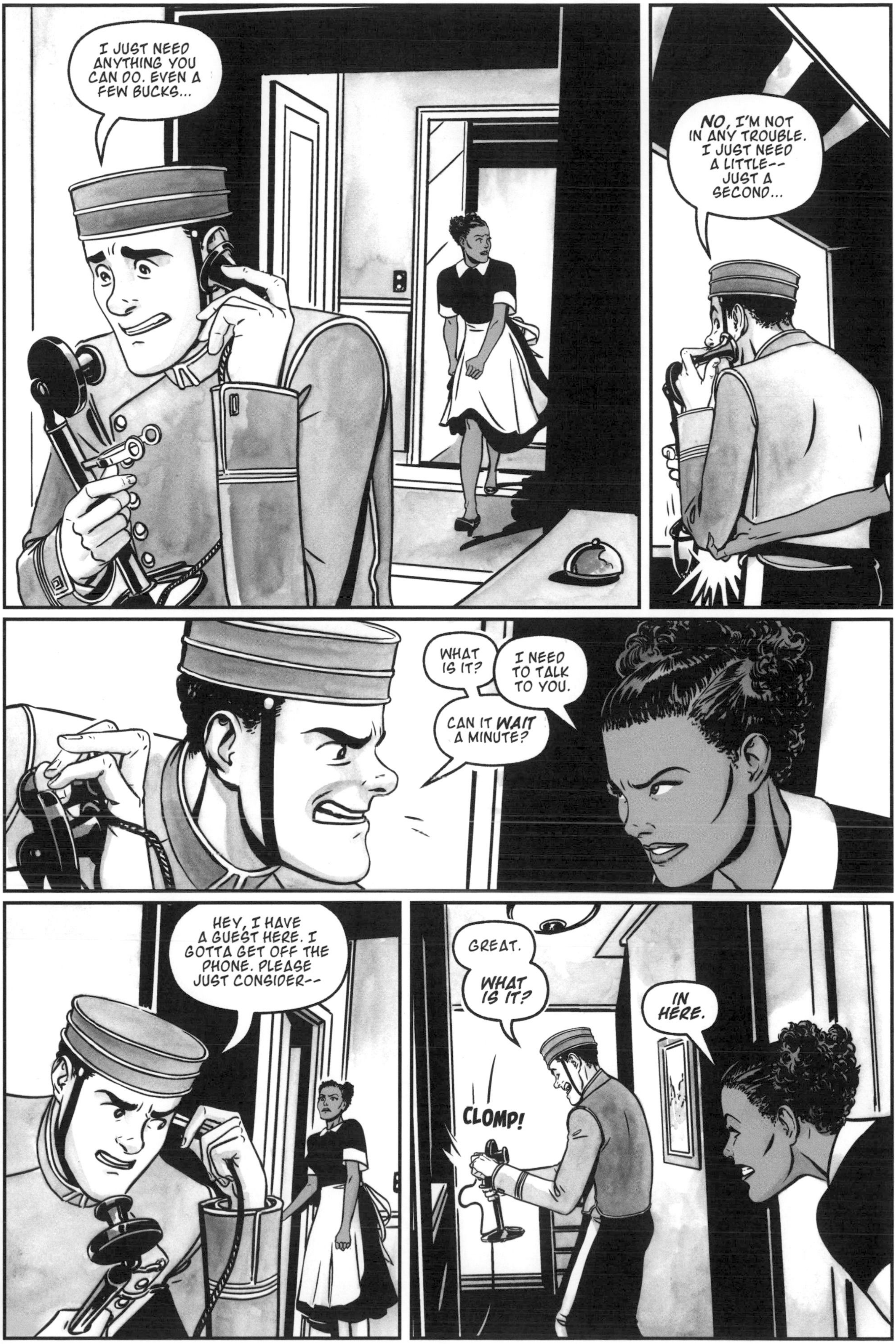
I JUST NEED ANYTHING YOU CAN DO. EVEN A FEW BUCKS...
NO, I'M NOT IN ANY TROUBLE. I JUST NEED A LITTLE-- JUST A SECOND...
WHAT IS IT?
I NEED TO TALK TO YOU.
CAN IT WAIT A MINUTE?
HEY, I HAVE A GUEST HERE. I GOTTA GET OFF THE PHONE. PLEASE JUST CONSIDER--
GREAT.
WHAT IS IT?
CLOMP!
IN HERE.

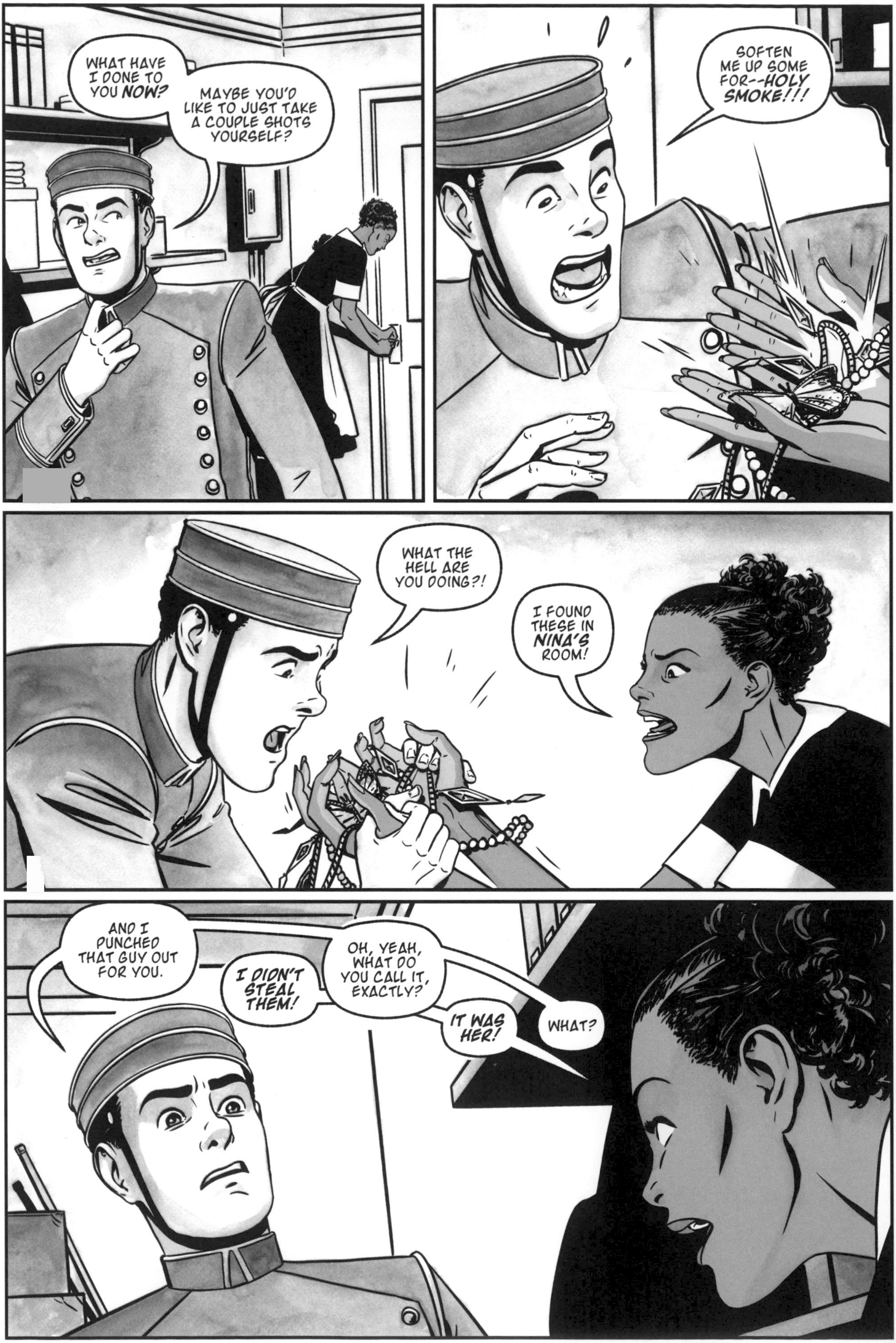
WHAT HAVE I DONE TO YOU NOW?
MAYBE YOU'D LIKE TO JUST TAKE A COUPLE SHOTS YOURSELF?
SOFTEN ME UP SOME FOR--HOLY SMOKE!!!
WHAT THE HELL ARE YOU DOING?!
I FOUND THESE IN NINA'S ROOM!
AND I PUNCHED THAT GUY OUT FOR YOU.
I DIDN'T STEAL THEM!
OH, YEAH, WHAT DO YOU CALL IT, EXACTLY?
IT WAS HER!
WHAT?

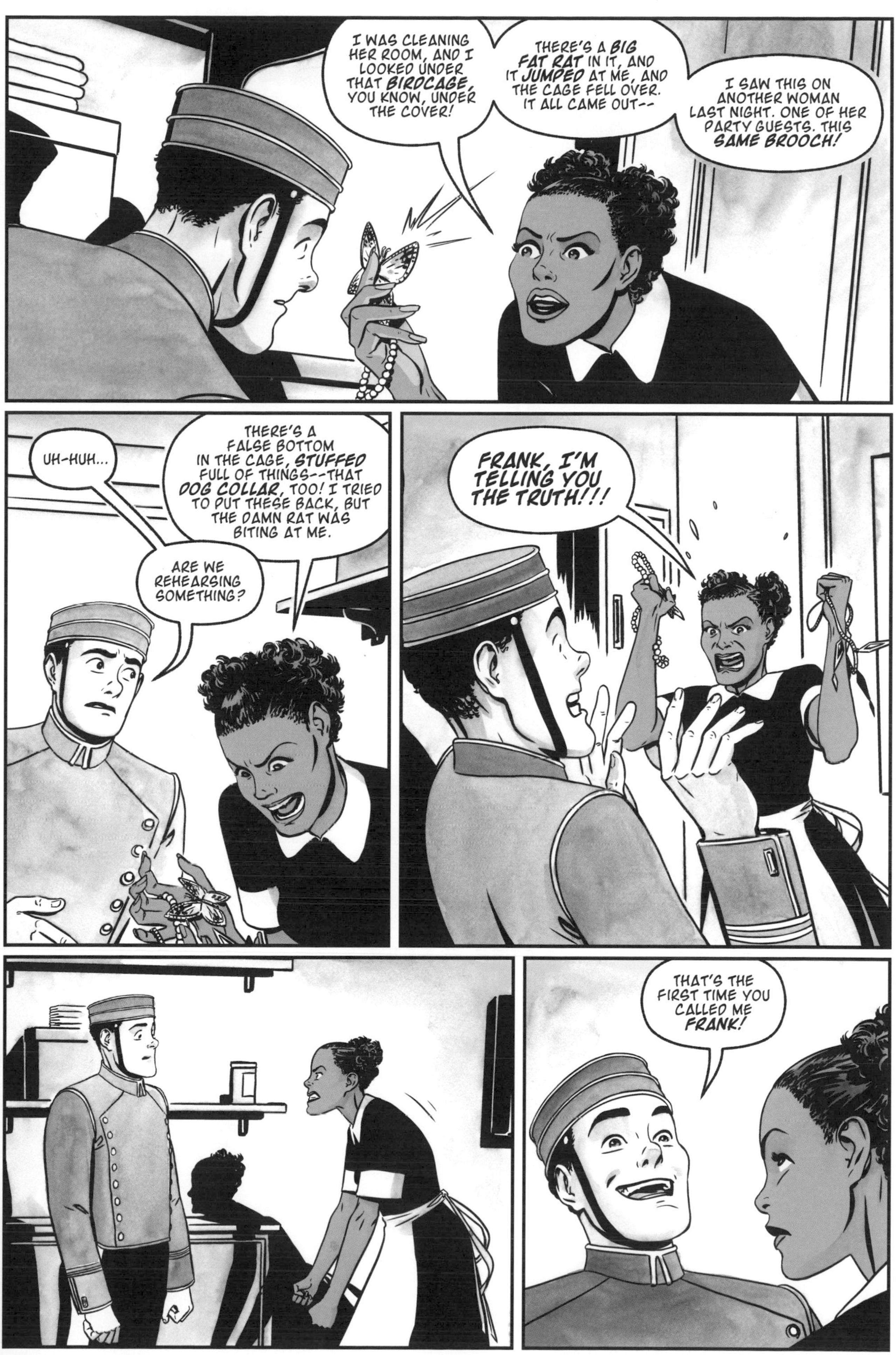
I WAS CLEANING HER ROOM, AND I LOOKED UNDER THAT BIRDCAGE, YOU KNOW, UNDER THE COVER!
THERE'S A BIG FAT RAT IN IT, AND IT JUMPED AT ME, AND THE CAGE FELL OVER. IT ALL CAME OUT--
I SAW THIS ON ANOTHER WOMAN LAST NIGHT. ONE OF HER PARTY GUESTS. THIS SAME BROOCH!
UH-HUH...
THERE'S A FALSE BOTTOM IN THE CAGE, STUFFED FULL OF THINGS--THAT DOG COLLAR, TOO! I TRIED TO PUT THESE BACK, BUT THE DAMN RAT WAS BITING AT ME.
ARE WE REHEARSING SOMETHING?
FRANK, I'M TELLING YOU THE TRUTH!!!
THAT'S THE FIRST TIME YOU CALLED ME FRANK!

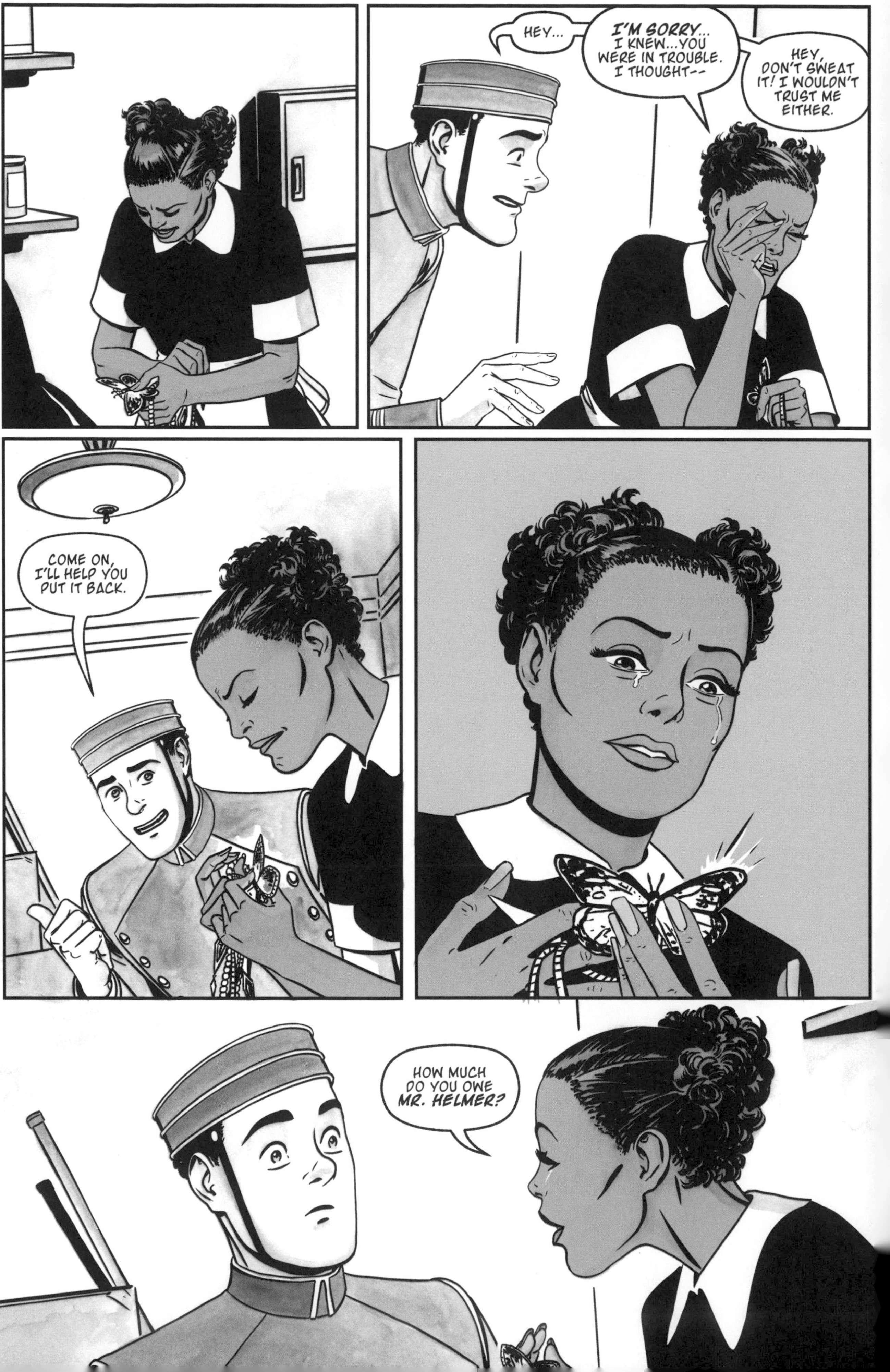
HEY...
I'M SORRY... I KNEW...YOU WERE IN TROUBLE. I THOUGHT--
HEY, DON'T SWEAT IT! I WOULDN'T TRUST ME EITHER.
COME ON, I'LL HELP YOU PUT IT BACK.
HOW MUCH DO YOU OWE MR. HELMER?

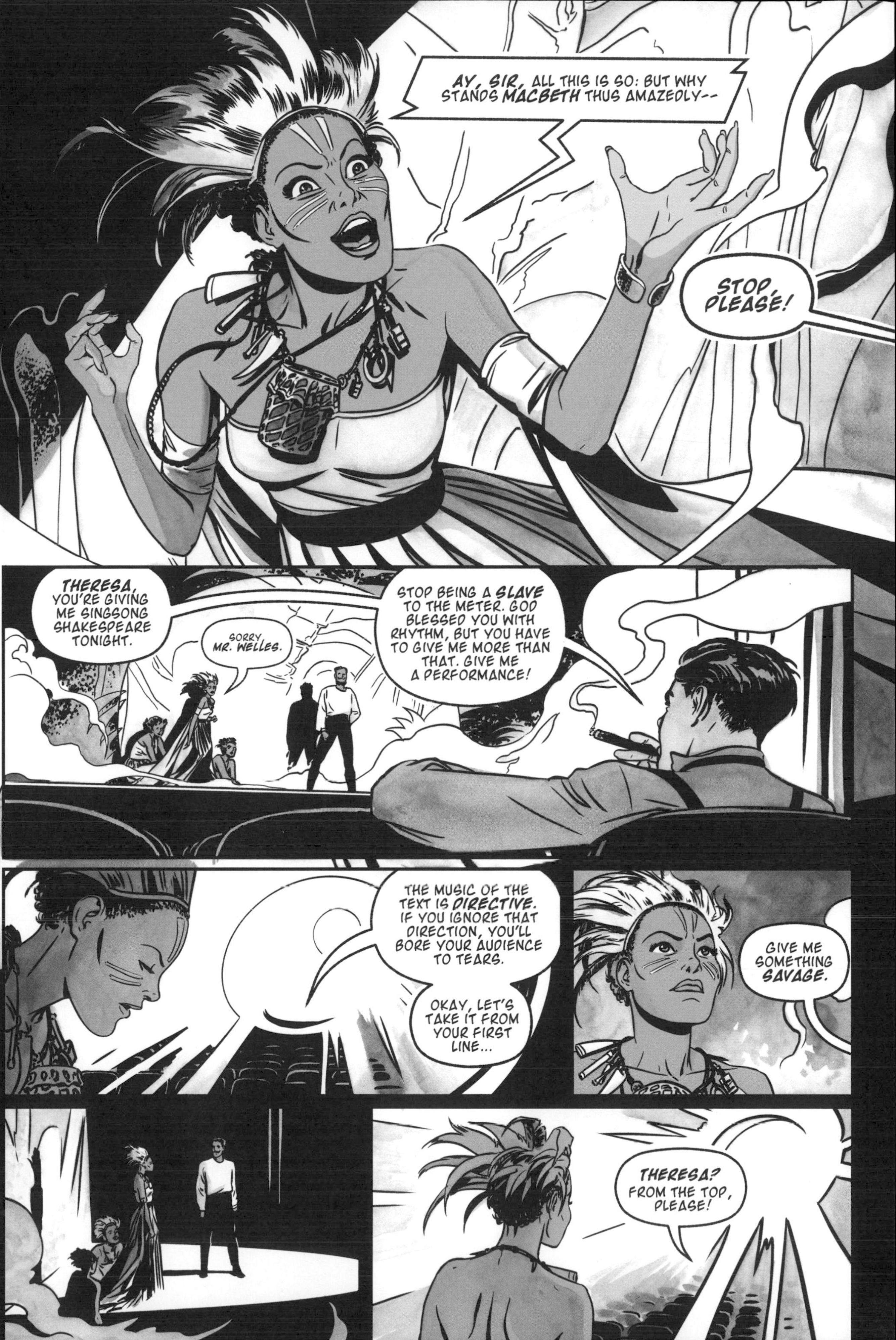
AY, SIR, ALL THIS IS SO: BUT WHY STANDS MACBETH THUS AMAZEDLY--
STOP, PLEASE!
THERESA, YOU'RE GIVING ME SINGSONG SHAKESPEARE TONIGHT.
SORRY MR. WELLES.
STOP BEING A SLAVE TO THE METER. GOD BLESSED YOU WITH RHYTHM, BUT YOU HAVE TO GIVE ME MORE THAN THAT. GIVE ME A PERFORMANCE!
THE MUSIC OF THE TEXT IS DIRECTIVE. IF YOU IGNORE THAT DIRECTION, YOU'LL BORE YOUR AUDIENCE TO TEARS.
OKAY, LET'S TAKE IT FROM YOUR FIRST LINE...
GIVE ME SOMETHING SAVAGE.
THERESA? FROM THE TOP, PLEASE!

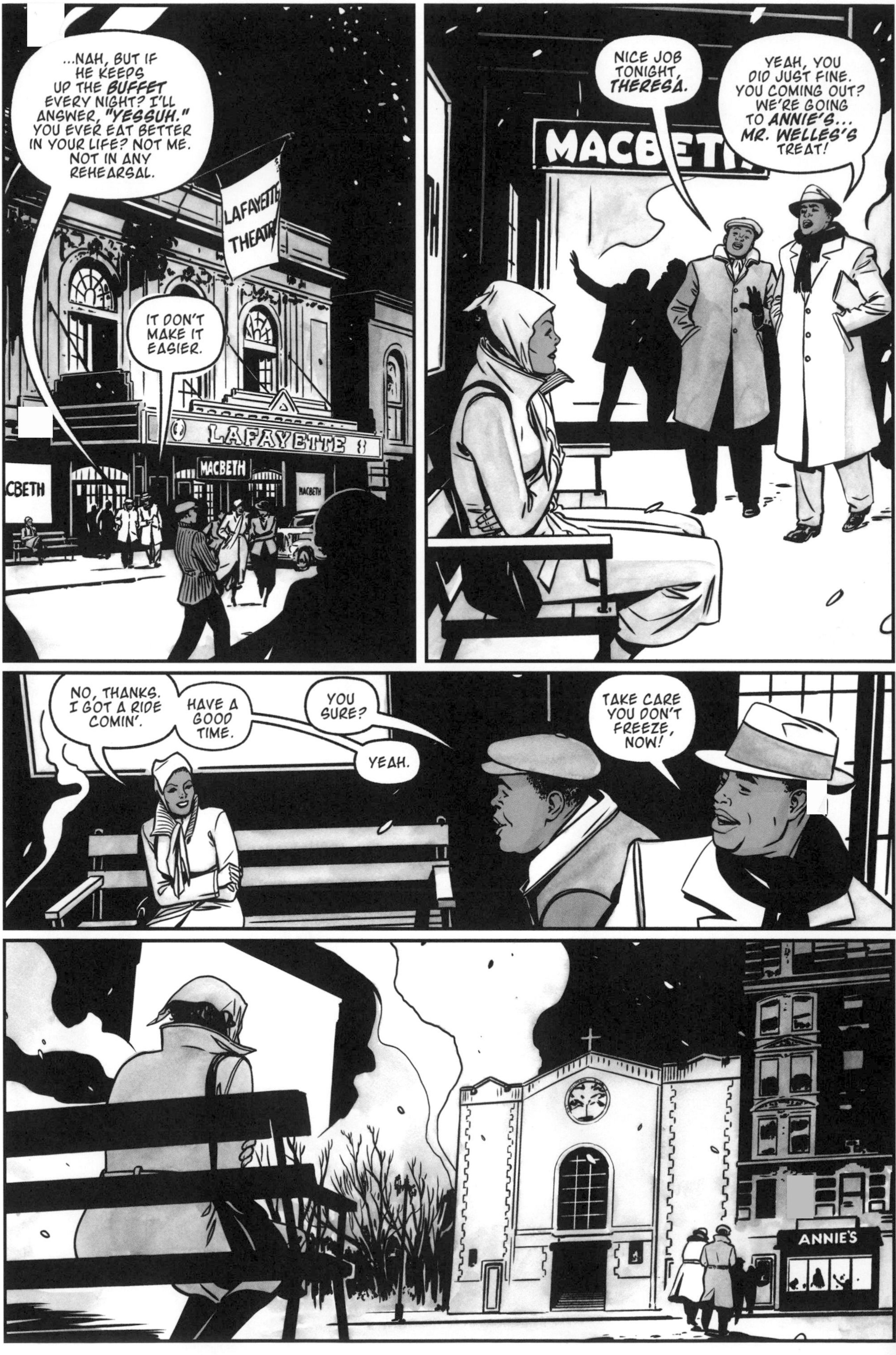
...NAH, BUT IF HE KEEPS UP THE BUFFET EVERY NIGHT? I'LL ANSWER, "YESSUH." YOU EVER EAT BETTER IN YOUR LIFE? NOT ME. NOT IN ANY REHEARSAL.
LAFAYETTE THEATRE
IT DON'T MAKE IT EASIER.
LAFAYETTE
MACBETH
CBETH
NICE JOB TONIGHT, THERESA.
YEAH, YOU DID JUST FINE. YOU COMING OUT? WE'RE GOING TO ANNIE'S... MR. WELLES'S TREAT!
MACBETH
NO, THANKS. I GOT A RIDE COMIN'.
HAVE A GOOD TIME.
YOU SURE?
YEAH.
TAKE CARE YOU DON'T FREEZE, NOW!
ANNIE'S

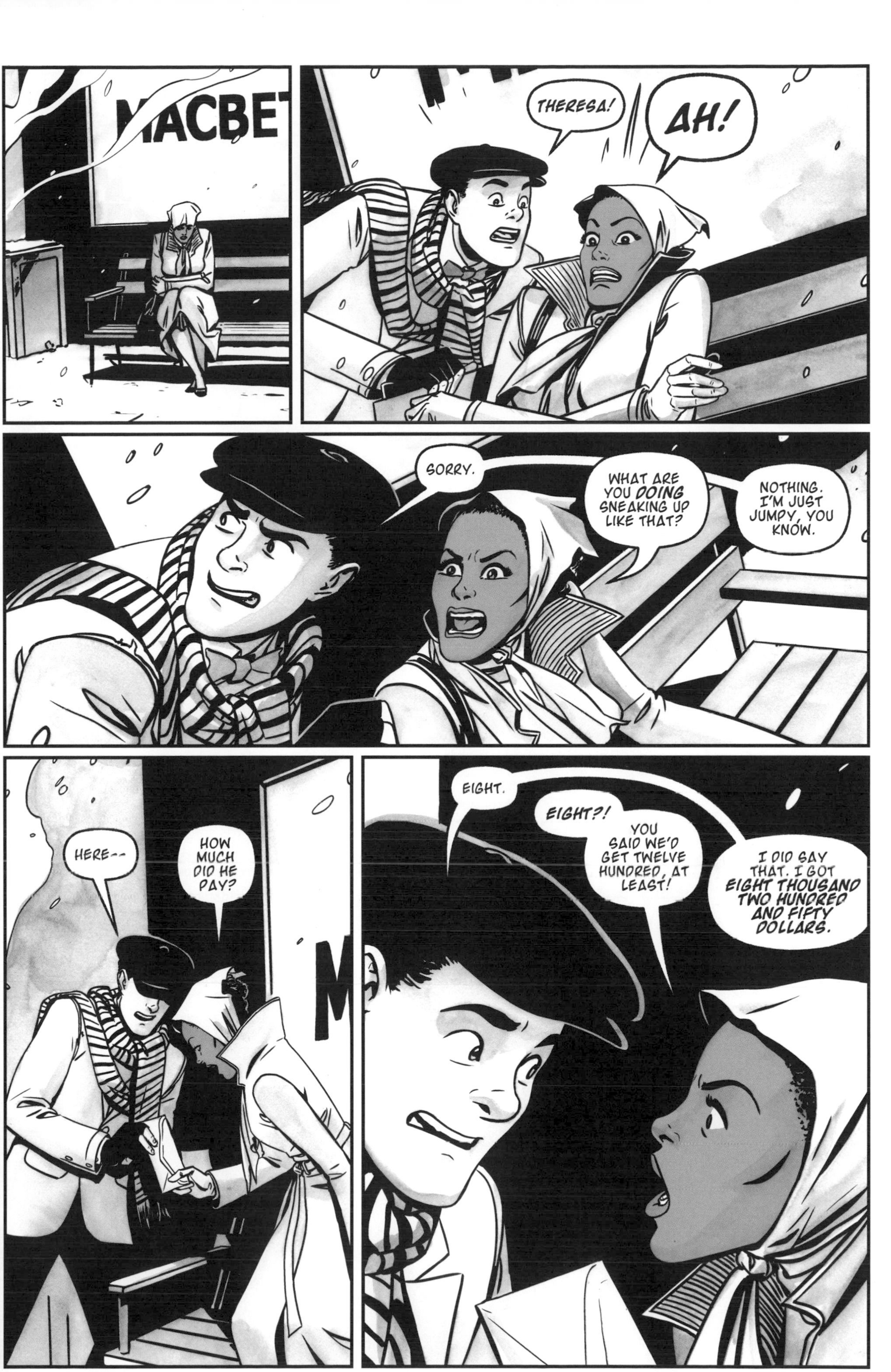
MACBET
THERESA!
AH!
SORRY.
WHAT ARE YOU DOING SNEAKING UP LIKE THAT?
NOTHING. I'M JUST JUMPY, YOU KNOW.
HERE--
HOW MUCH DID HE PAY?
EIGHT.
EIGHT?!
YOU SAID WE'D GET TWELVE HUNDRED, AT LEAST!
I DID SAY THAT. I GOT EIGHT THOUSAND TWO HUNDRED AND FIFTY DOLLARS.

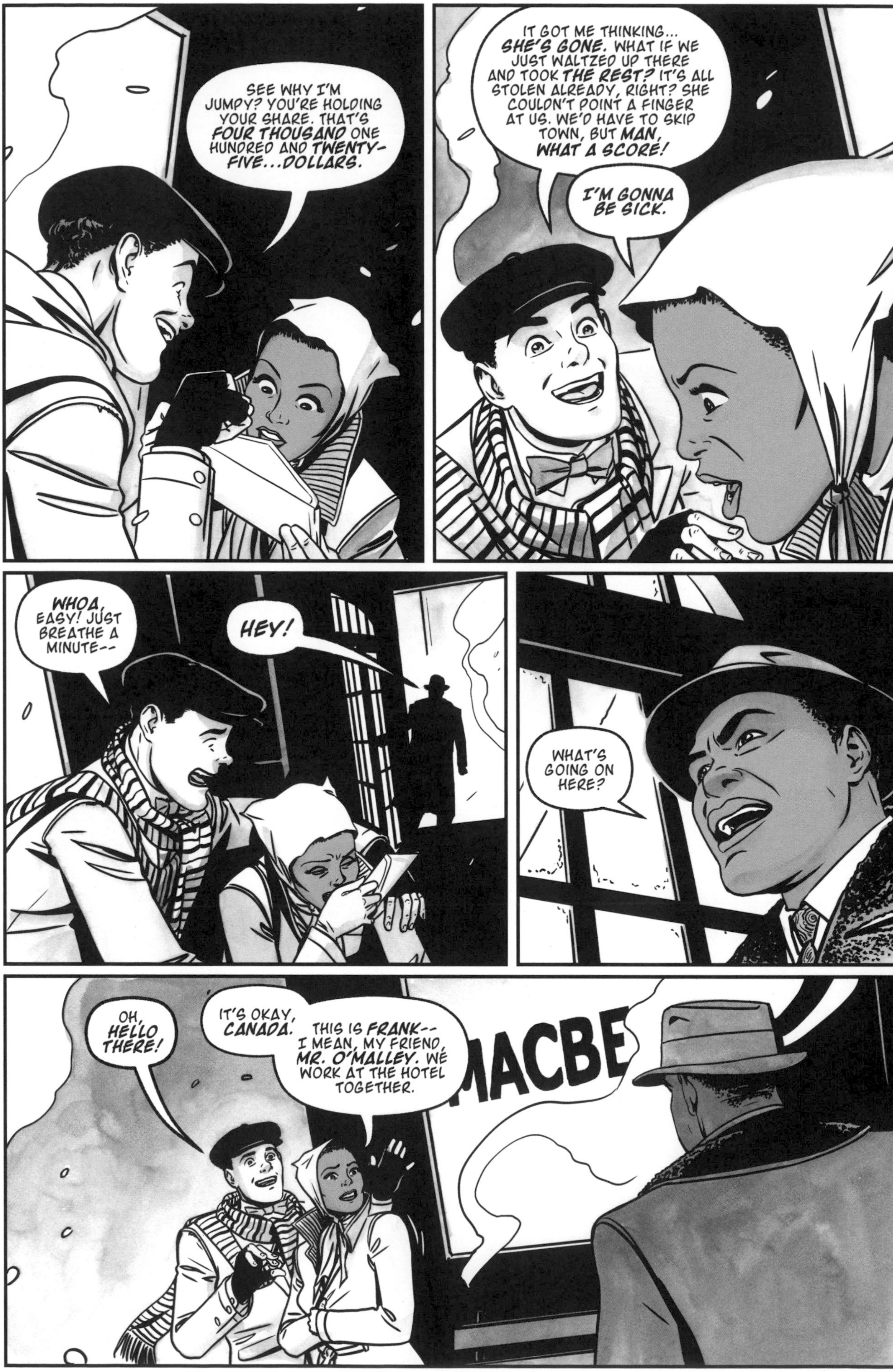
SEE WHY I'M JUMPY? YOU'RE HOLDING YOUR SHARE. THAT'S FOUR THOUSAND ONE HUNDRED AND TWENTY-FIVE...DOLLARS.
IT GOT ME THINKING... SHE'S GONE. WHAT IF WE JUST WALTZED UP THERE AND TOOK THE REST? IT'S ALL STOLEN ALREADY, RIGHT? SHE COULDN'T POINT A FINGER AT US. WE'D HAVE TO SKIP TOWN, BUT MAN, WHAT A SCORE!
I'M GONNA BE SICK.
WHOA, EASY! JUST BREATHE A MINUTE--
HEY!
WHAT'S GOING ON HERE?
OH, HELLO THERE!
IT'S OKAY, CANADA.
THIS IS FRANK-- I MEAN, MY FRIEND, MR. O'MALLEY. WE WORK AT THE HOTEL TOGETHER.
MACBE

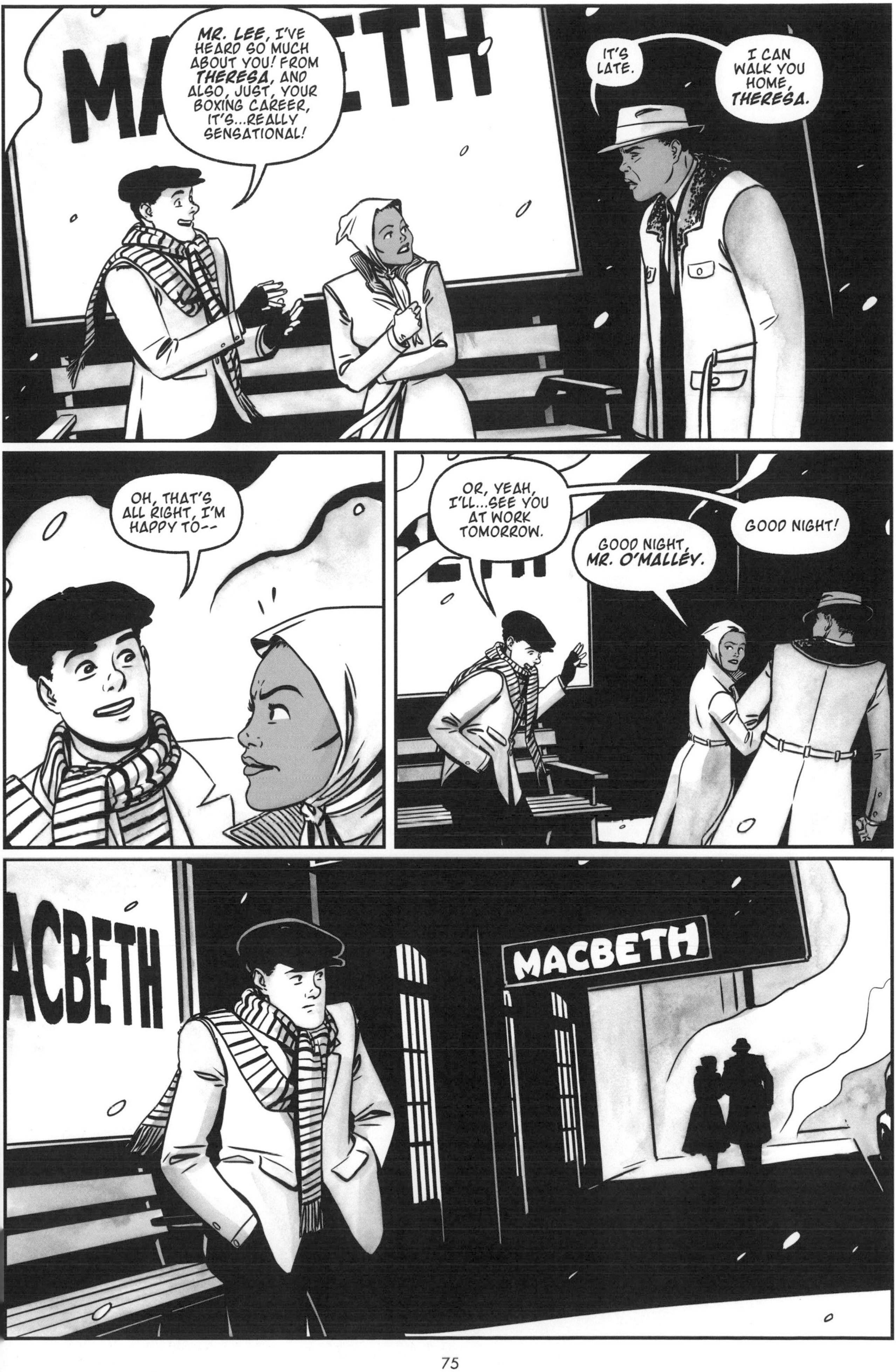
MACBETH
MR. LEE, I'VE HEARD SO MUCH ABOUT YOU! FROM THERESA, AND ALSO, JUST, YOUR BOXING CAREER, IT'S...REALLY SENSATIONAL!
IT'S LATE.
I CAN WALK YOU HOME, THERESA.
OH, THAT'S ALL RIGHT, I'M HAPPY TO--
OR, YEAH, I'LL...SEE YOU AT WORK TOMORROW.
GOOD NIGHT, MR. O'MALLEY.
GOOD NIGHT!
ACBETH
MACBETH

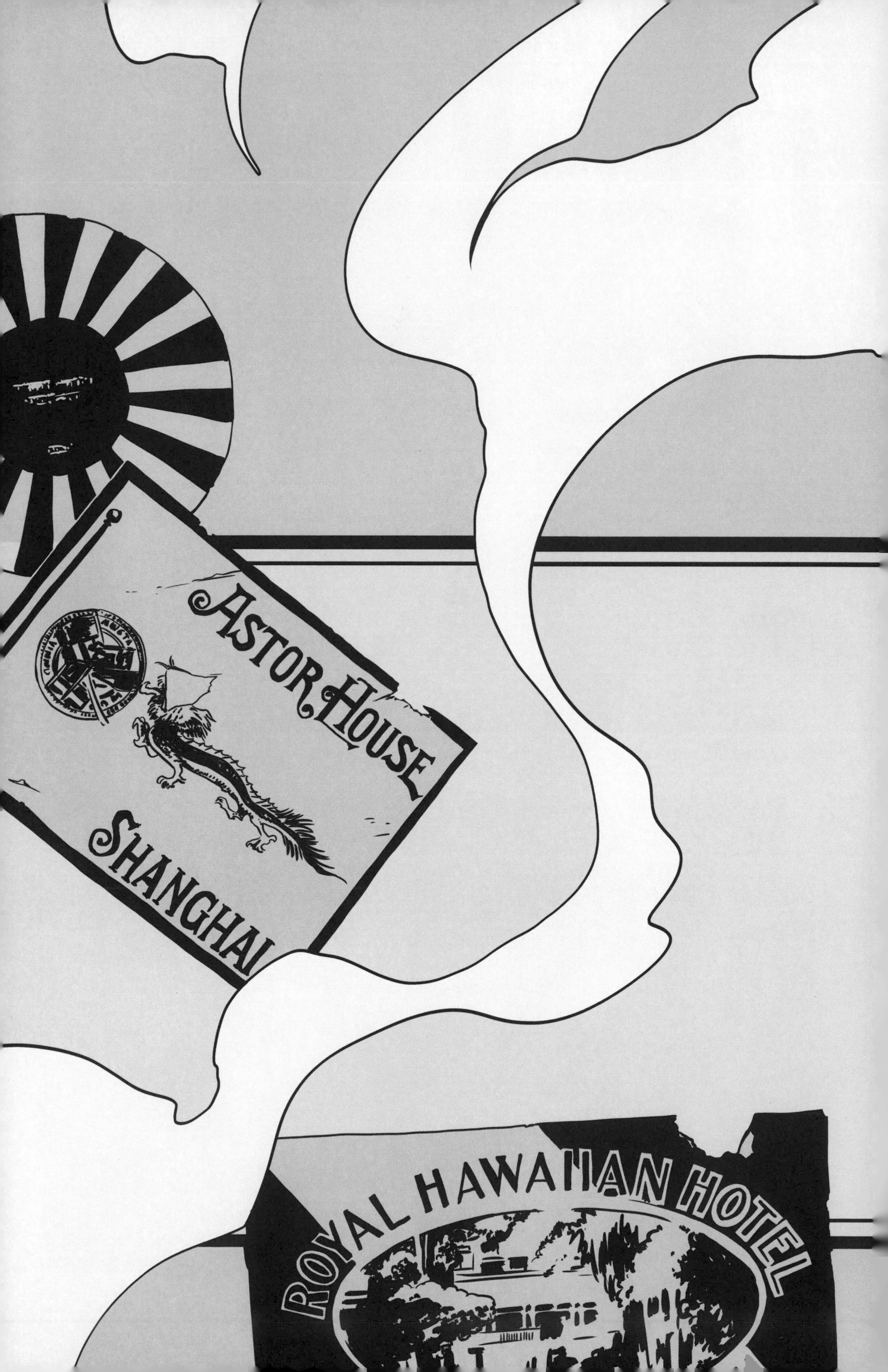
ASTOR HOUSE
SHANGHAI
ROYAL HAWAIIAN HOTEL

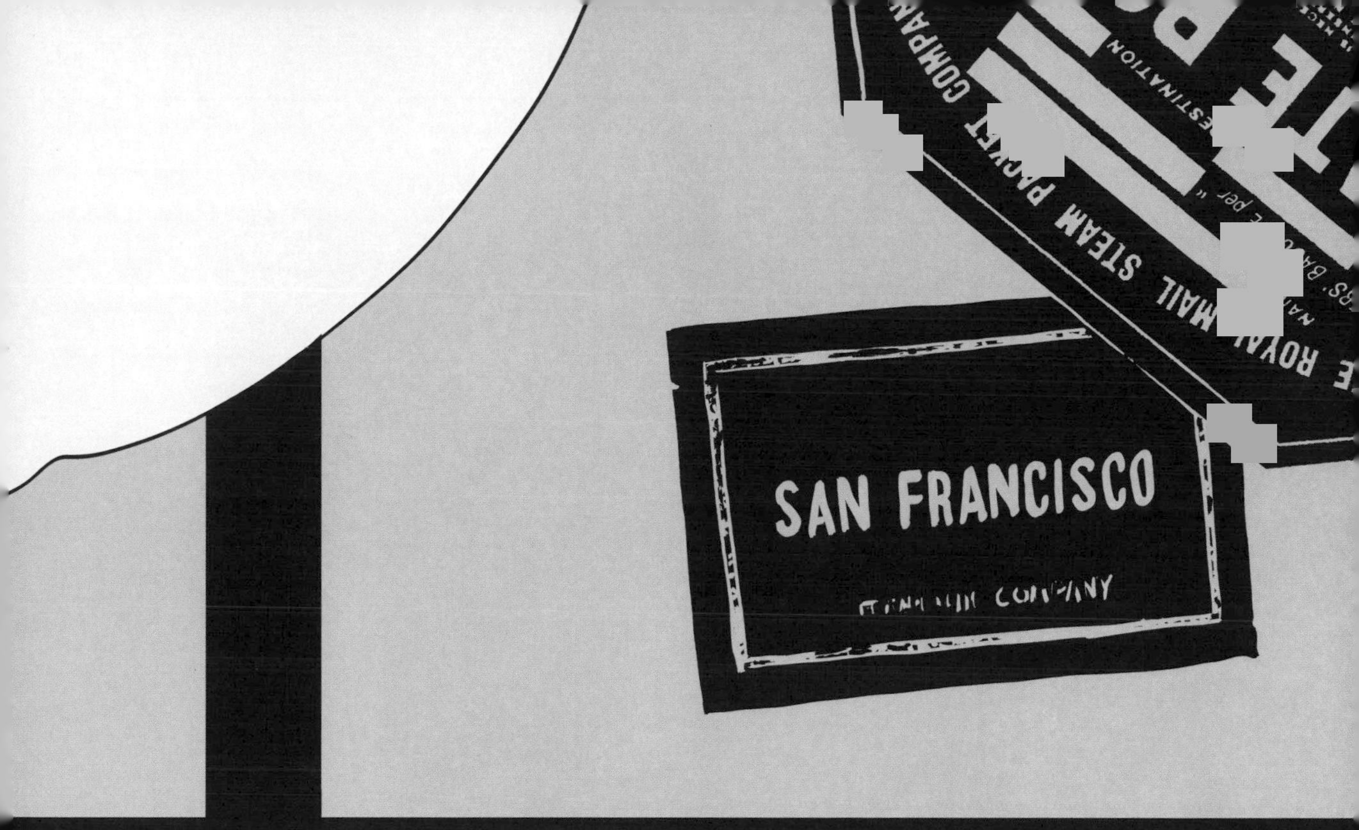
SAN FRANCISCO

CHAPTER 4

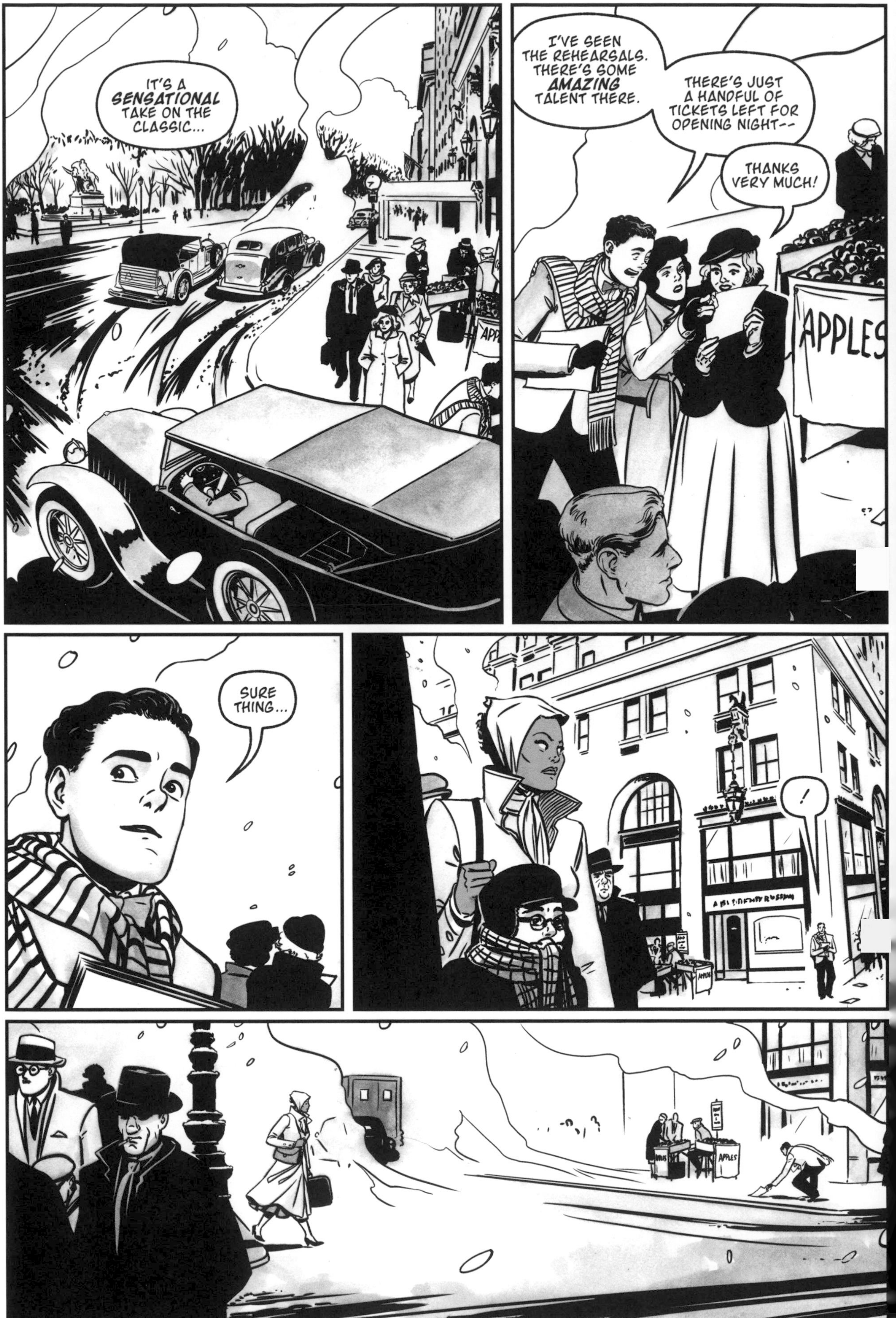
IT'S A SENSATIONAL TAKE ON THE CLASSIC...
I'VE SEEN THE REHEARSALS. THERE'S SOME AMAZING TALENT THERE.
THERE'S JUST A HANDFUL OF TICKETS LEFT FOR OPENING NIGHT--
THANKS VERY MUCH!
APPLES
SURE THING...
!
APPLES

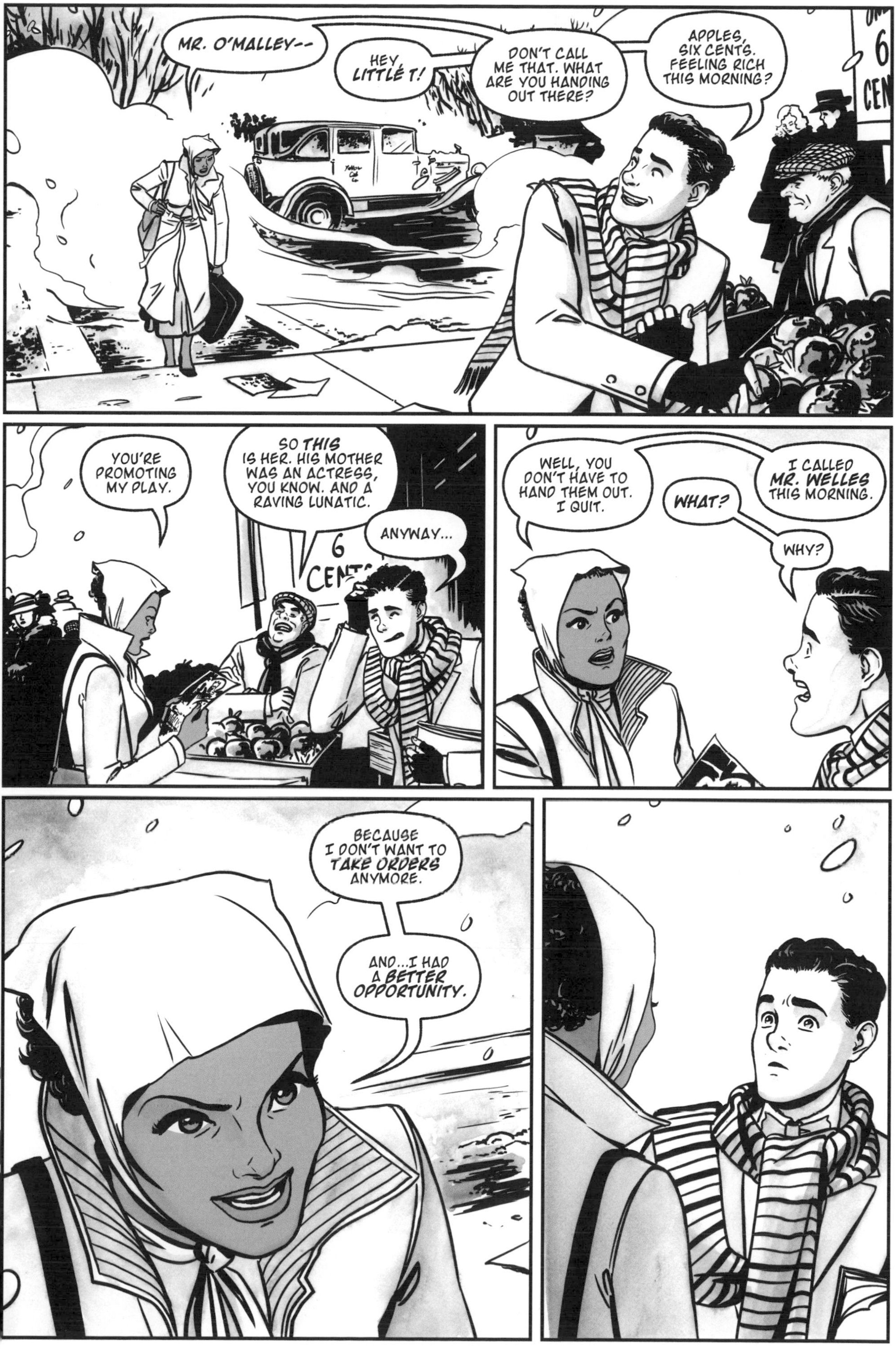

MR. O'MALLEY--
HEY, LITTLE T!
DON'T CALL ME THAT. WHAT ARE YOU HANDING OUT THERE?
APPLES, SIX CENTS. FEELING RICH THIS MORNING?
6 CEN
YOU'RE PROMOTING MY PLAY.
SO THIS IS HER. HIS MOTHER WAS AN ACTRESS, YOU KNOW. AND A RAVING LUNATIC.
6 CENTS
ANYWAY...
WELL, YOU DON'T HAVE TO HAND THEM OUT. I QUIT.
I CALLED MR. WELLES THIS MORNING.
WHAT?
WHY?
BECAUSE I DON'T WANT TO TAKE ORDERS ANYMORE.
AND...I HAD A BETTER OPPORTUNITY.

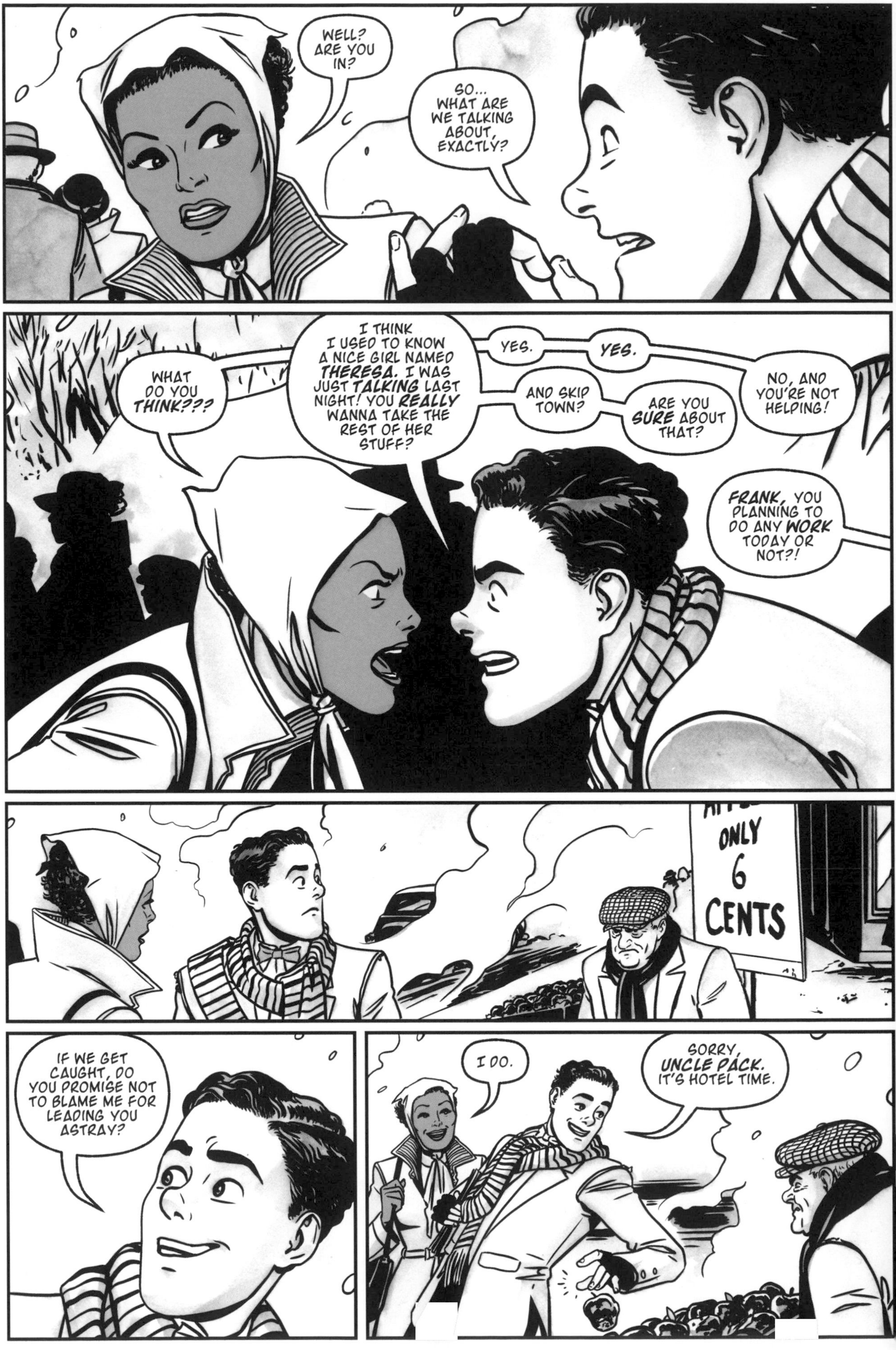
WELL? ARE YOU IN?
SO... WHAT ARE WE TALKING ABOUT, EXACTLY?
WHAT DO YOU THINK???
I THINK I USED TO KNOW A NICE GIRL NAMED THERESA. I WAS JUST TALKING LAST NIGHT! YOU REALLY WANNA TAKE THE REST OF HER STUFF?
YES.
AND SKIP TOWN?
YES.
ARE YOU SURE ABOUT THAT?
NO, AND YOU'RE NOT HELPING!
FRANK, YOU PLANNING TO DO ANY WORK TODAY OR NOT?!
ONLY 6 CENTS
IF WE GET CAUGHT, DO YOU PROMISE NOT TO BLAME ME FOR LEADING YOU ASTRAY?
I DO.
SORRY, UNCLE PACK. IT'S HOTEL TIME.

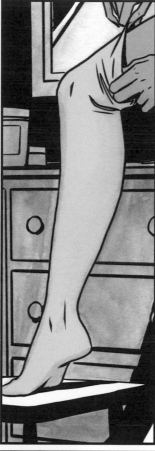

GOOD MORNING THERESA!

GOOD MORNING!

IF YOU'RE BLUE AND YOU BA-DAH BUM BUM BUM BUM...

TOWER ELEVATORS

...WHY DON'T YOU TRY WHERE DYAH DUM DUM-- PUTTIN' ON THE RITZ!

DING!

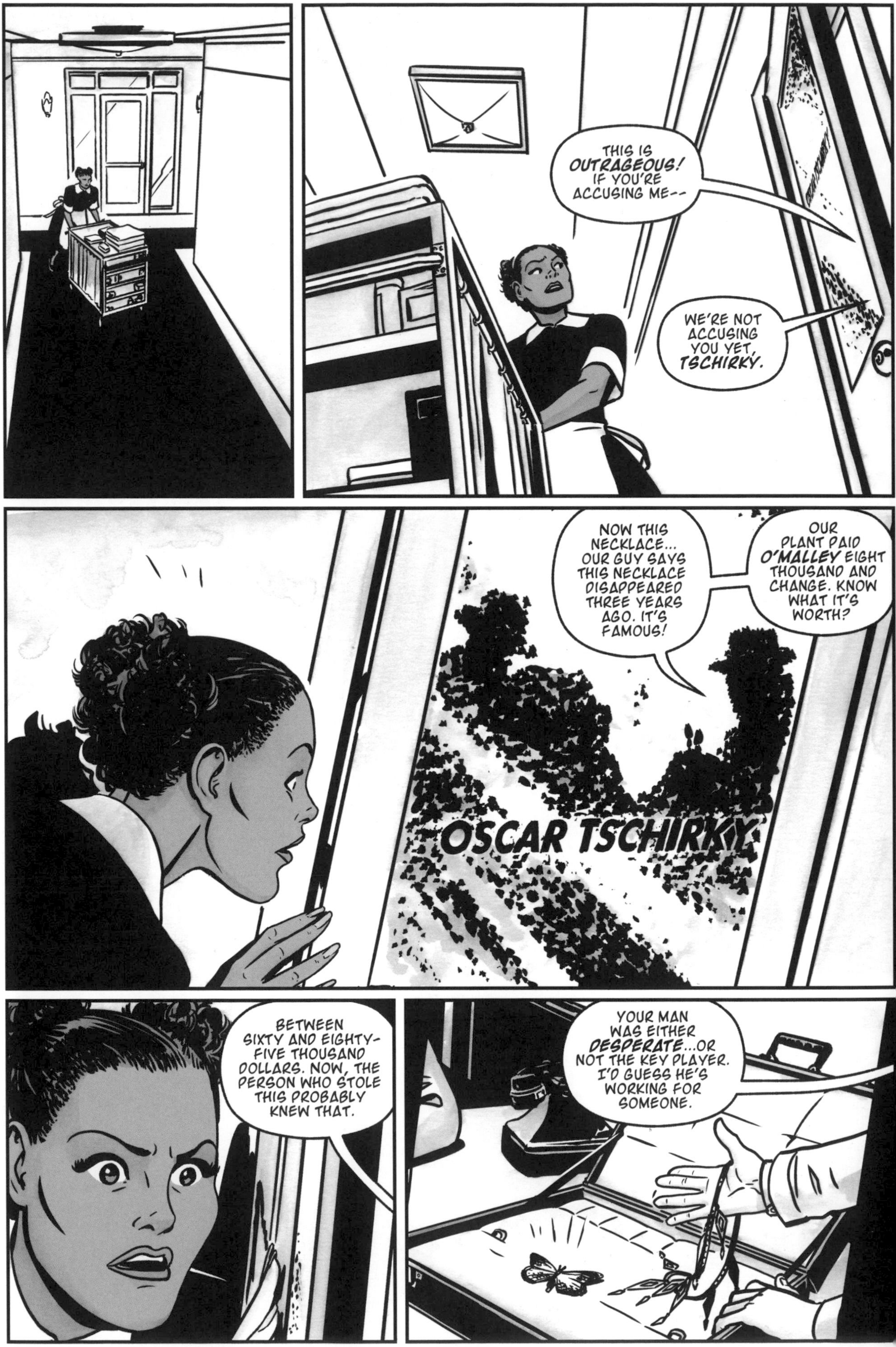
THIS IS OUTRAGEOUS! IF YOU'RE ACCUSING ME--
WE'RE NOT ACCUSING YOU YET, TSCHIRKY.
NOW THIS NECKLACE... OUR GUY SAYS THIS NECKLACE DISAPPEARED THREE YEARS AGO. IT'S FAMOUS!
OUR PLANT PAID O'MALLEY EIGHT THOUSAND AND CHANGE. KNOW WHAT IT'S WORTH?
OSCAR TSCHIRKY
BETWEEN SIXTY AND EIGHTY-FIVE THOUSAND DOLLARS. NOW, THE PERSON WHO STOLE THIS PROBABLY KNEW THAT.
YOUR MAN WAS EITHER DESPERATE...OR NOT THE KEY PLAYER. I'D GUESS HE'S WORKING FOR SOMEONE.

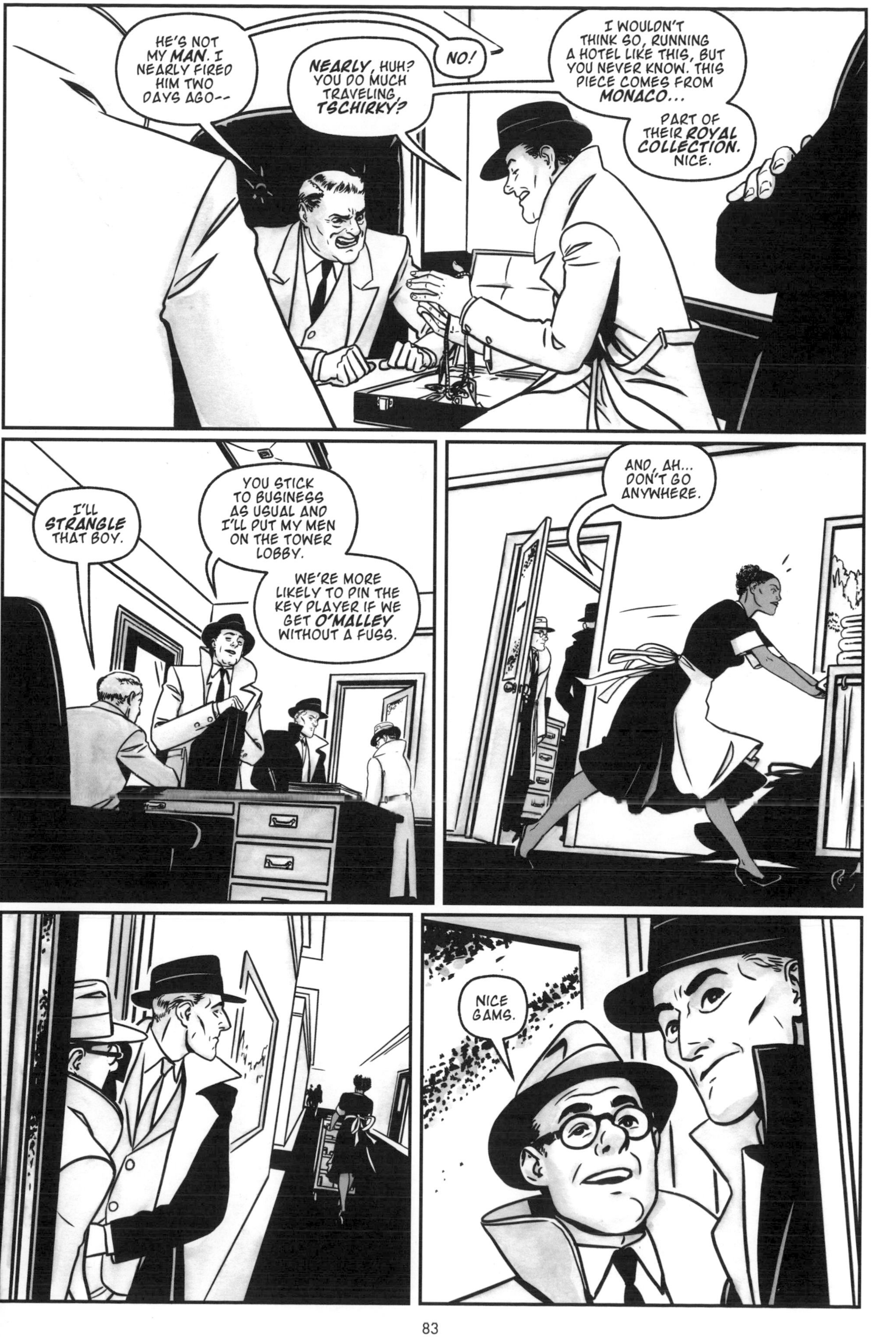
HE'S NOT MY **MAN**. I NEARLY FIRED HIM TWO DAYS AGO--
NEARLY, HUH? YOU DO MUCH TRAVELING **TSCHIRKY?**
NO!
I WOULDN'T THINK SO, RUNNING A HOTEL LIKE THIS, BUT YOU NEVER KNOW. THIS PIECE COMES FROM **MONACO...**
PART OF THEIR **ROYAL COLLECTION.** NICE.
I'LL **STRANGLE** THAT BOY.
YOU STICK TO BUSINESS AS USUAL AND I'LL PUT MY MEN ON THE TOWER LOBBY.
WE'RE MORE LIKELY TO PIN THE KEY PLAYER IF WE GET **O'MALLEY** WITHOUT A FUSS.
AND, AH... DON'T GO ANYWHERE.
NICE GAMS.

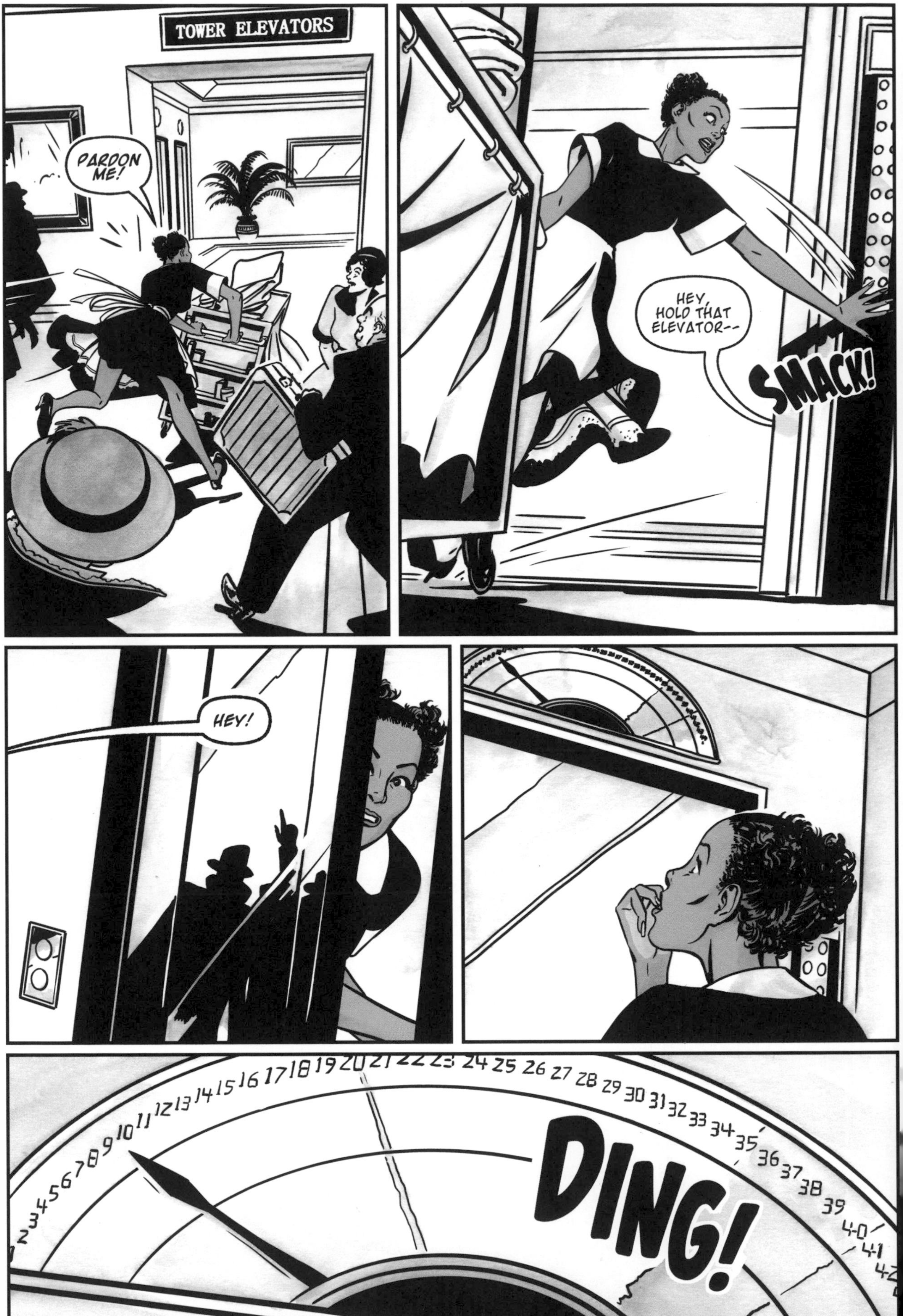
TOWER ELEVATORS
PARDON ME!
HEY, HOLD THAT ELEVATOR--
SMACK!
HEY!
DING!

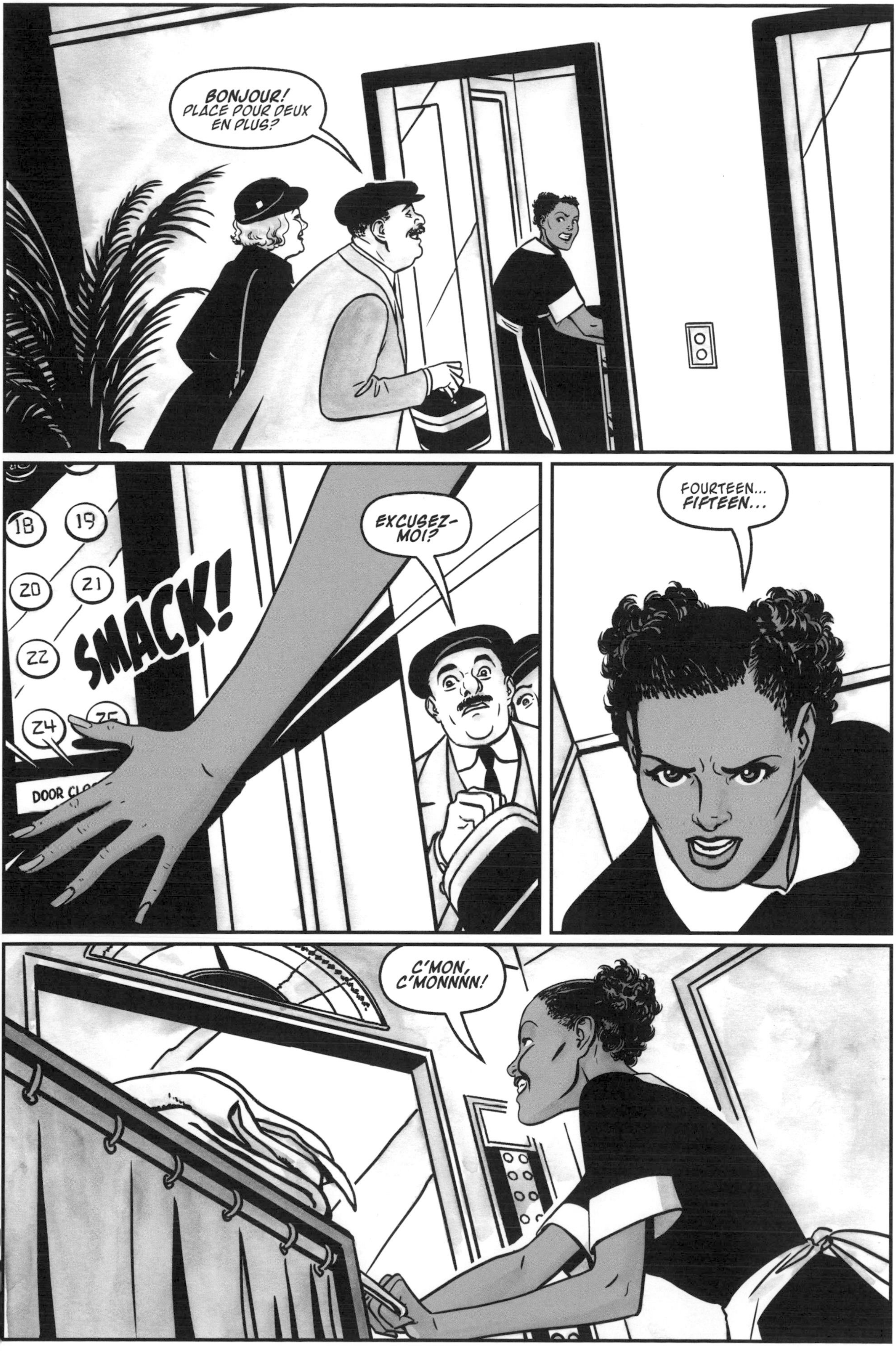
BONJOUR! PLACE POUR DEUX EN PLUS?
18
19
20
21
22
24
SMACK!
EXCUSEZ-MOI?
FOURTEEN... FIFTEEN...
C'MON, C'MONNNN!

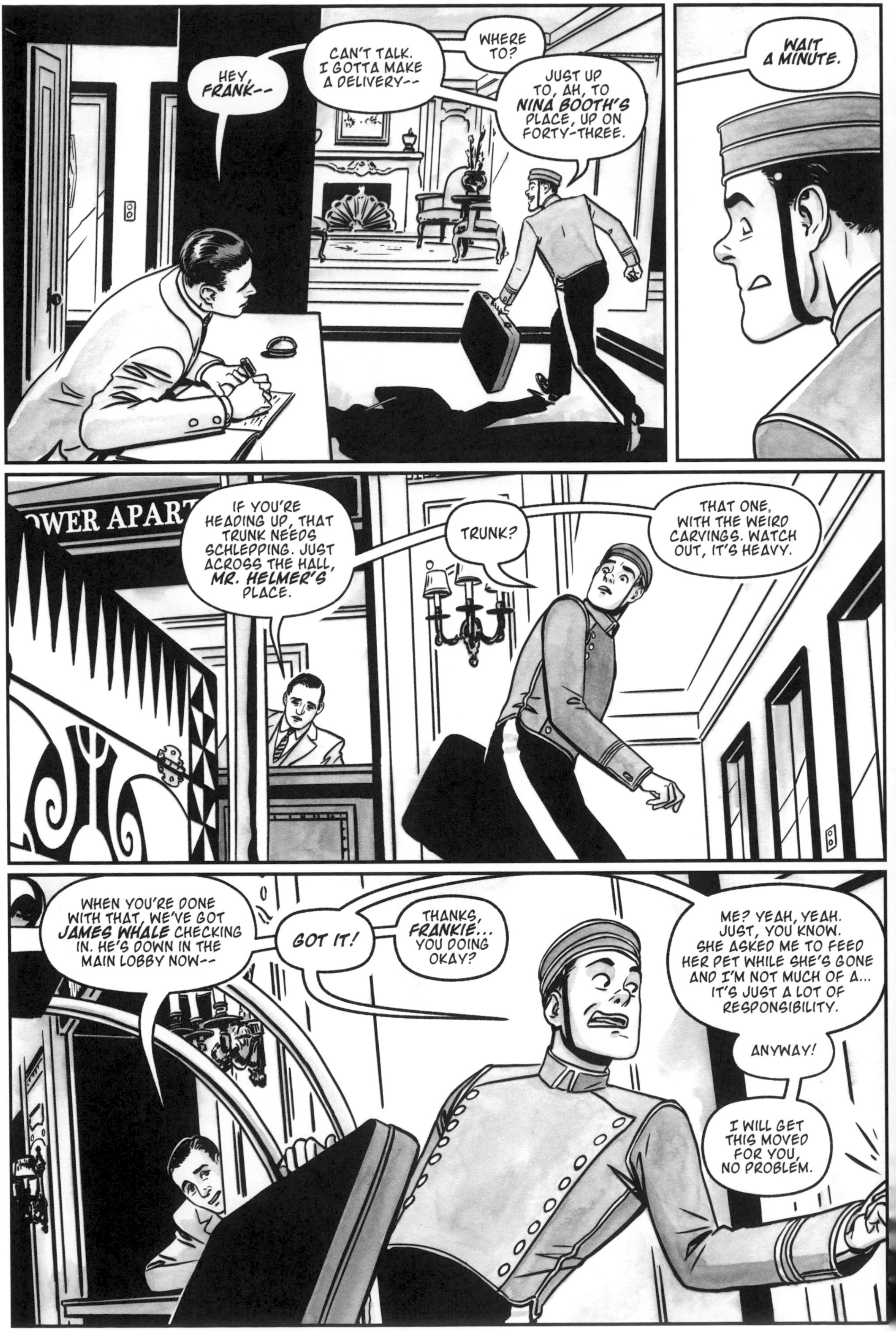
HEY, FRANK--
CAN'T TALK. I GOTTA MAKE A DELIVERY--
WHERE TO?
JUST UP TO, AH, TO NINA BOOTH'S PLACE, UP ON FORTY-THREE.
WAIT A MINUTE.
OWER APART
IF YOU'RE HEADING UP, THAT TRUNK NEEDS SCHLEPPING. JUST ACROSS THE HALL, MR. HELMER'S PLACE.
TRUNK?
THAT ONE, WITH THE WEIRD CARVINGS. WATCH OUT, IT'S HEAVY.
WHEN YOU'RE DONE WITH THAT, WE'VE GOT JAMES WHALE CHECKING IN. HE'S DOWN IN THE MAIN LOBBY NOW--
GOT IT!
THANKS, FRANKIE... YOU DOING OKAY?
ME? YEAH, YEAH. JUST, YOU KNOW. SHE ASKED ME TO FEED HER PET WHILE SHE'S GONE AND I'M NOT MUCH OF A... IT'S JUST A LOT OF RESPONSIBILITY.
ANYWAY!
I WILL GET THIS MOVED FOR YOU, NO PROBLEM.

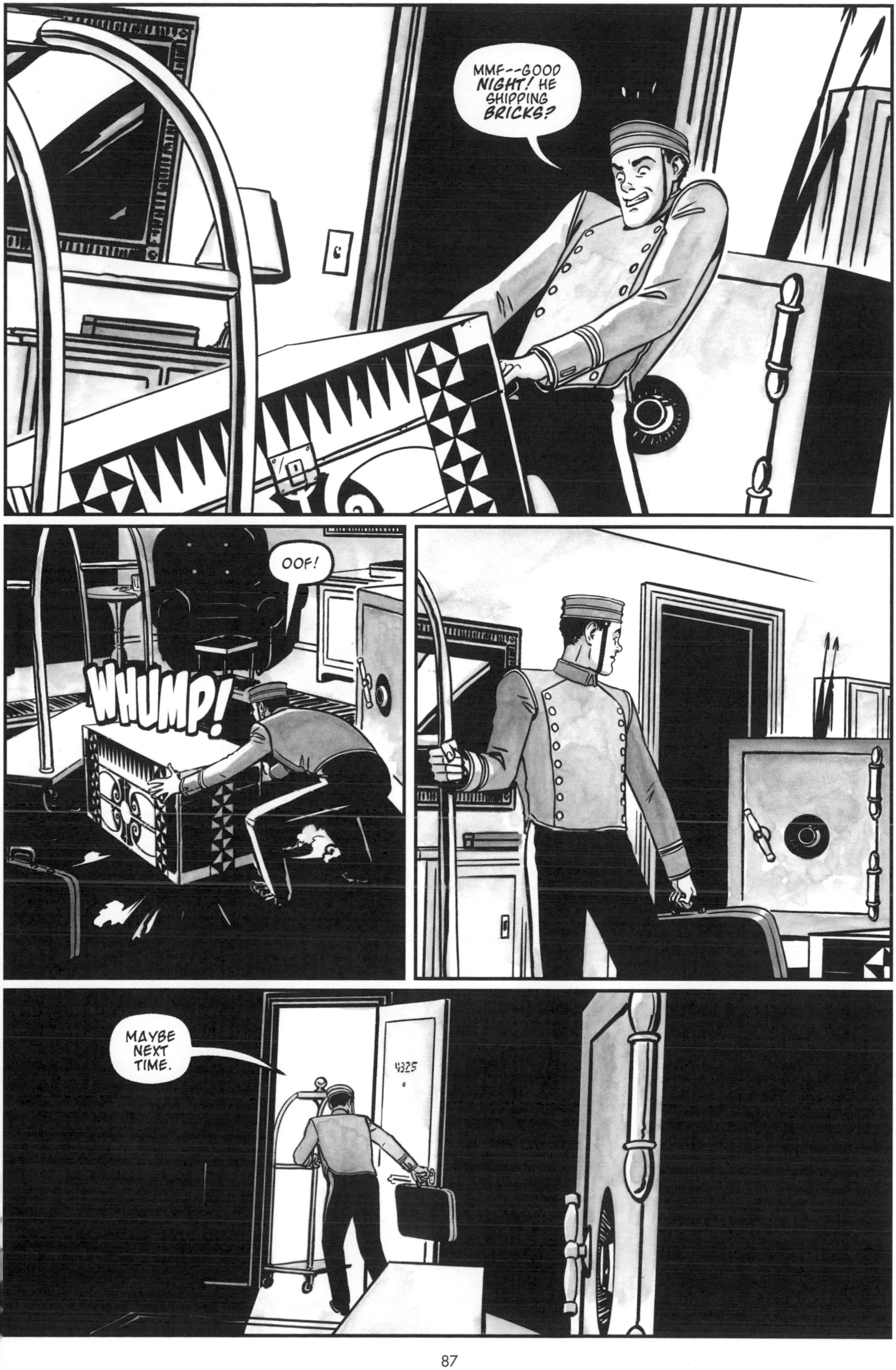
MMF--GOOD NIGHT! HE SHIPPING BRICKS?
OOF!
WHUMP!
MAYBE NEXT TIME.
4325

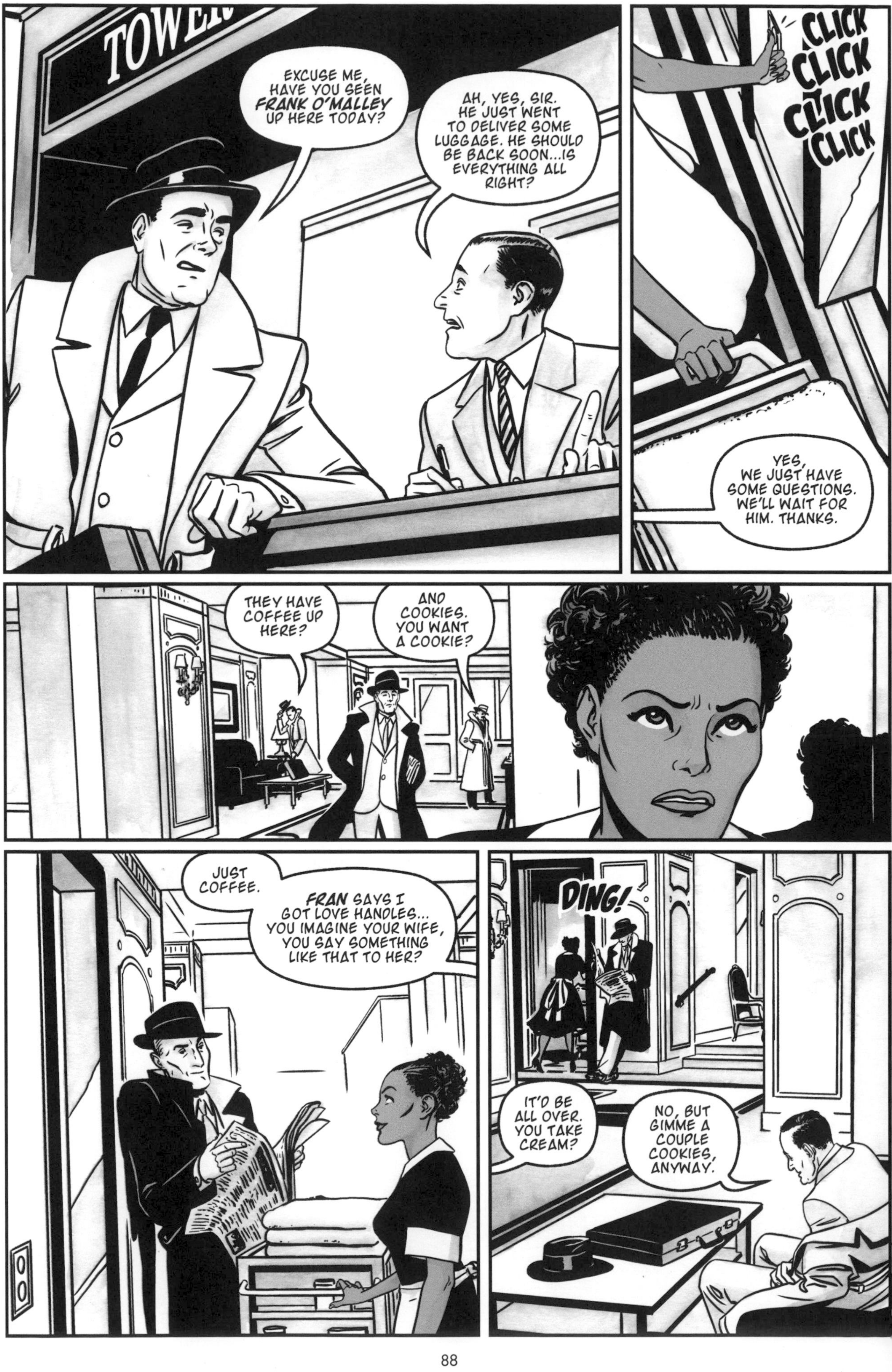
TOWER
EXCUSE ME, HAVE YOU SEEN FRANK O'MALLEY UP HERE TODAY?
AH, YES, SIR. HE JUST WENT TO DELIVER SOME LUGGAGE. HE SHOULD BE BACK SOON...IS EVERYTHING ALL RIGHT?
CLICK CLICK CLICK CLICK
YES, WE JUST HAVE SOME QUESTIONS. WE'LL WAIT FOR HIM. THANKS.
THEY HAVE COFFEE UP HERE?
AND COOKIES. YOU WANT A COOKIE?
JUST COFFEE.
FRAN SAYS I GOT LOVE HANDLES... YOU IMAGINE YOUR WIFE, YOU SAY SOMETHING LIKE THAT TO HER?
DING!
IT'D BE ALL OVER. YOU TAKE CREAM?
NO, BUT GIMME A COUPLE COOKIES, ANYWAY.

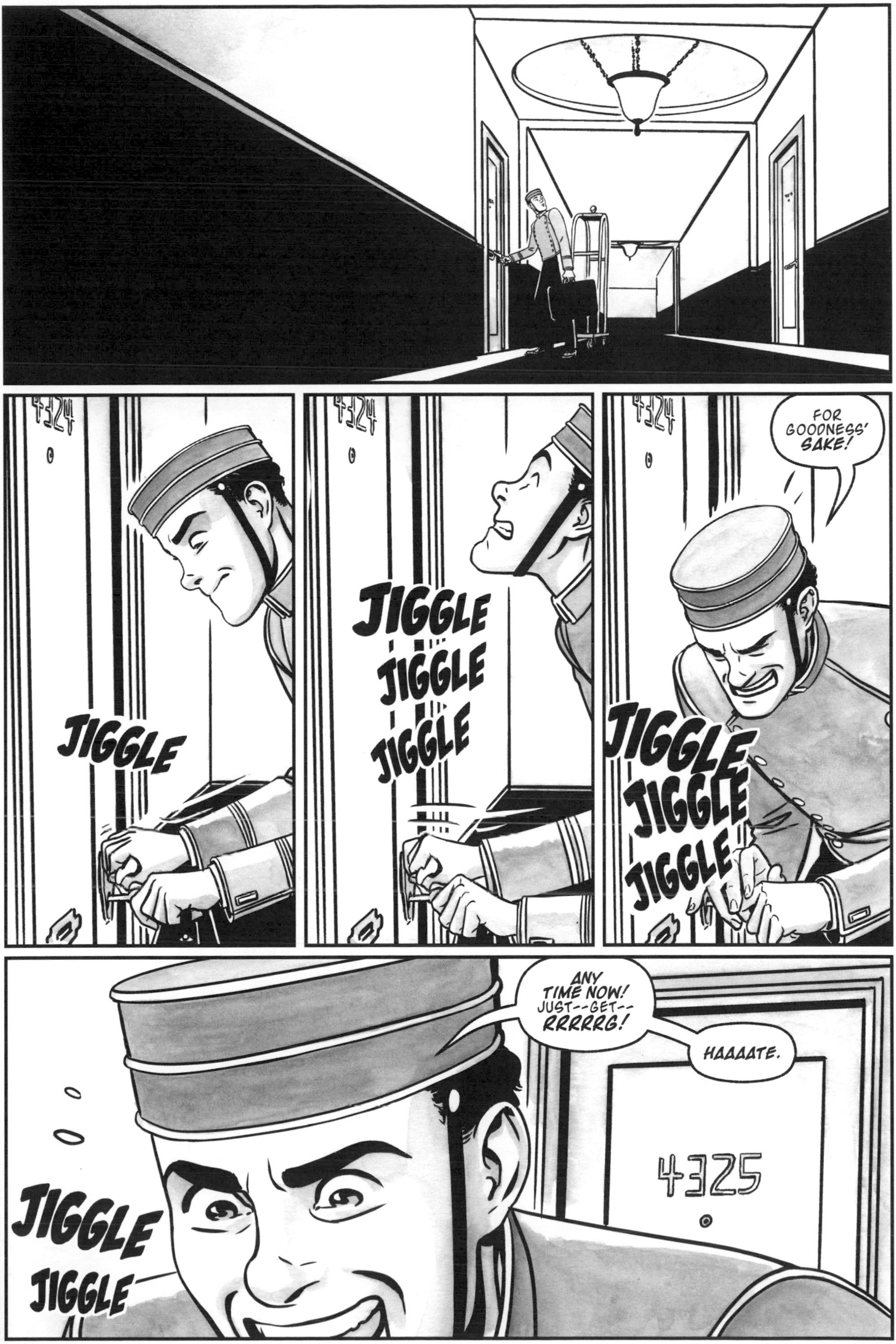
JIGGLE
JIGGLE
JIGGLE
JIGGLE
FOR GOODNESS' SAKE!
JIGGLE
JIGGLE
JIGGLE
ANY TIME NOW! JUST--GET--RRRRRG!
HAAAATE.
4325
JIGGLE
JIGGLE

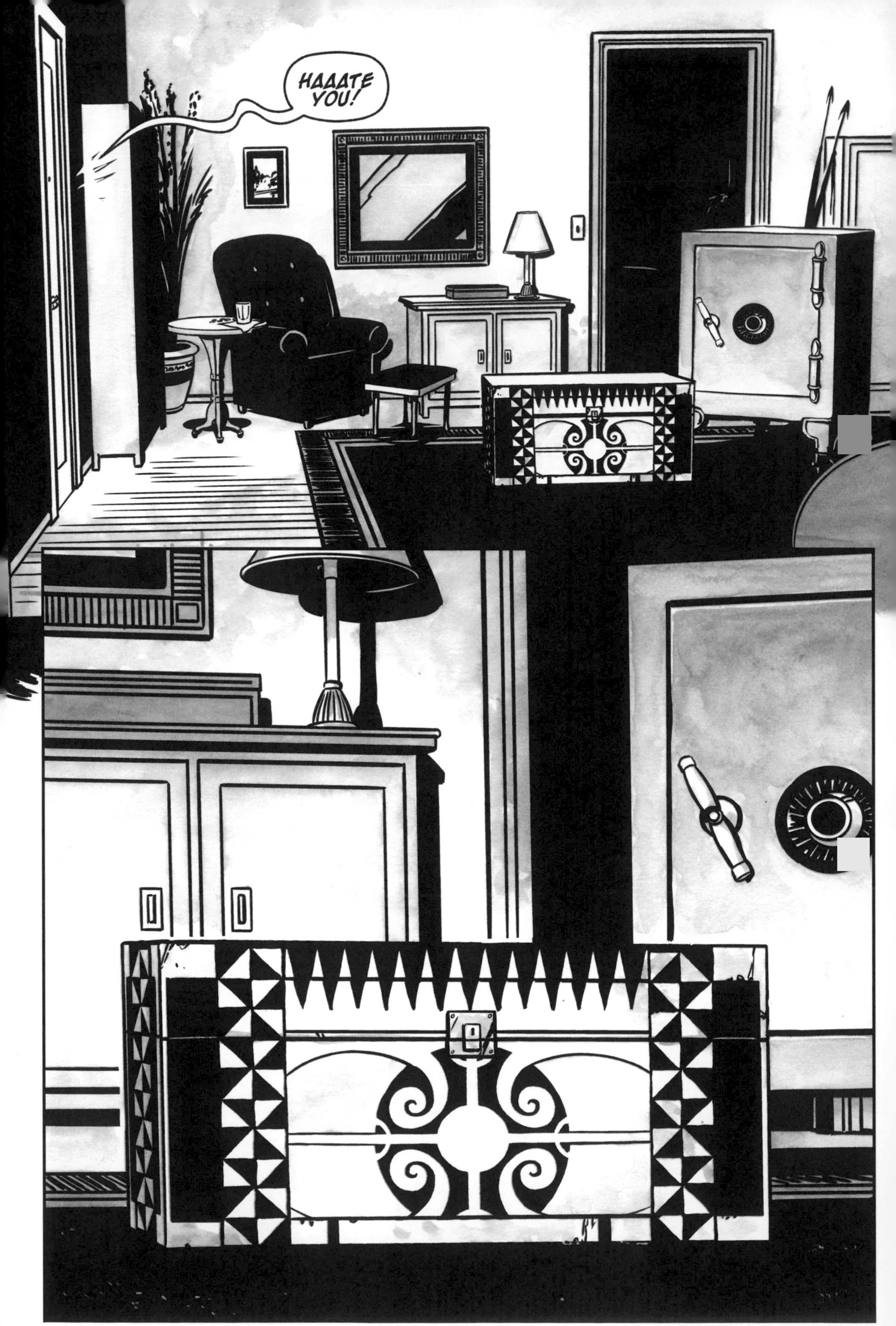
HAAATE YOU!

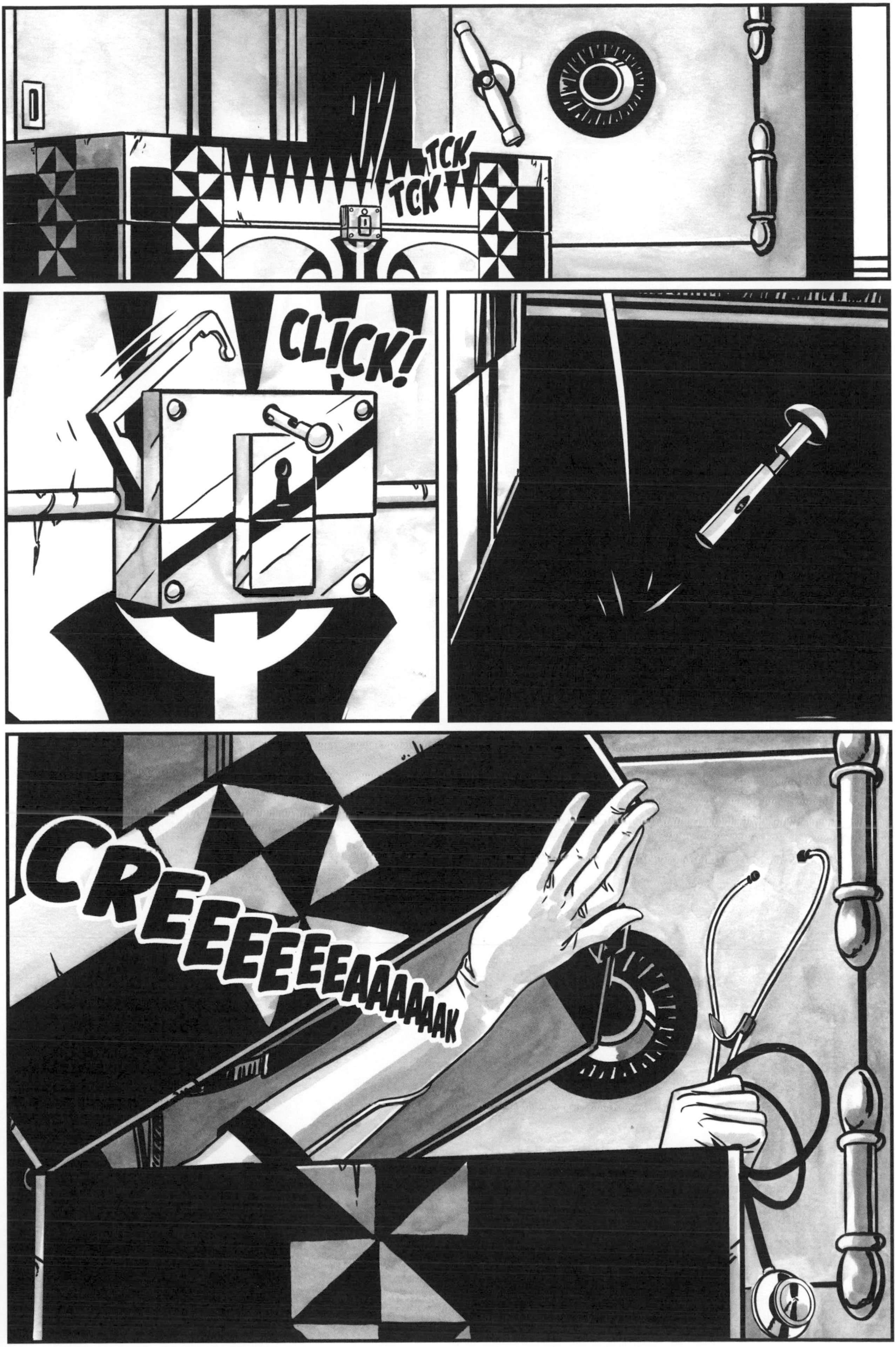
TCK
TCK
CLICK!
CREEEEEEEAAAAAAAK

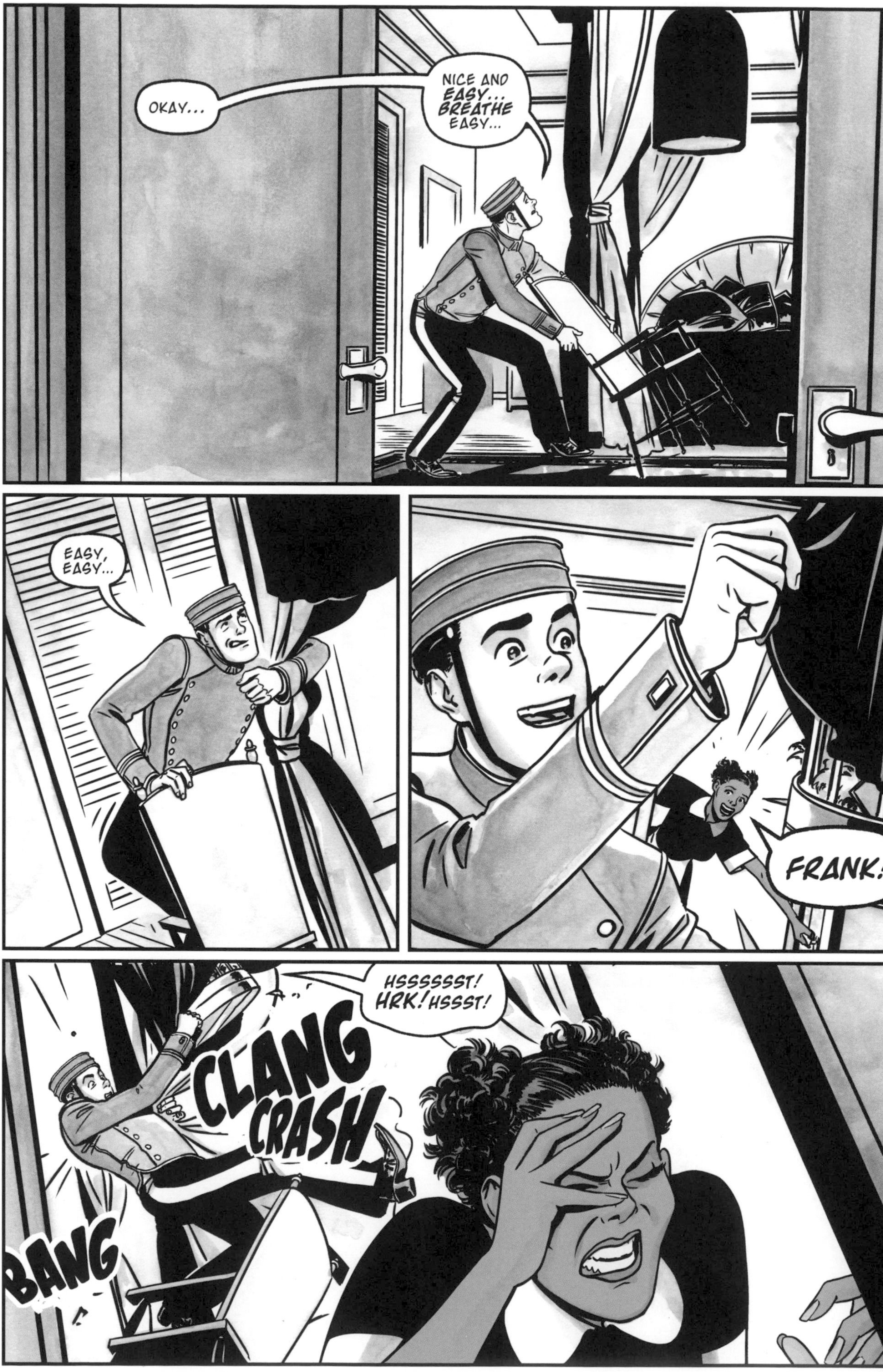
OKAY...
NICE AND EASY... BREATHE EASY...
EASY, EASY...
FRANK!
HSSSSSST! HRK! HSSST!
CLANG
CRASH
BANG

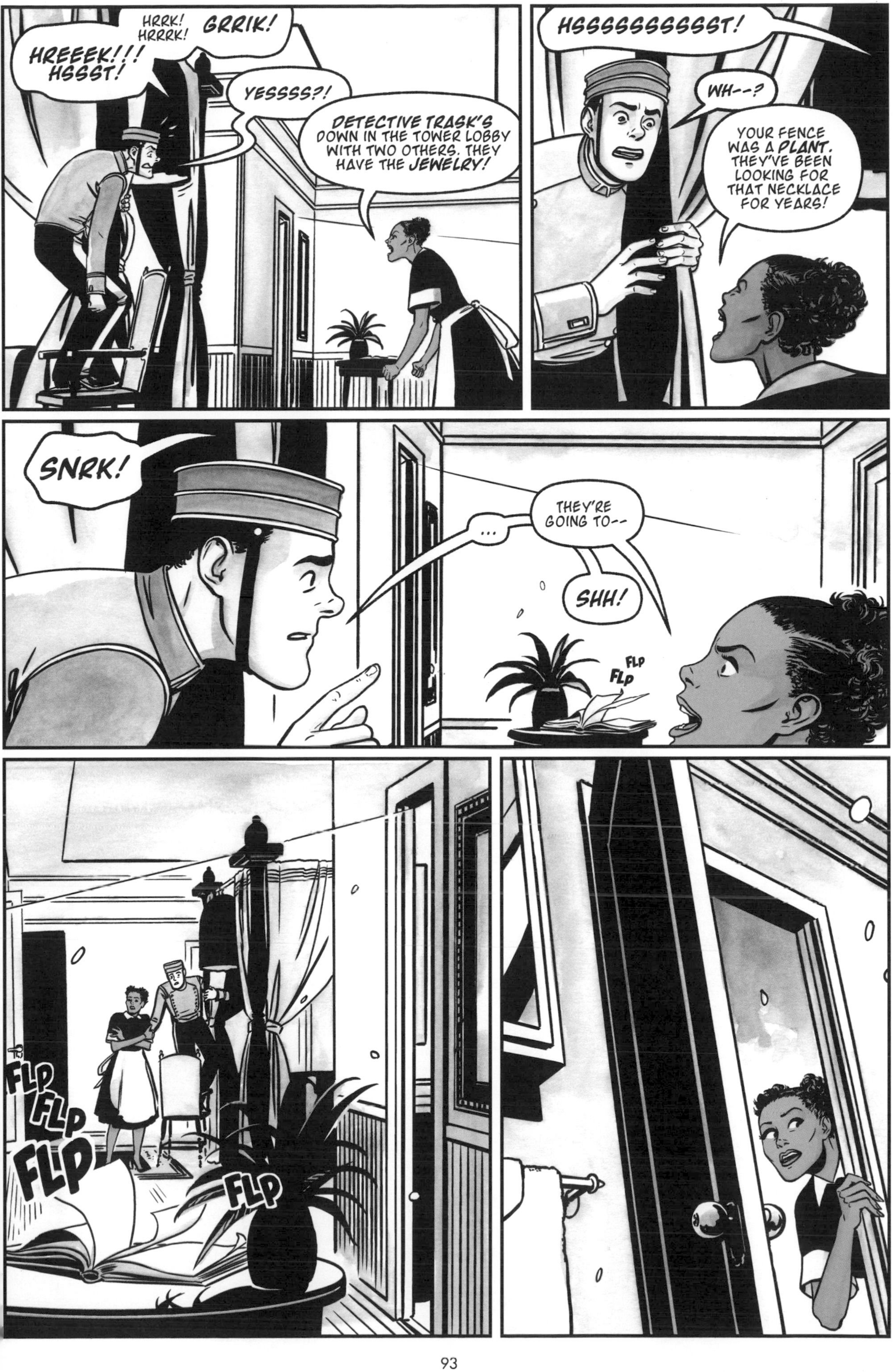
HREEEK!!!
HSSST!
HRRK!
HRRRK!
GRRIK!
YESSSS?!
DETECTIVE TRASK'S DOWN IN THE TOWER LOBBY WITH TWO OTHERS. THEY HAVE THE JEWELRY!
HSSSSSSSSSSST!
WH--?
YOUR FENCE WAS A PLANT. THEY'VE BEEN LOOKING FOR THAT NECKLACE FOR YEARS!
SNRK!
THEY'RE GOING TO--
...
SHH!
FLP
FLP
FLP
FLP
FLP
FLP

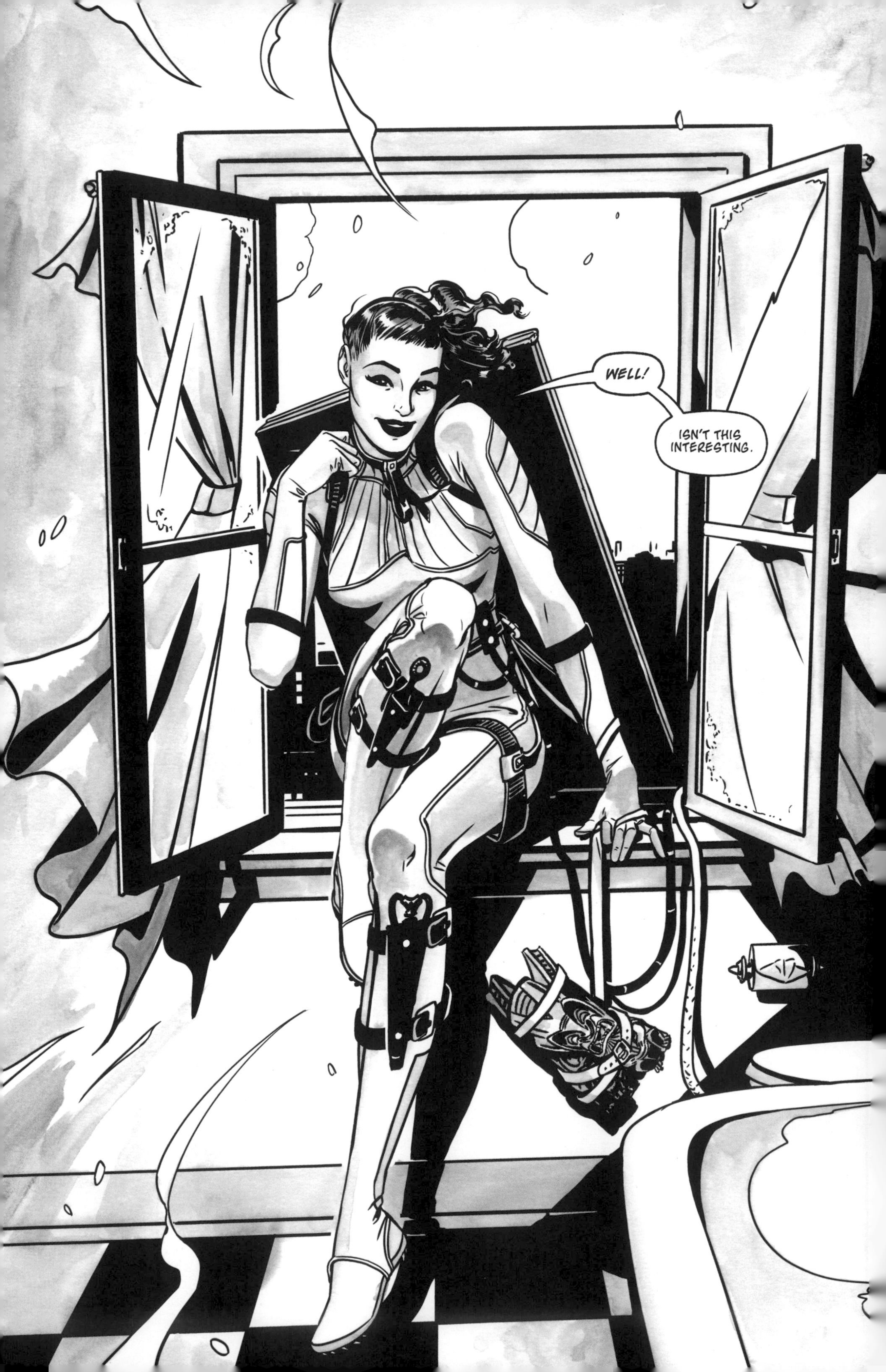
WELL!
ISN'T THIS INTERESTING.

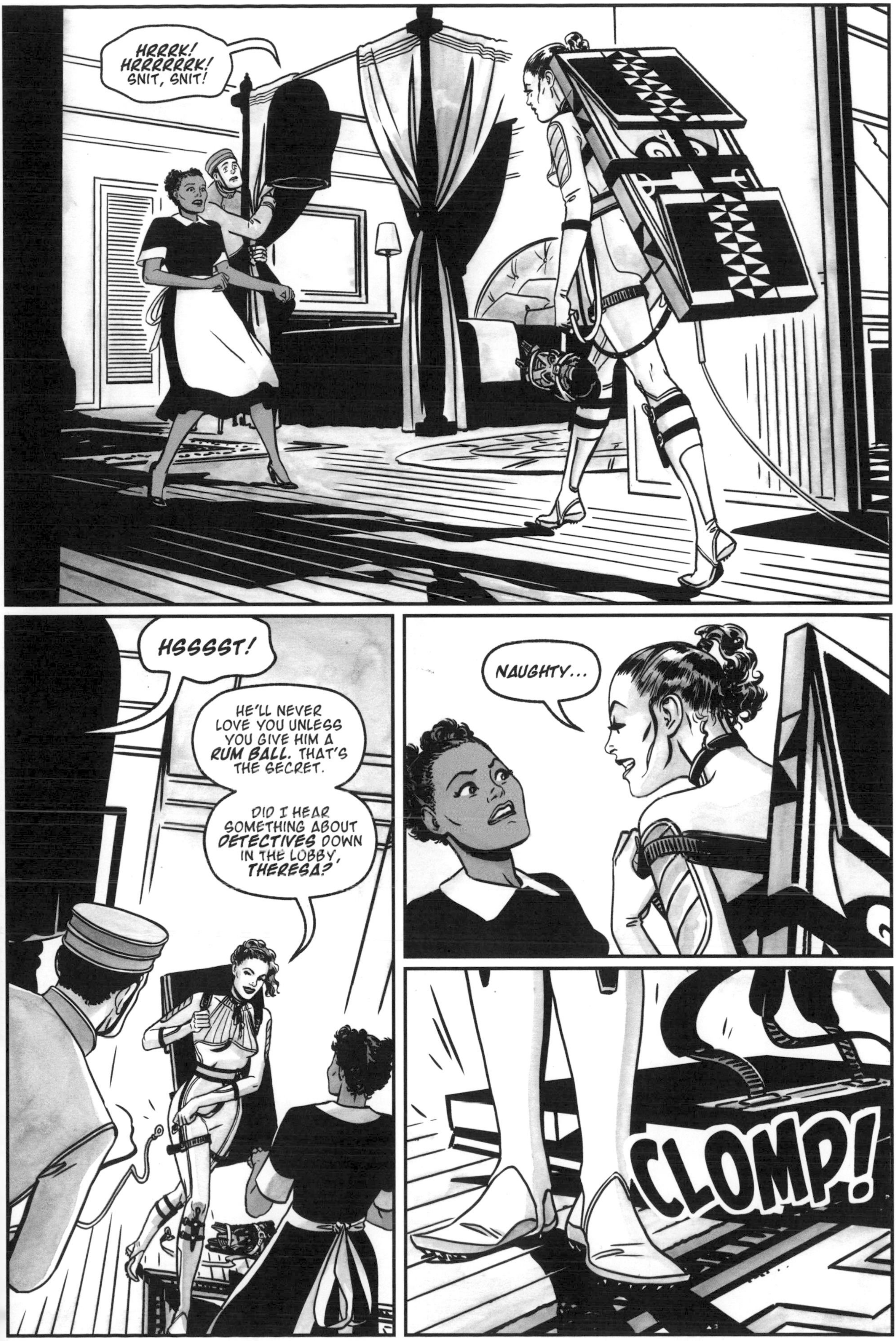
HRRRK! HRRRRRRK! SNIT, SNIT!
HSSSST!
HE'LL NEVER LOVE YOU UNLESS YOU GIVE HIM A RUM BALL. THAT'S THE SECRET.
DID I HEAR SOMETHING ABOUT DETECTIVES DOWN IN THE LOBBY, THERESA?
NAUGHTY...
CLOMP!

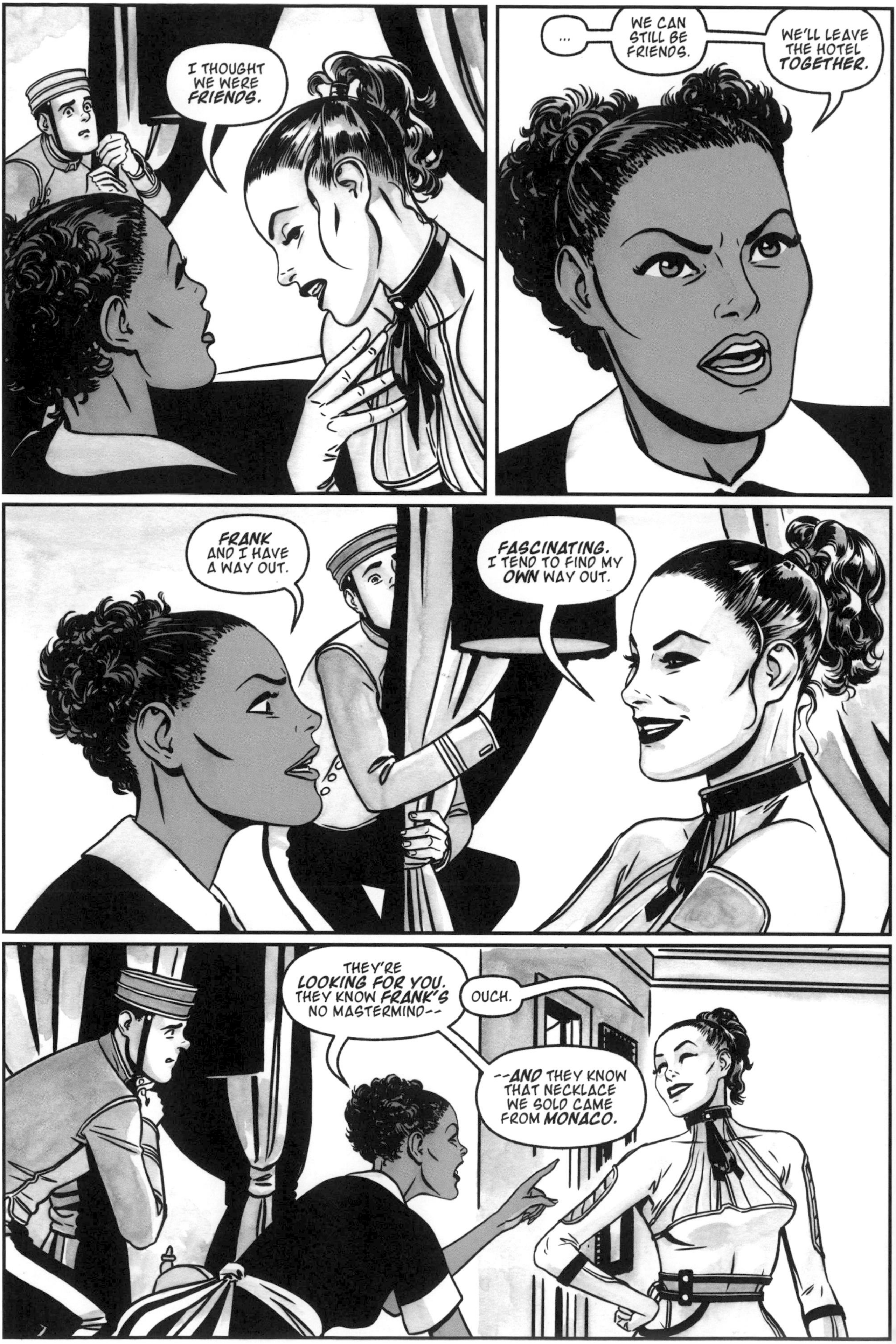
I THOUGHT WE WERE FRIENDS.
...
WE CAN STILL BE FRIENDS.
WE'LL LEAVE THE HOTEL TOGETHER.
FRANK AND I HAVE A WAY OUT.
FASCINATING. I TEND TO FIND MY OWN WAY OUT.
THEY'RE LOOKING FOR YOU. THEY KNOW FRANK'S NO MASTERMIND--
OUCH.
--AND THEY KNOW THAT NECKLACE WE SOLD CAME FROM MONACO.

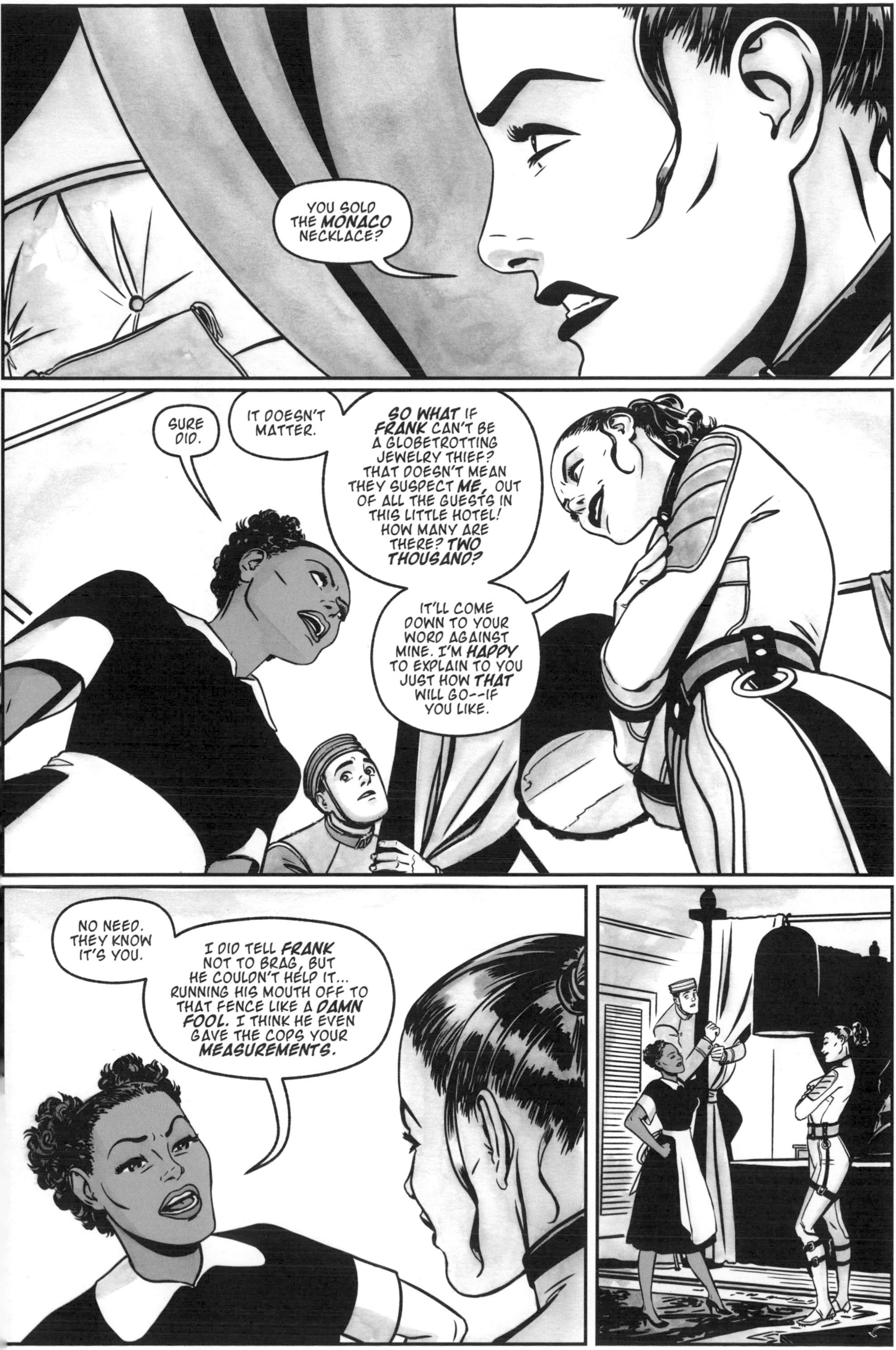
YOU SOLD THE MONACO NECKLACE?
SURE DID.
IT DOESN'T MATTER.
SO WHAT IF FRANK CAN'T BE A GLOBETROTTING JEWELRY THIEF? THAT DOESN'T MEAN THEY SUSPECT ME, OUT OF ALL THE GUESTS IN THIS LITTLE HOTEL! HOW MANY ARE THERE? TWO THOUSAND?
IT'LL COME DOWN TO YOUR WORD AGAINST MINE. I'M HAPPY TO EXPLAIN TO YOU JUST HOW THAT WILL GO--IF YOU LIKE.
NO NEED. THEY KNOW IT'S YOU.
I DID TELL FRANK NOT TO BRAG, BUT HE COULDN'T HELP IT... RUNNING HIS MOUTH OFF TO THAT FENCE LIKE A DAMN FOOL. I THINK HE EVEN GAVE THE COPS YOUR MEASUREMENTS.

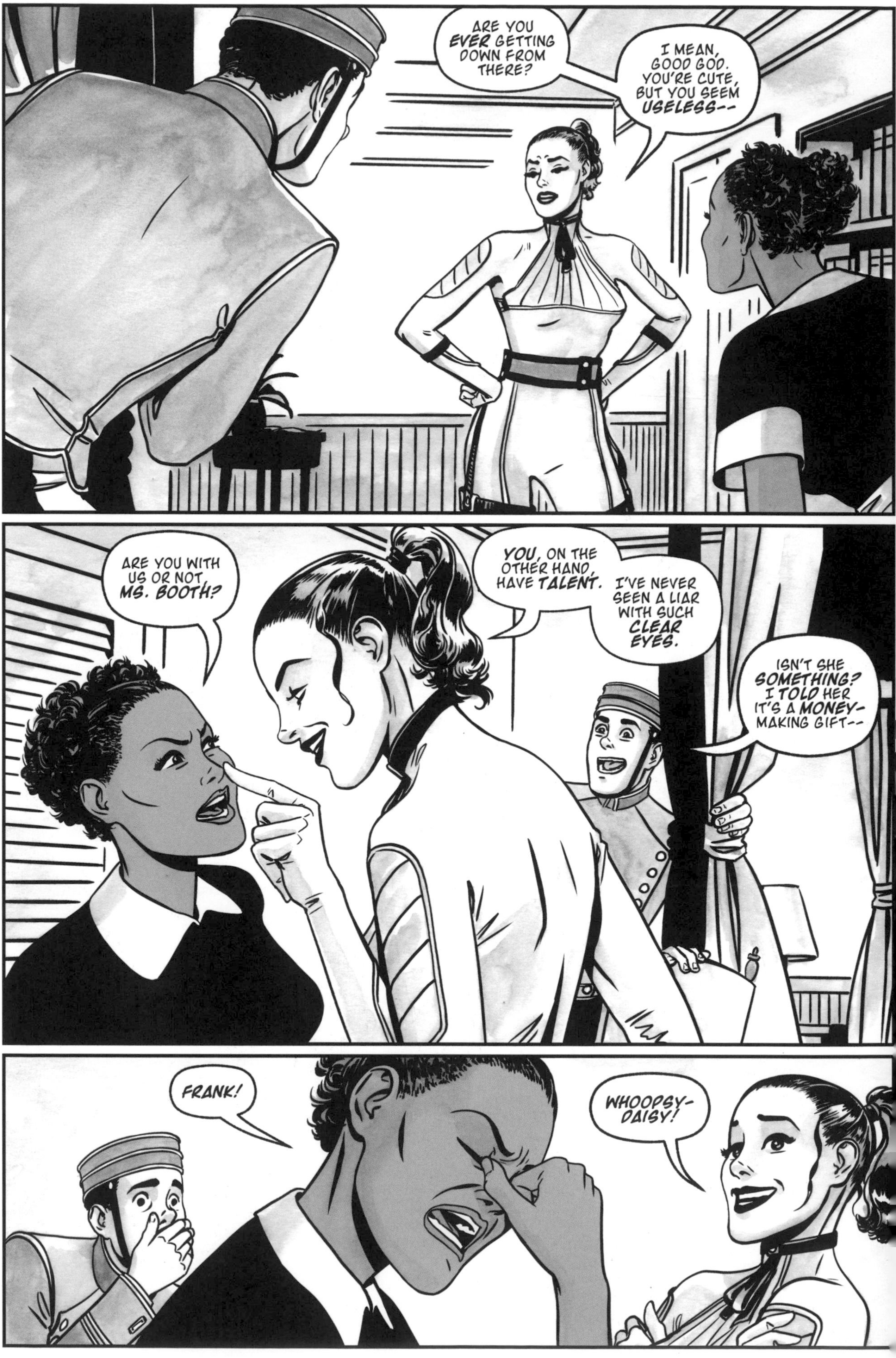
ARE YOU EVER GETTING DOWN FROM THERE?
I MEAN, GOOD GOD. YOU'RE CUTE, BUT YOU SEEM USELESS--
ARE YOU WITH US OR NOT, MS. BOOTH?
YOU, ON THE OTHER HAND, HAVE TALENT.
I'VE NEVER SEEN A LIAR WITH SUCH CLEAR EYES.
ISN'T SHE SOMETHING? I TOLD HER IT'S A MONEY-MAKING GIFT--
FRANK!
WHOOPSY-DAISY!

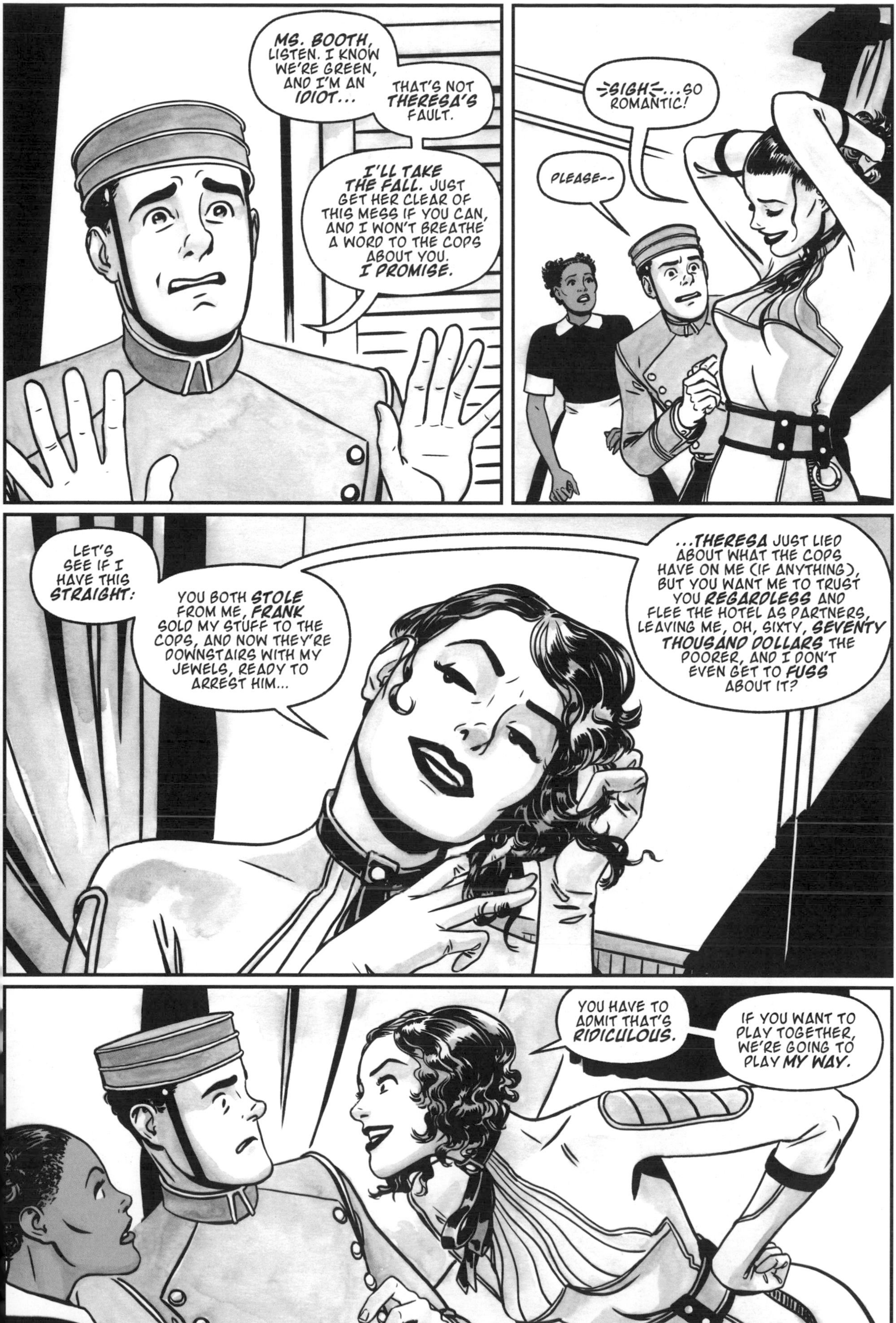
MS. BOOTH, LISTEN. I KNOW WE'RE GREEN, AND I'M AN IDIOT...
THAT'S NOT THERESA'S FAULT.
I'LL TAKE THE FALL. JUST GET HER CLEAR OF THIS MESS IF YOU CAN, AND I WON'T BREATHE A WORD TO THE COPS ABOUT YOU. I PROMISE.
PLEASE--
SIGH...SO ROMANTIC!
LET'S SEE IF I HAVE THIS STRAIGHT:
YOU BOTH STOLE FROM ME, FRANK SOLD MY STUFF TO THE COPS, AND NOW THEY'RE DOWNSTAIRS WITH MY JEWELS, READY TO ARREST HIM...
...THERESA JUST LIED ABOUT WHAT THE COPS HAVE ON ME (IF ANYTHING), BUT YOU WANT ME TO TRUST YOU REGARDLESS AND FLEE THE HOTEL AS PARTNERS, LEAVING ME, OH, SIXTY, SEVENTY THOUSAND DOLLARS THE POORER, AND I DON'T EVEN GET TO FUSS ABOUT IT?
YOU HAVE TO ADMIT THAT'S RIDICULOUS.
IF YOU WANT TO PLAY TOGETHER, WE'RE GOING TO PLAY MY WAY.

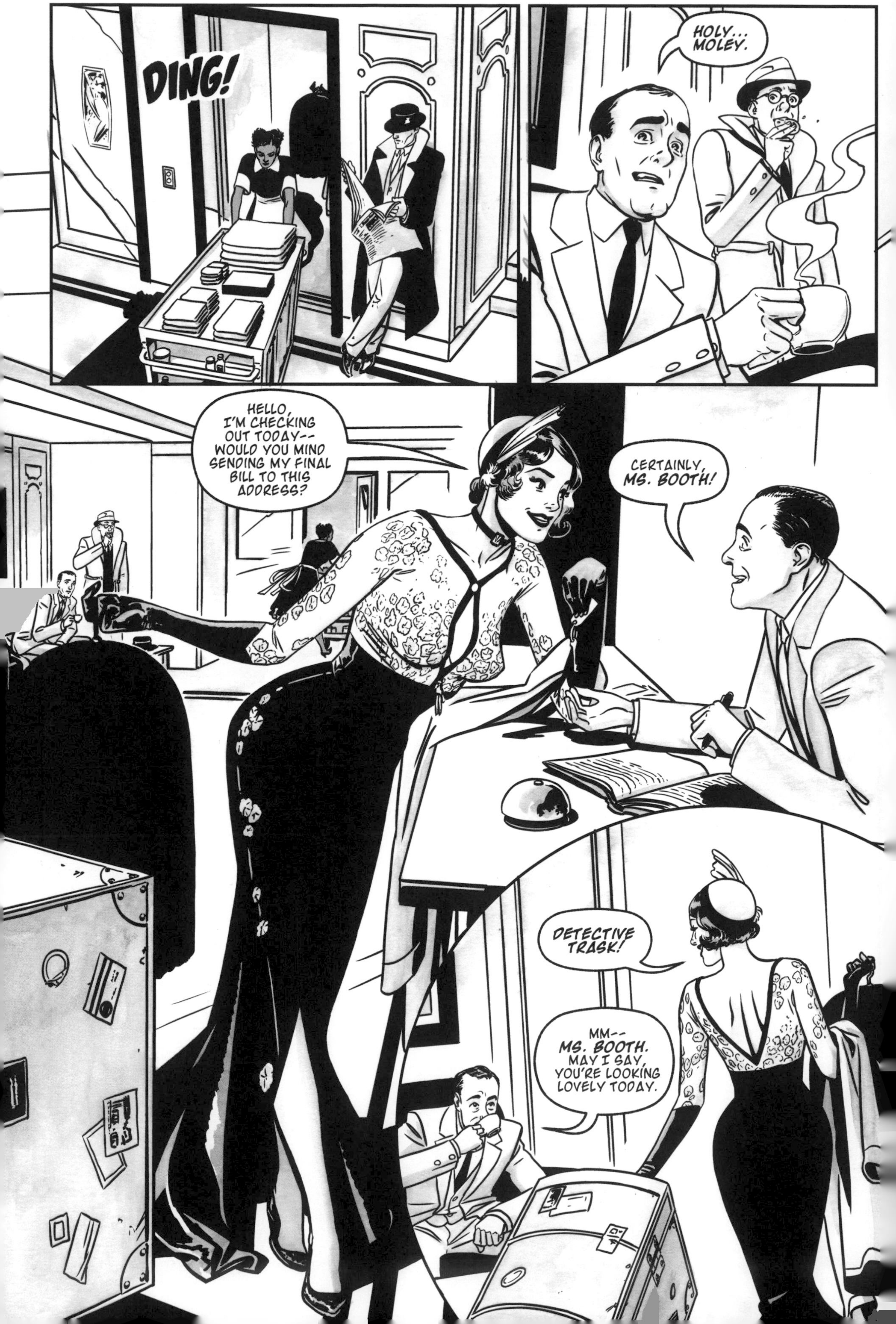
DING!
HOLY... MOLEY.
HELLO, I'M CHECKING OUT TODAY-- WOULD YOU MIND SENDING MY FINAL BILL TO THIS ADDRESS?
CERTAINLY, MS. BOOTH!
DETECTIVE TRASK!
MM-- MS. BOOTH. MAY I SAY, YOU'RE LOOKING LOVELY TODAY.

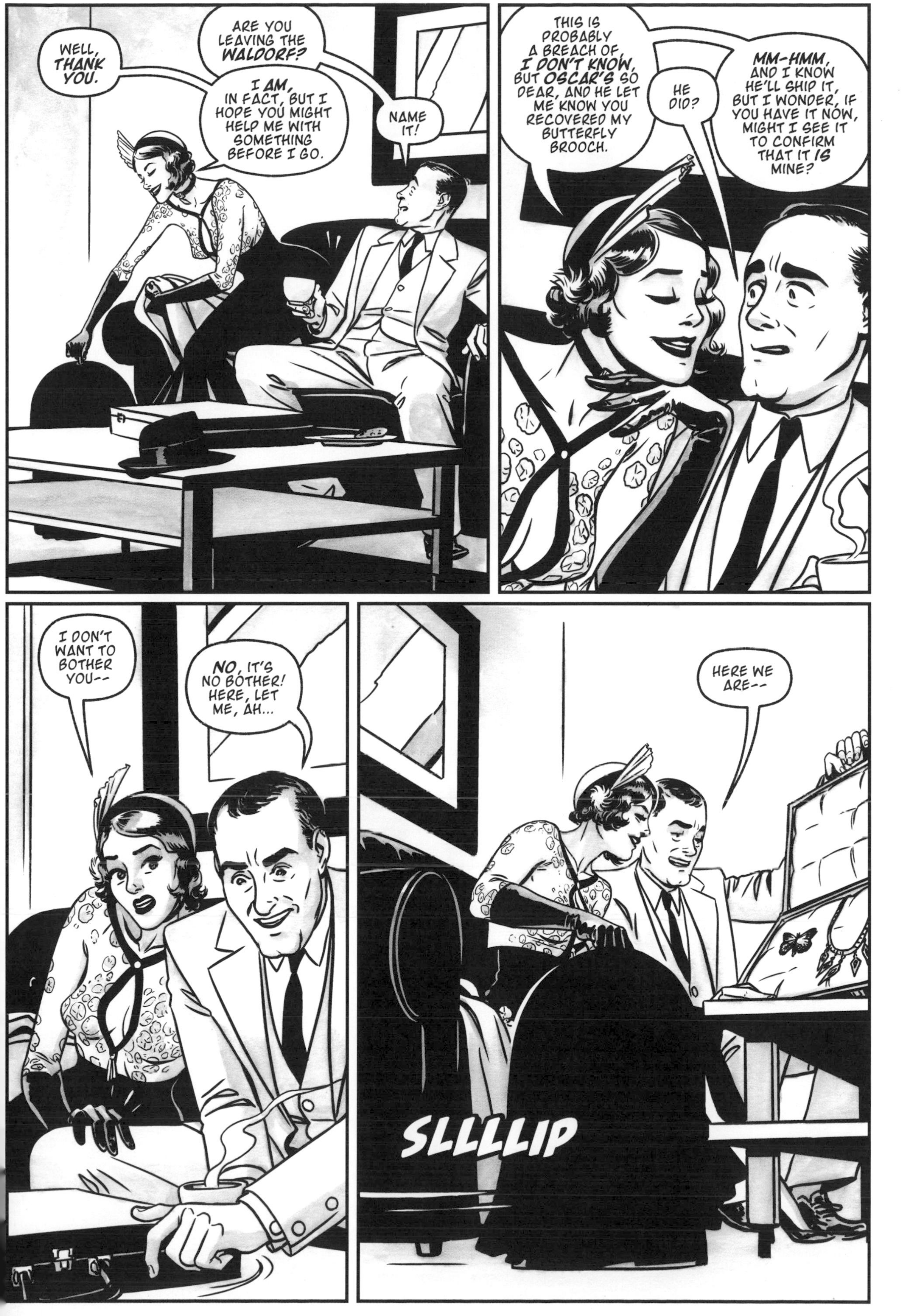
WELL, THANK YOU.
ARE YOU LEAVING THE WALDORF?
I AM, IN FACT, BUT I HOPE YOU MIGHT HELP ME WITH SOMETHING BEFORE I GO.
NAME IT!
THIS IS PROBABLY A BREACH OF, I DON'T KNOW, BUT OSCAR'S SO DEAR, AND HE LET ME KNOW YOU RECOVERED MY BUTTERFLY BROOCH.
HE DID?
MM-HMM, AND I KNOW HE'LL SHIP IT, BUT I WONDER, IF YOU HAVE IT NOW, MIGHT I SEE IT TO CONFIRM THAT IT IS MINE?
I DON'T WANT TO BOTHER YOU--
NO, IT'S NO BOTHER! HERE, LET ME, AH...
HERE WE ARE--
SLLLLIP

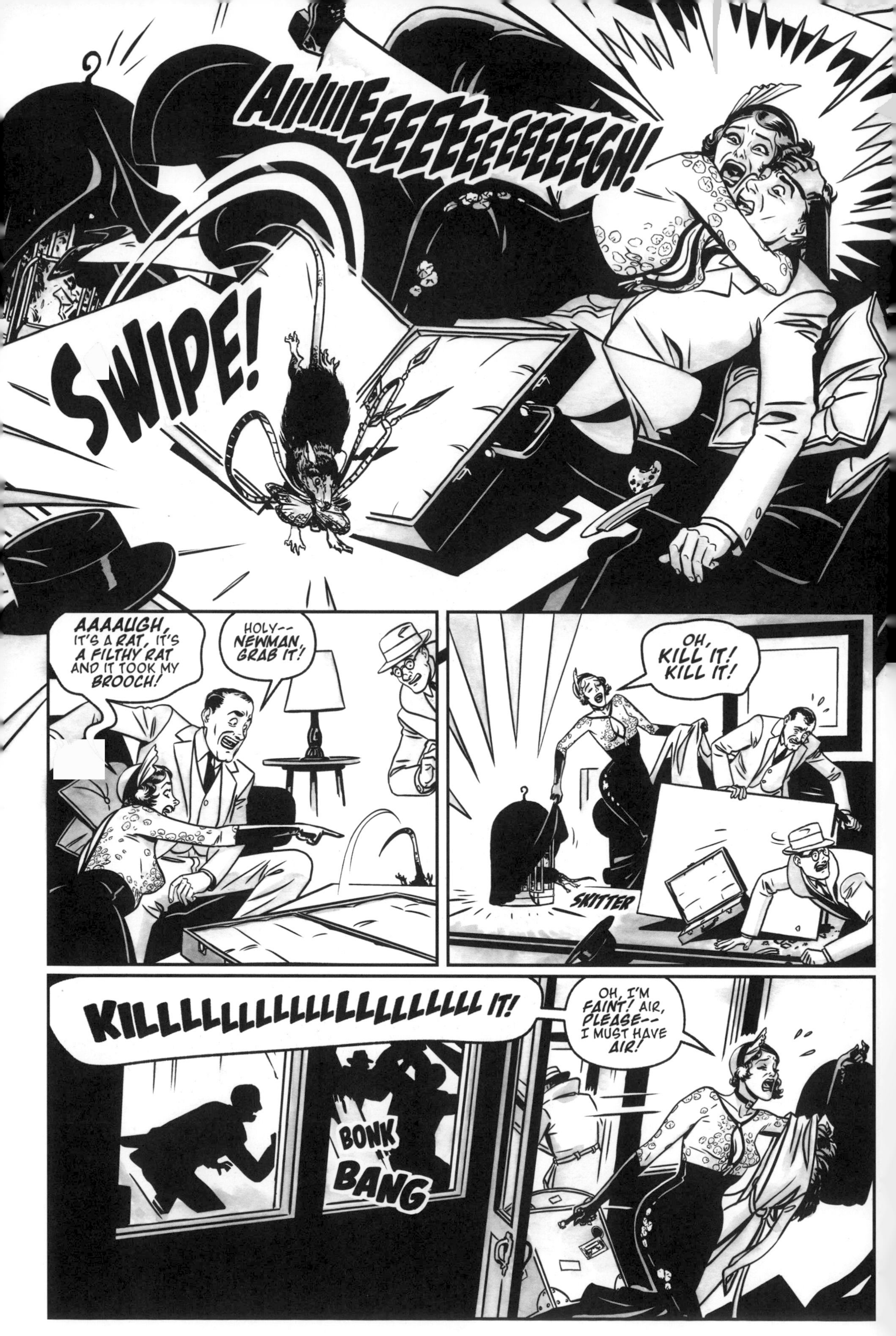

AIIIIIEEEEEEEEEEEEEGH!
SWIPE!
AAAAUGH, IT'S A RAT, IT'S A FILTHY RAT AND IT TOOK MY BROOCH!
HOLY-- NEWMAN, GRAB IT!
OH, KILL IT! KILL IT!
SKITTER
KILLLLLLLLLLLLLLLLLLLL IT!
BONK
BANG
OH, I'M FAINT! AIR, PLEASE-- I MUST HAVE AIR!

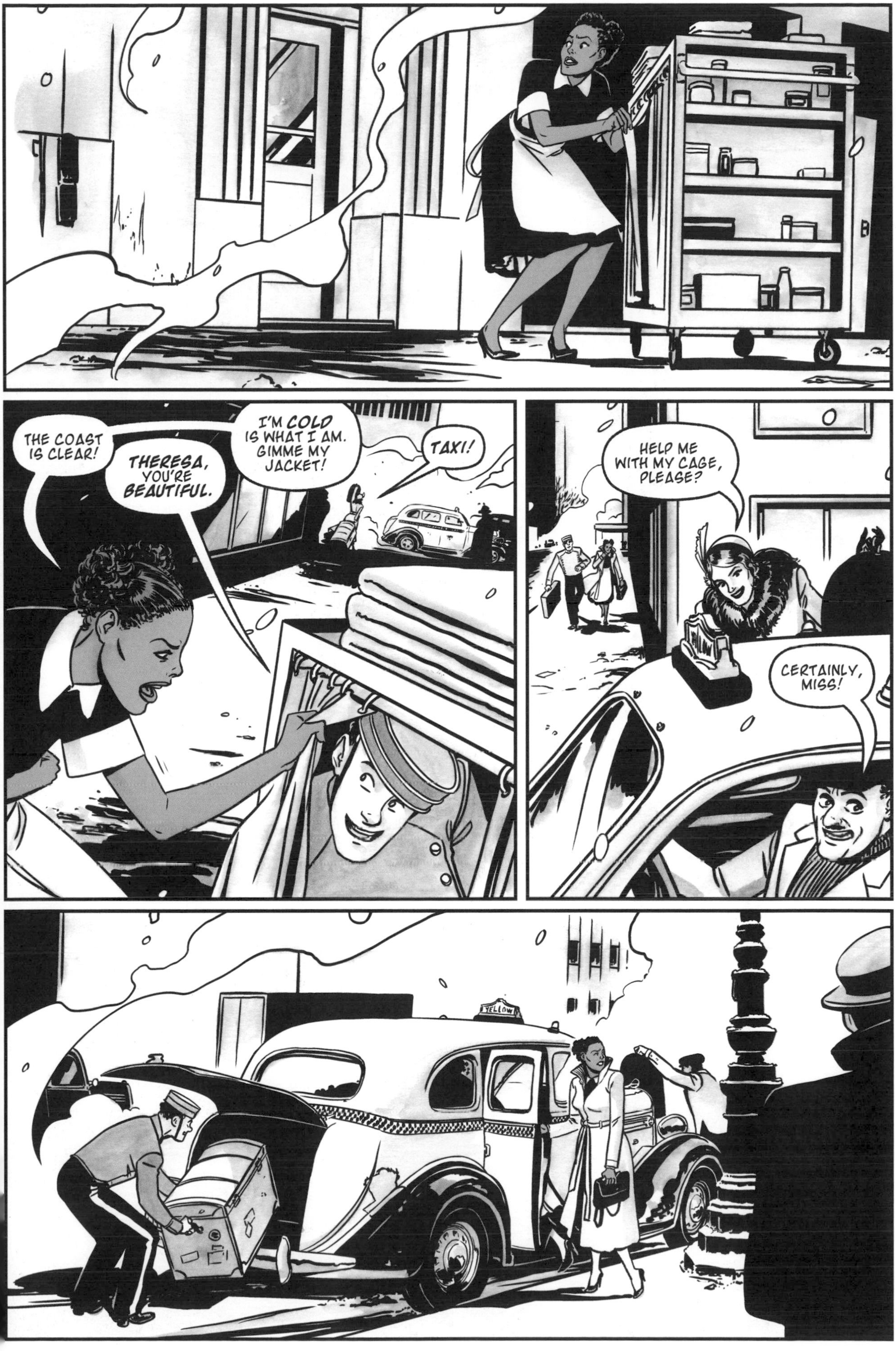

THE COAST IS CLEAR!
THERESA, YOU'RE BEAUTIFUL.
I'M COLD IS WHAT I AM. GIMME MY JACKET!
TAXI!
HELP ME WITH MY CAGE, PLEASE?
CERTAINLY, MISS!

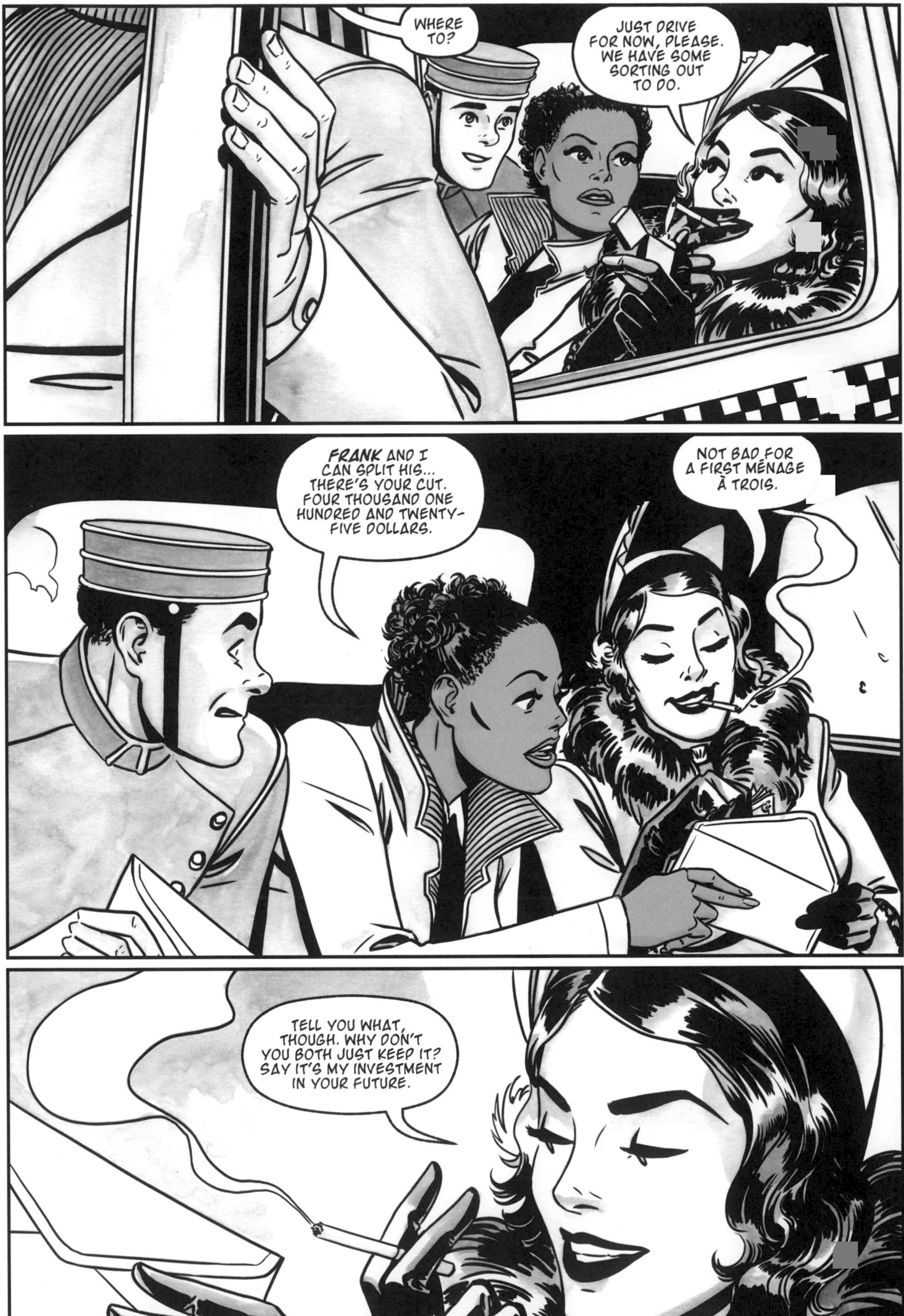
WHERE TO?
JUST DRIVE FOR NOW, PLEASE. WE HAVE SOME SORTING OUT TO DO.
FRANK AND I CAN SPLIT HIS... THERE'S YOUR CUT. FOUR THOUSAND ONE HUNDRED AND TWENTY-FIVE DOLLARS.
NOT BAD FOR A FIRST MÉNAGE À TROIS.
TELL YOU WHAT, THOUGH. WHY DON'T YOU BOTH JUST KEEP IT? SAY IT'S MY INVESTMENT IN YOUR FUTURE.

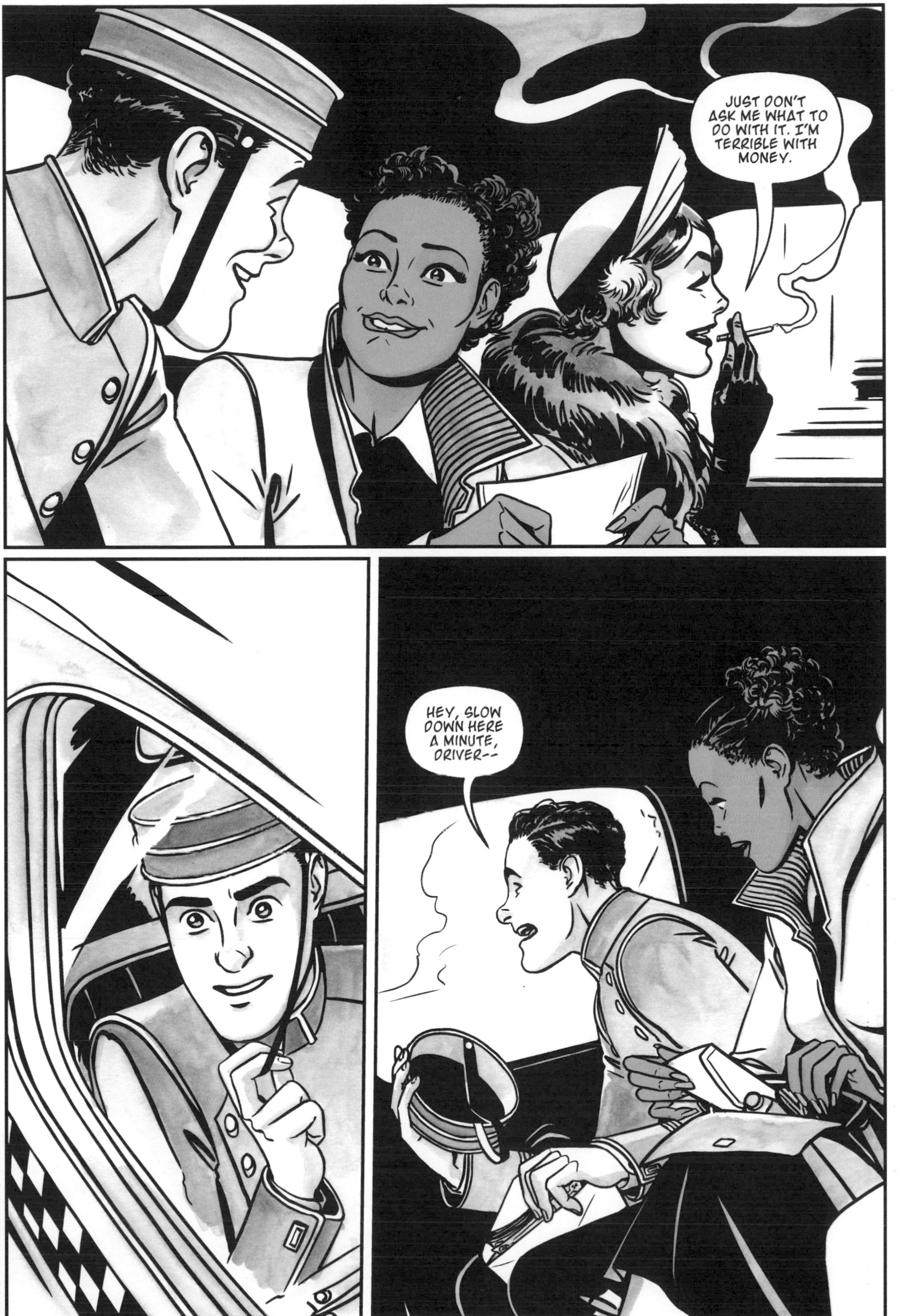
JUST DON'T ASK ME WHAT TO DO WITH IT. I'M TERRIBLE WITH MONEY.
HEY, SLOW DOWN HERE A MINUTE, DRIVER--

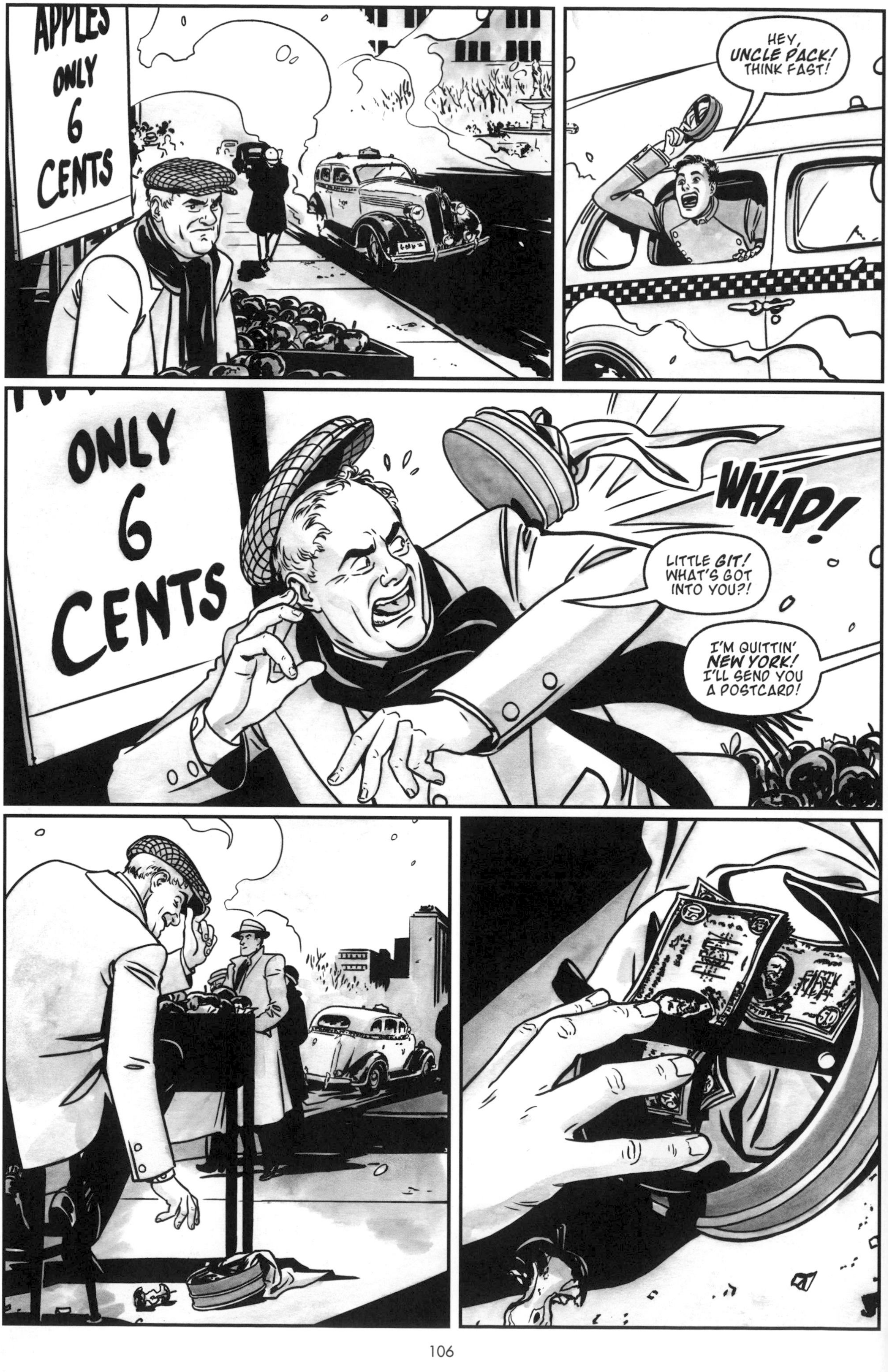
APPLES ONLY 6 CENTS
HEY, UNCLE PACK! THINK FAST!
ONLY 6 CENTS
WHAP!
LITTLE GIT! WHAT'S GOT INTO YOU?!
I'M QUITTIN' NEW YORK! I'LL SEND YOU A POSTCARD!

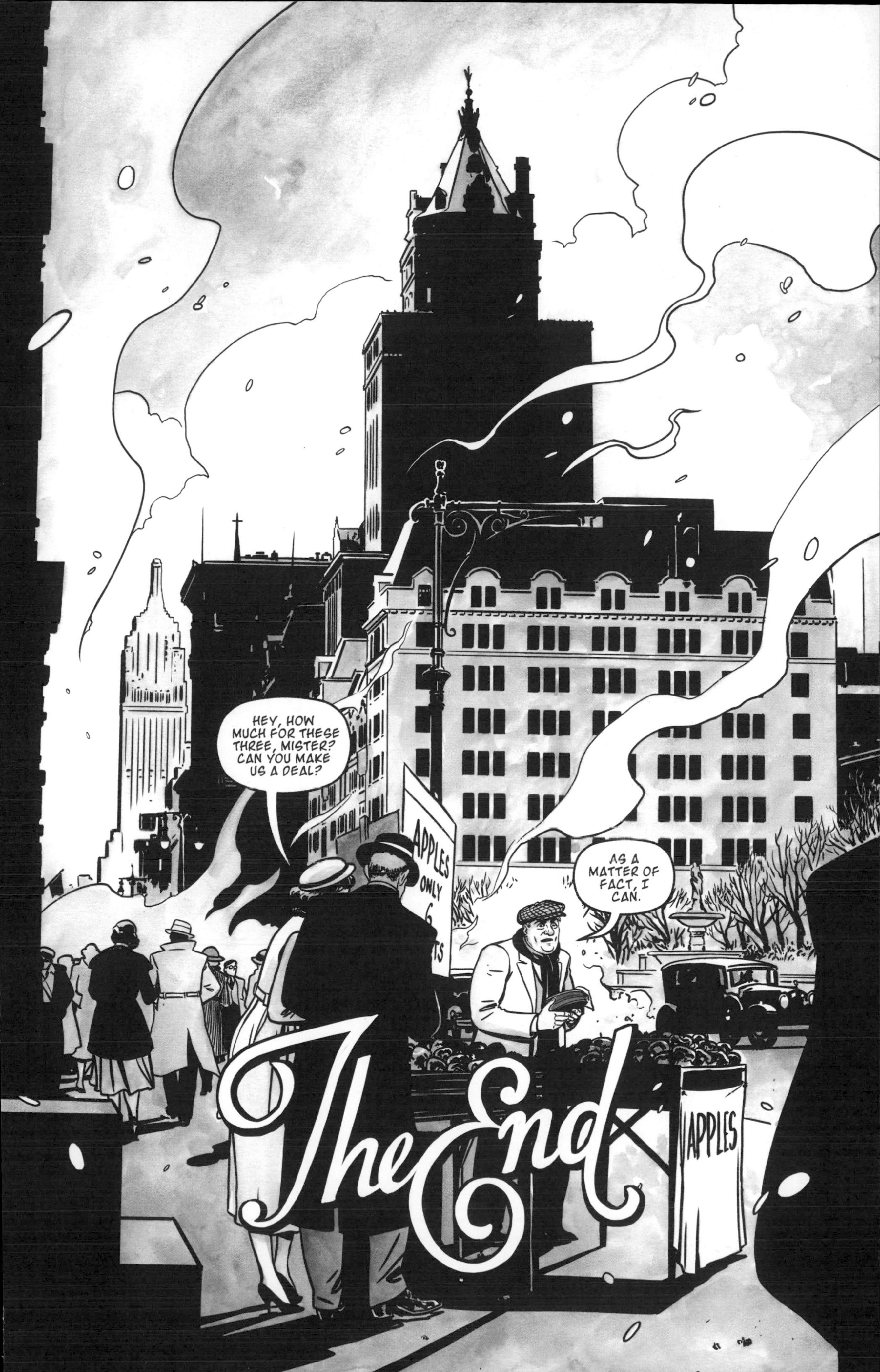

HEY, HOW MUCH FOR THESE THREE, MISTER? CAN YOU MAKE US A DEAL?
APPLES ONLY
AS A MATTER OF FACT, I CAN.
The End
APPLES

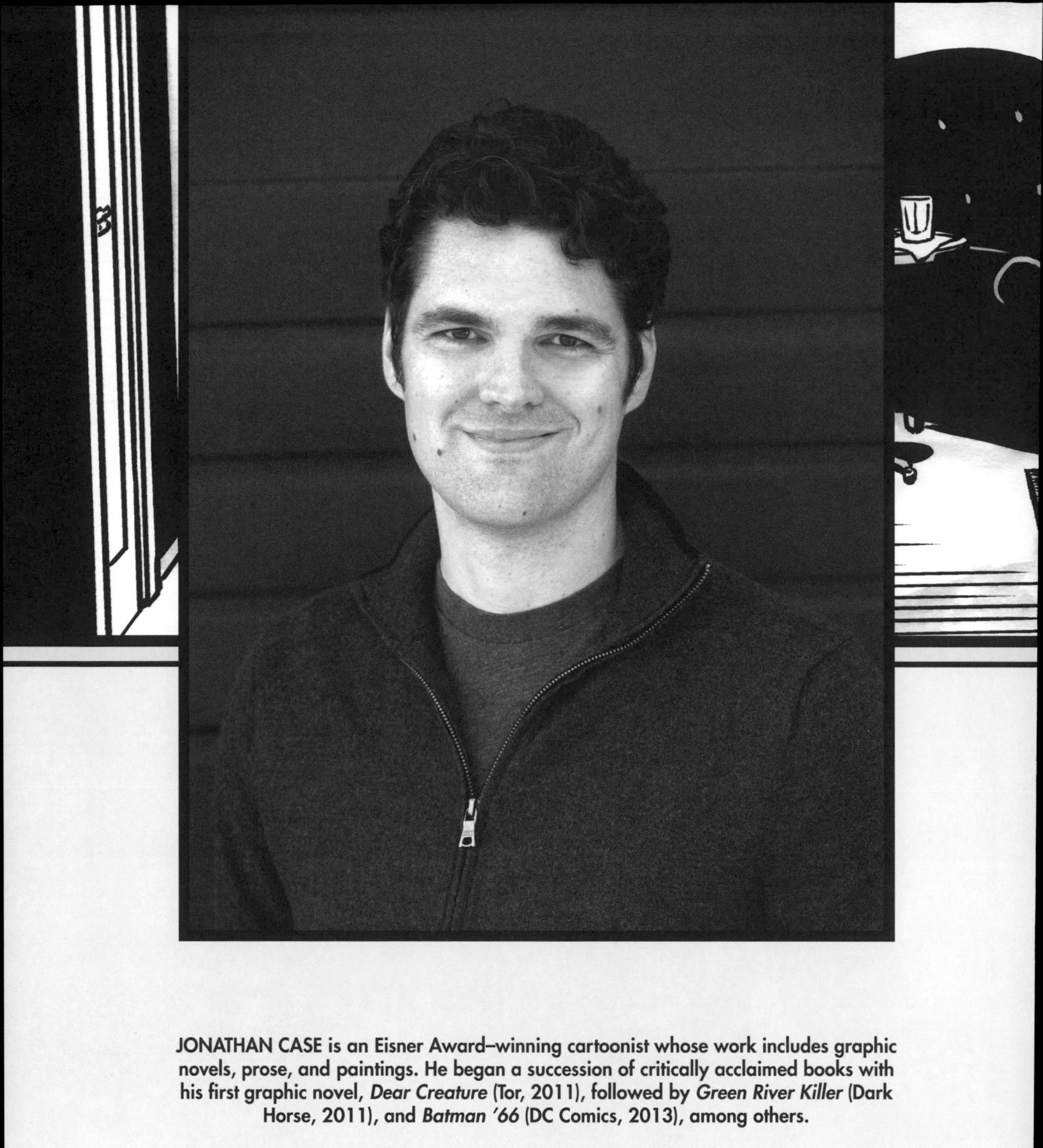

JONATHAN CASE is an Eisner Award–winning cartoonist whose work includes graphic novels, prose, and paintings. He began a succession of critically acclaimed books with his first graphic novel, *Dear Creature* (Tor, 2011), followed by *Green River Killer* (Dark Horse, 2011), and *Batman '66* (DC Comics, 2013), among others.

An Oregon native, Jonathan has dozens of paintings and murals throughout Portland hotspots. In 2015, the city's TEDx event honored him as their featured artist.

He lives in Portland with his wife, Sarah, and their children, Dorothy and Otis.

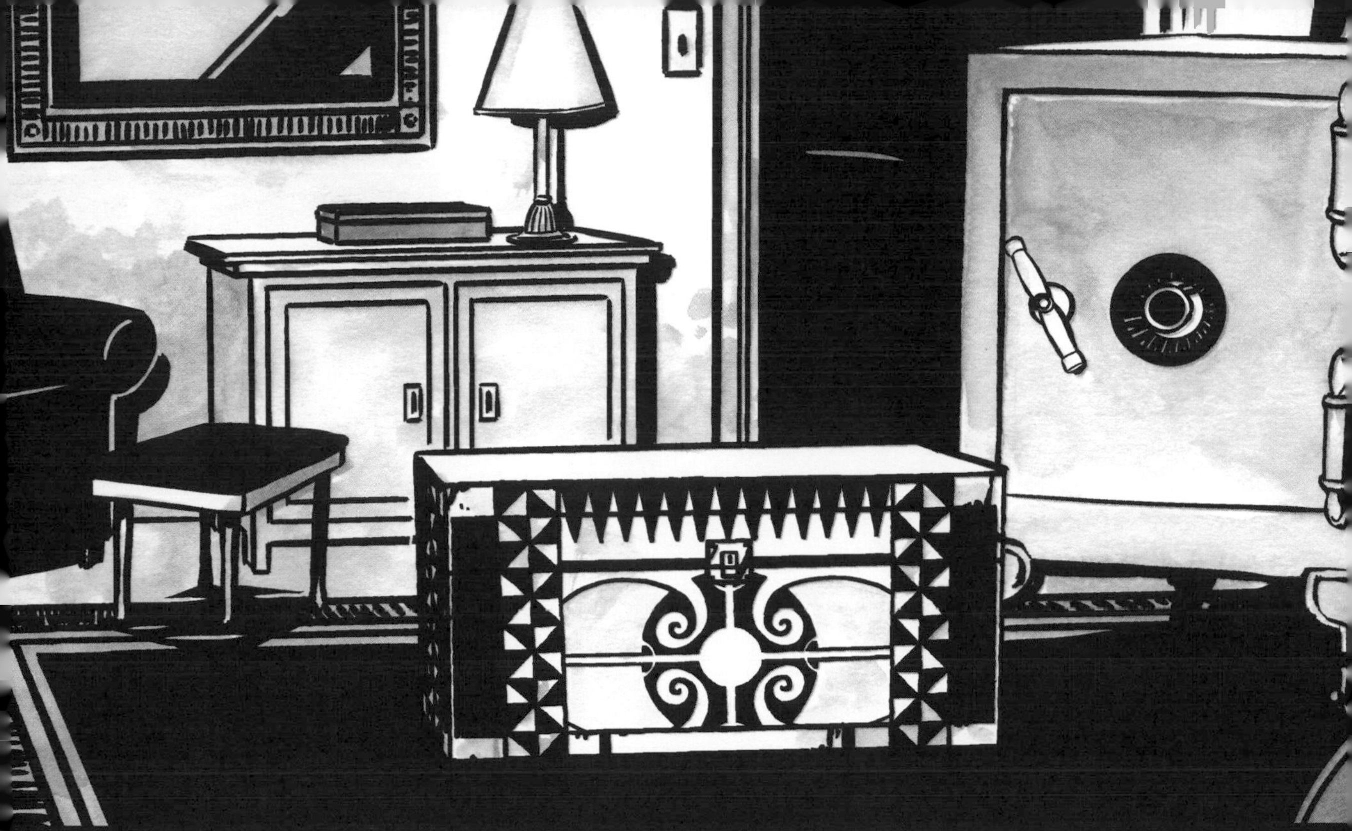

MORE BY JONATHAN CASE

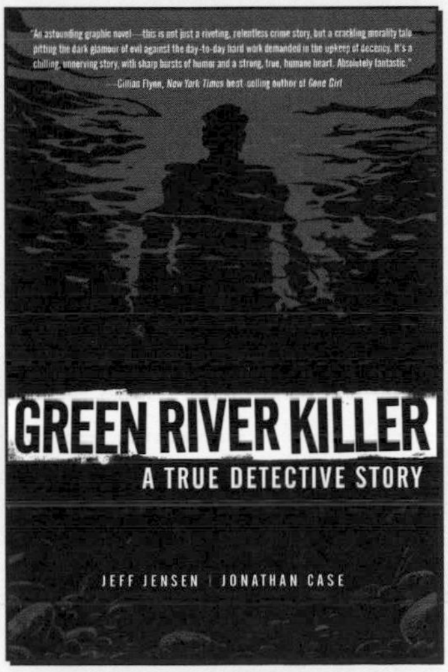
"An astounding graphic novel—this is not just a riveting, relentless crime story, but a crackling morality tale pitting the dark glamour of evil against the day-to-day hard work demanded in the upkeep of decency. It's a chilling, unnerving story, with sharp bursts of humor and a strong, true, humane heart. Absolutely fantastic."
—Gillian Flynn, New York Times best-selling author of Gone Girl
GREEN RIVER KILLER
A TRUE DETECTIVE STORY
JEFF JENSEN | JONATHAN CASE

GREEN RIVER KILLER: A TRUE DETECTIVE STORY
Jeff Jensen, Jonathan Case
Softcover: 978-1-61655-812-3 | **$19.99**
Hardcover: 978-1-59582-560-5 | **$24.99**

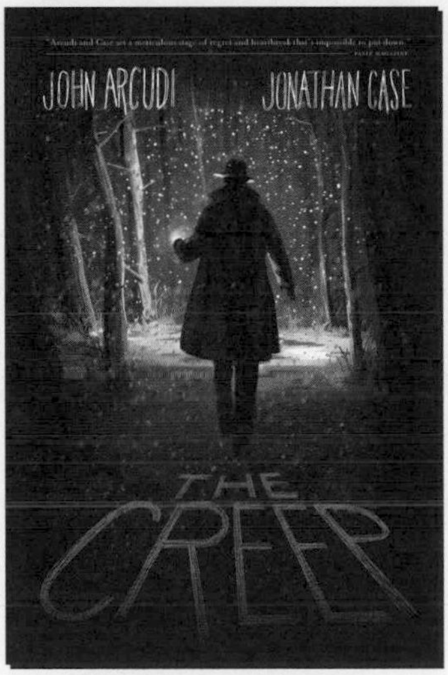
JOHN ARCUDI
JONATHAN CASE
THE CREEP

THE CREEP
John Arcudi, Jonathan Case
Hardcover: 978-1-61655-061-5 | **$19.99**

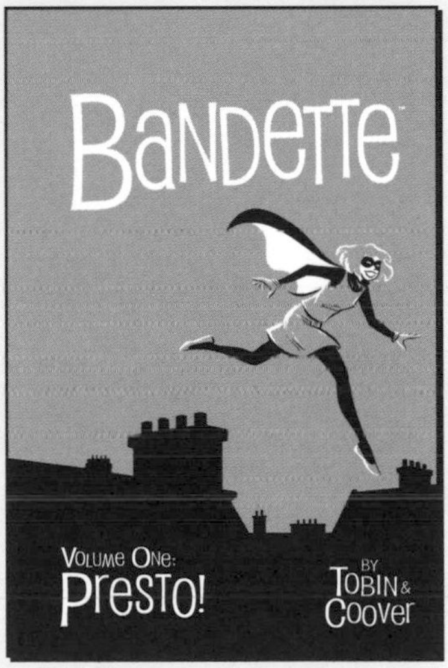
BANDETTE
VOLUME ONE:
PRESTO!
BY
TOBIN & COOVER

BANDETTE VOLUME 1: PRESTO!
Paul Tobin, Alberto J. Alburquerque,
Colleen Coover, Steve Lieber,
Erika Moen, Jonathan Case, Jennifer Meyer
Hardcover: 978-1-61655-279-4 | **$14.99**

BEFORE TOMORROWLAND
Jeff Jensen, Jonathan Case,
Brad Bird, Damon Lindelof
978-1-48470-421-9

DEAR CREATURE
Jonathan Case,
978-0-76533-111-3

ALSO FROM

darkhorseoriginals | great creators original visions

2 sisters
by Matt Kindt

MIND MGMT
matt kindt
volume one: THE MANAGER
"Best comic I have read in many, many, MANY months. Exquisitely dense in all the right ways. Bravo."
—DAMON LINDELOF, CO-CREATOR OF LOST

"Terrific. It's got the scariest opening sequence I've read in years, and the novel as a whole makes compelling stay-up-late reading. Great, creepy stuff."
—STEPHEN KING
GREEN RIVER KILLER
A TRUE DETECTIVE STORY
DO NOT CROSS CRIME SCENE DO NOT CROSS
JEFF JENSEN | JONATHAN CASE

BRIAN WOOD
CHANNEL ZERO
THE COMPLETE COLLECTION
WITH BECKY CLOONAN
INTRODUCTION BY WARREN ELLIS

THE AWARD-WINNING INTERNATIONAL BESTSELLER
DARK HORSE BOOKS presents
BLACKSAD
DÍAZ CANALES GUARNIDO
"As good as it gets!"
—Stan Lee

SPEAK OF THE DEVIL
GILBERT HERNANDEZ

2 SISTERS
Matt Kindt
ISBN 978-1-61655-721-8 | $27.99

MIND MGMT VOLUME 1
Matt Kindt
ISBN 978-1-59582-797-5 | $19.99

CITIZEN REX
Gilbert Hernandez, Mario Hernandez
ISBN 978-1-59582-556-8 | $19.99

SPEAK OF THE DEVIL
Gilbert Hernandez
ISBN 978-1-59582-193-5 | $19.99

BLACKSAD
Juan Díaz Canales, Juanjo Guarnido
ISBN 978-1-59582-393-9 | $29.99

BLACKSAD: A SILENT HELL
Juan Díaz Canales, Juanjo Guarnido
ISBN 978-1-59582-931-3 | $19.99

BLACKSAD: AMARILLO
Juan Díaz Canales, Juanjo Guarnido
ISBN 978-1-61655-525-2 | $17.99

CHANNEL ZERO
Brian Wood, Becky Cloonan
ISBN 978-1-59582-936-8 | $19.99

GREEN RIVER KILLER
Jeff Jensen, Jonathan Case
ISBN 978-1-59582-560-5 | $24.99

DE:TALES
Gabriel Bá, Fábio Moon
ISBN 978-1-59307-485-2 | $14.95

JAYBIRD
Jaakko and Lauri Ahonen
ISBN 978-1-61655-469-9 | $19.99

AVAILABLE AT YOUR LOCAL COMICS SHOP OR BOOKSTORE! • To find a comics shop in your area, call 1-888-266-4226.
For more information or to order direct visit DarkHorse.com or call 1-800-862-0052 Mon.–Fri. 9 AM to 5 PM Pacific Time. Prices and availability subject to change without notice.

DarkHorse.com

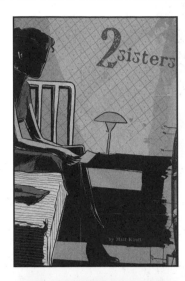

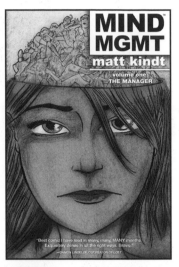

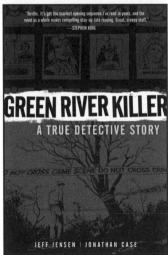

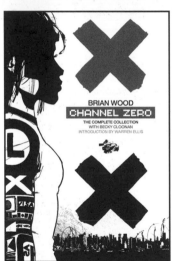

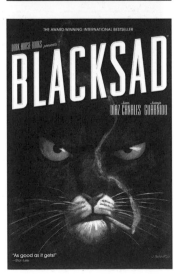

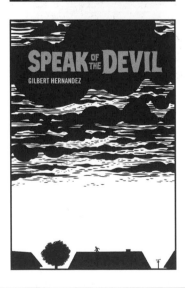

ALSO FROM

darkhorseoriginals | great creators original visions

TWO BROTHERS
Fábio Moon Gabriel Bá

JONATHAN CASE
THE NEW DEAL

THE COMPLETE
MATT KINDT JASON HALL
PISTOL WHIP

BAD HOUSES
SARA RYAN
CARLA SPEED MCNEIL

APOCALYPTIGIRL
AN ARIA FOR THE END TIMES
ANDREW MACLEAN

Sabertooth Swordsman
GENTRY
CONLEY

TWO BROTHERS
Gabriel Bá, Fábio Moon
ISBN 978-1-61655-856-7 | $24.99

THE NEW DEAL
Jonathan Case
ISBN 978-1-61655-731-7 | $16.99

THE COMPLETE PISTOLWHIP
Jason Hall, Matt Kindt
ISBN 978-1-61655-720-1 | $27.99

BAD HOUSES
Sara Ryan, Carla Speed McNeil
ISBN 978-1-59582-993-1 | $19.99

APOCALYPTIGIRL: AN ARIA FOR THE END TIMES
Andrew MacLean
ISBN 978-1-61655-566-5 | $9.99

SABERTOOTH SWORDSMAN
Damon Gentry, Aaron Conley
ISBN 978-1-61655-176-6 | $17.99

SIN TITULO
Cameron Stewart
ISBN 978-1-61655-248-0 | $19.99

THE TRUE LIVES OF THE FABULOUS KILLJOYS
Gerard Way, Shaun Simon, Becky Cloonan
ISBN 978-1-59582-462-2 | $19.99

DEMO
Brian Wood, Becky Cloonan
ISBN 978-1-61655-682-2 | $24.99

MOTEL ART IMPROVEMENT SERVICE
Jason Little
ISBN 978-1-59582-550-6 | $19.99

AVAILABLE AT YOUR LOCAL COMICS SHOP OR BOOKSTORE! • To find a comics shop in your area, call 1-888-266-4226.
For more information or to order direct visit DarkHorse.com or call 1-800-862-0052 Mon.–Fri. 9 AM to 5 PM Pacific Time. Prices and availability subject to change without notice.

DarkHorse.com

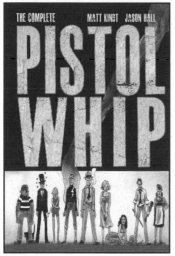

GABRIEL BÁ AND FÁBIO MOON!

"Twin Brazilian artists Fábio Moon and Gabriel Bá have made a huge mark on comics." *–Publisher's Weekly*

TWO BROTHERS
Story and art by Gabriel Bá
and Fábio Moon
ISBN 978-1-61655-856-7 | $24.99

DE:TALES
Story and art by Gabriel Bá and Fábio Moon
ISBN 978-1-59582-557-5 | $19.99

**THE UMBRELLA ACADEMY:
APOCALYPSE SUITE**
Story by Gerard Way
Art by Gabriel Bá
TPB ISBN: 978-1-59307-978-9 | $17.99
Ltd. Ed. HC ISBN: 978-1-59582-163-8 | $79.95

THE UMBRELLA ACADEMY: DALLAS
Story by Gerard Way
Art by Gabriel Bá
TPB ISBN: 978-1-59582-345-8 | $17.99
Ltd. Ed. HC ISBN: 978-1-59582-344-1 | $79.95

PIXU: THE MARK OF EVIL
Story and art by Gabriel Bá, Becky Cloonan,
Vasilis Lolos, and Fábio Moon
ISBN 978-1-61655-813-0 | $14.99

B.P.R.D.: VAMPIRE
Story by Mike Mignola, Fábio Moon, and Gabriel Bá
Art by Fábio Moon and Gabriel Bá
ISBN 978-1-61655-196-4 | $19.99

B.P.R.D.: 1946–1948
Story by Mike Mignola, Joshua Dysart, and John Arcudi
Art by Fábio Moon, Gabriel Bá, Paul Azaceta, and Max Fiumara
ISBN 978-1-61655-646-4 | $34.99